50 HIKES
IN PENNSYLVANIA

50 HIKES

IN PENNSYLVANIA

FIRST EDITION

Matthew Cathcart

THE COUNTRYMAN PRESS

A Division of W. W. Norton & Company

Independent Publishers Since 1923

AN INVITATION TO THE READER

Over time trails can be rerouted and signs and landmarks altered. If you find that changes have occurred on the routes described in this book, please let us know so that corrections may be made in future editions. The author and publisher also welcome other comments and suggestions.

Address all correspondence to:
Editor, 50 Hikes Series
The Countryman Press
500 Fifth Avenue
New York, NY 10110

For information about permission to reproduce selections from this book, write to Permissions, The Countryman Press, 500 Fifth Avenue, New York, NY 10110

For information about special discounts for bulk purchases, please contact W. W. Norton Special Sales at specialsales@wwnorton.com or 800-233-4830

Manufacturing by Versa Press
Series book design by Chris Welch
Maps by Michael Borop (sitesatlas.com)
Production manager: Gwen Cullen

The Countryman Press
www.countrymanpress.com

A division of W. W. Norton & Company, Inc.
500 Fifth Avenue, New York, NY 10110
www.wwnorton.com

978-1-68268-523-5 (pbk.)

10 9 8 7 6 5 4 3 2 1

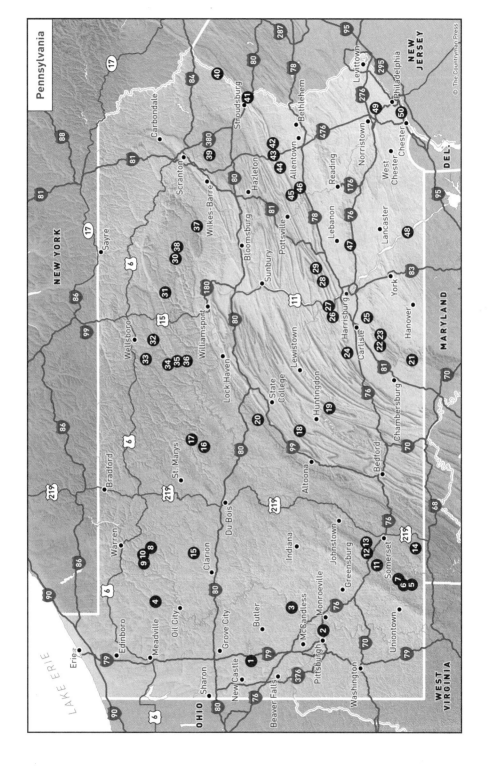

Contents

III. EASTERN PENNSYLVANIA | 229

Hikes at a Glance

	Hike	Region	Distance (miles)	Difficulty
Western	1. McConnells Mill State Park	Western	7.1	Difficult
	2. Frick Park Falls Loop	Western	2.4	Easy
	3. Rachel Carson Trail Harrison Hills Loop	Western	5.3	Moderate
	4. Oil Creek State Park	Western	8	Difficult
	5. Meadow Run Loop	Western	2.1	Moderate
	6. Ferncliff Loop	Western	2	Easy
	7. Bear Run Nature Reserve	Western	5.2	Moderate
	8. Minister Creek North Loop	Western	6.6	Very Difficult
	9. Hickory Creek Wilderness Trail	Western	13.5	Difficult
	10. Hearts Content National Scenic Area	Western	1.1	Easy
	11. Roaring Run Natural Area	Western	8.5	Difficult
	12. Wolf Rocks Loop	Western	4.5	Moderate
	13. Beam Rocks	Western	0.9	Easy
	14. Mount Davis High Point	Western	6	Difficult
	15. Cook Forest Ancient Forest Loop	Western	2.9	Moderate
Central	16. Teaberry and Lincoln Loops	Central	5.4	Difficult
	17. Fred Woods Trail	Central	5	Easy
	18. Little Juniata Natural Area	Central	3.3	Difficult
	19. Thousand Steps	Central	2.8	Very Difficult
	20. Ralph's Views	Central	6.9	Moderate
	21. Chimney Rocks Loop	Central	5.3	Difficult
	22. Sunset Rocks Loop	Central	8.2	Difficult
	23. Pole Steeple Loop	Central	6	Moderate
	24. Flat Rock	Central	4.6	Difficult
	25. White Rocks Trail and Center Point Knob	Central	3	Difficult

Good for Kids	Dogs Allowed	Camping	Waterfalls	Historic Interest	Scenic Views	Type
	✓		✓	✓	✓	Loop
✓	✓		✓			Loop
✓	✓				✓	Loop
	✓		✓	✓	✓	Loop
✓	✓		✓			Loop
✓	✓		✓		✓	Loop
	✓	✓	✓			Loop
	✓	✓			✓	Loop
	✓					Loop
✓	✓			✓		Loop
	✓			✓		Loop
✓	✓				✓	Loop
✓	✓				✓	Out and Back
	✓			✓	✓	Loop
✓	✓			✓		Loop
	✓				✓	Loop
✓	✓			✓	✓	Loop
	✓				✓	Out and Back
	✓			✓	✓	Out and Back
✓	✓	✓			✓	Out and Back
	✓	✓			✓	Loop
	✓	✓		✓	✓	Loop
✓	✓			✓	✓	Loop
	✓	✓			✓	Out and Back
	✓			✓	✓	Out and Back

	Hike	Region	Distance (miles)	Difficulty
Central	26. Hawk Rock	Central	1.7	Difficult
	27. Clarks Ferry Loop	Central	4	Difficult
	28. Stony Mountain Lookout Tower	Central	7.3	Difficult
	29. Yellow Springs Loop	Central	8.1	Difficult
	30. Worlds End State Park	Central	6.1	Difficult
	31. Rock Run	Central	3	Moderate
	32. Haunted Vista	Central	3.9	Difficult
	33. West Rim Trail Day Hike	Central	14.6	Very Difficult
	34. Black Forest Trail Day Hike	Central	15.6	Very Difficult
	35. Golden Eagle Trail	Central	9.6	Very Difficult
	36. Bob Webber Trail	Central	3.7	Very Difficult
Eastern	37. Ricketts Glen Falls Trail	Eastern	6.9	Difficult
	38. The Haystacks and Dutchman Falls	Eastern	4.5	Moderate
	39. Big Pine Hill Loop	Eastern	5.8	Moderate
	40. Pocono Environmental Education Center	Eastern	6.7	Difficult
	41. Mount Minsi	Eastern	4	Difficult
	42. Lehigh Gap Appalachian Trail Winter Loop	Eastern	2.7	Very Difficult
	43. North Trail Loop	Eastern	6.8	Difficult
	44. Bear Rocks and Knife's Edge	Eastern	4.3	Moderate
	45. Hawk Mountain Sanctuary	Eastern	5.1	Very Difficult
	46. Pulpit Rock and The Pinnacle	Eastern	9.2	Difficult
	47. Governor Dick Park	Eastern	5.7	Moderate
	48. Kellys Run Loop	Eastern	5.9	Difficult
	49. Wissahickon North Gorge Loop	Eastern	5.2	Moderate
	50. John Heinz National Wildlife Refuge	Eastern	4	Easy

Good for Kids	Dogs Allowed	Camping	Waterfalls	Historic Interest	Scenic Views	Type
✓	✓				✓	Out and Back
	✓			✓	✓	Loop
	✓			✓	✓	Loop
	✓	✓		✓		Loop
	✓	✓	✓		✓	Loop
✓	✓	✓	✓			Out and Back
	✓			✓	✓	Out and Back
	✓	✓			✓	Loop
	✓	✓	✓		✓	Loop
	✓		✓		✓	Loop
	✓				✓	Out and Back
	✓		✓			Loop
✓	✓	✓	✓			Loop
✓	✓				✓	Loop
✓	✓		✓	✓	✓	Loop
	✓				✓	Out and Back
	✓				✓	Loop
	✓				✓	Loop
✓	✓	✓			✓	Out and Back
					✓	Loop
	✓	✓			✓	Loop
✓	✓			✓	✓	Loop
	✓		✓		✓	Loop
✓	✓		✓	✓		Loop
✓	✓				✓	Loop

Introduction

"Nope, it still moves a little bit. We'll have to dig it out and try again."

I leaned on my pry bar, exhausted. I let out a defeated sigh, hanging my head for a brief moment. I had been watching a retired man stand on a rock the size of a minifridge that sat in an 8-inch-deep hole. The blazing sun that beat down on the leaves warmed the humid forest air below the dense canopy, making it feel more like the middle of July than early September. Sweat rolled down my face and dripped off my chin. My safety glasses fogged up unceremoniously. Despite the heat, I was dressed in long pants, plastic catcher-style shin guards, thick leather work gloves, and a hard hat. It was 2013 and my wife and I were participating in an Appalachian Trail Crew, a volunteer-based workforce that performs manual labor with primitive hand tools, refurbishing and repairing the tread of the historic 2,000-mile footpath that runs from Georgia to Maine. My wife had discovered the opportunity while browsing online and we both decided that it seemed like a fun way to give back. At that moment, however, as I stood in the half-sun of a September afternoon, tired, hungry, sticky,

GAZING OVER THE VALLEY FROM ATOP THE KNIFE'S EDGE

filthy, and frustrated, "fun" seemed like a foreign concept.

The man I had been watching was my crew leader. The other volunteers and I had just spent over an hour leveraging the massive rock into and then back out of the shallow pit, trying over and over again to dig a hole that fit the uneven bottom side of the rock snugly, so it would not move. Seemingly in spite of this hard work, our crew leader was trying with all his might to wiggle the 400-pound rock. It moved no more than the width of two nickels.

The volunteers went back to the task at hand, reluctant but determined, while our crew leader, confident in our abilities, started scoping out the nearby forest for other rocks that might work well as stepping stones. We were working on a creekside section of trail near Eckville, Pennsylvania, that was prone to flooding and the subsequent erosion that went along with it. The work we were doing would provide hikers with a dry alternative to slogging through the mud, and this section would now be resistant to flowing floodwaters. With any luck, the stones we dug into the ground would not need to be replaced for 10 or 15, maybe 20 years. The thought of building such a long-standing structure with a few hand tools, the collective brute strength of a few sweaty individuals, and (quite literally) some grit was immensely satisfying. But to stand the test of time, the stepping stones had to be held perfectly in place by the ground around them. Hikers carrying heavy packs generate a lot of force when they traipse downhill, and the sloping trail that led down to the creek would see thousands of visitors over the years. If it wasn't set perfectly in place, the stepping stone would wiggle more and more every year, slowly enlarging the

hole it sat in. After that, water would be able to seep into any loose space around the rock, and the freeze-thaw cycle that Pennsylvania experiences in the spring and fall would lift the stepping stone out of place and blow out the trail.

As I worked I reflected on several unavoidable truths. The eroding of the trail was inevitable of course, as the forces of nature and the pounding of footsteps took their toll on the trail. For a trail to have any staying power, it would need to be maintained or else it would fade into the ether, under duff and brush, or fall apart due to overuse, essentially crumbling under the weight of its own popularity. It is easy to take a good hiking trail for granted, I surmised. Anyone who has been hiking is familiar with the experience: You show up at the trailhead, exit your vehicle, and instantly step into the woods on winding trails that appear to have existed since time immemorial. Sometimes, where many trails exist, the path intersects with others, which forces hikers to make decisions about which way to go. Other times, as on large stretches of the Appalachian Trail, the way is fairly straightforward and the only options that exist are to go forward or turn around. Despite how they differ in philosophy, both scenarios occur seemingly of their own volition, unfolding with no effort or foresight required of those who choose to enjoy them. The Appalachian Trail, like all footpaths through the deep, dark woods, is inherently fragile. It is held together largely by the efforts of public servants who work tirelessly to protect the remaining undeveloped land we still have and by the never-ending labor of hardy volunteers who apparently get a kick out of banging rocks together to build something so rustic that it looks like it wasn't forged by human hands.

Why go to such great lengths to make something so thankless, so tenuous, so extravagantly Sisyphean?

I continued thinking as I worked, turning the ideas over in my head like a coin found on the ground. At sparse, random intervals a hiker or two would walk by. All of them were incredibly grateful for our work. They would usually survey our work and then let out a meek "thank you" as they continued. Our crew leader was typically the first to reply to passersby, always with the same retort. He would turn from whatever he was working on and say, "Thank you for hiking the trail! Otherwise we wouldn't have anything to do!" The half-cheeky, wholly sincere response caught me by surprise every time. I began to consider that, just maybe, doing anything or nothing in the woods and taking communion with a system that moved on its own set of wheels might be a special kind of medicine. But for what illness? Existential dread? The painfully blasé? The collective cultural ego? I couldn't say for sure.

At the end of the week, I stood back and looked at the work our team had managed to get done: two short log boardwalks, a couple of drainage ditches, and roughly 15 new stepping stones. In total, the stretch of trail we had reconditioned was no more than 300 feet long, a negligible distance compared to the 230 miles of the Appalachian Trail that meandered through Pennsylvania. That 300 feet went from scant to entirely laughable when I considered that the Appalachian Trail ran continuously for more than 2,000 miles, broken only by occasional road crossings. And yet, when I surveyed our work and thought about the amount of time it had taken, I felt a sense of accomplishment that I had not expected.

Consider for a moment the trail system in Pennsylvania. According to the Department of Conservation and Natural Resources, there are an estimated 12,000 miles of trailspace in the Keystone State. A good percentage of those miles follow repurposed railbeds or logging roads, but even if just 10 percent of the existing trails required as much sweaty, backbreaking work to build and maintain as what our small crew had done in a week's time, then there was some serious vigor and devotion behind the craft of meticulously shaping a forest path. I had hiked for years before I got my hands dirty learning what it took to build and maintain a trail, and in doing so I was beginning to understand the monumental outpouring of brotherly love that went into the whole ordeal.

I liked to imagine some nameless individual curiously walking through uncharted territory in the woods. I liked to think about them stumbling upon some surprising peculiarity, no matter how superficial, like an exposed ledge that offered a nice view, a small picturesque clearing beside a stream, a mossy rock that leaned at a specific angle, a stately tree that held their attention a split second longer than all the others that grew around it. I liked to envision them smiling at the thought of sharing the experience with a family member, a close friend, anyone, everyone. I felt humbled when I thought of the effort involved in preserving an area in its natural state and constructing a crude walkway across whatever terrain lay between point A and point B, just so a complete stranger might look at that same tilting stack of stone, crack a smile of their own, and think to themselves, "Yeah, that *is* a cool rock."

I have found endless pleasure in the minutiae of the forest. It has helped to remind me that a world exists outside of my own narrow scope of view, a world that is simultaneously both harmonious and dissonant, ordered and chaotic. Experiencing the wild has made me more aware of the wildness within my own head, the untamed nature of my thoughts, and the things I can do to reign them in. When the trail leads to solitude and silence, I have known the freedom to be myself more fully. At the end of a tiresome day, on a jaunt up a rocky hillside, when my body begs for me to be done, I have challenged myself to keep moving and learned that I am capable of even more than I think I am. The challenge, the beautiful and occasionally unforgiving setting, and close communion with strangers over shared difficulty have all helped me get outside of myself and consider the views of others more consistently, more thoroughly. I have been fortunate enough to experience the woods with so many different people, and I feel extremely proud and honored to call them my friends. Some of the closest relationships I have ever forged have grown stronger and more substantial in the forest through experiencing the negative and the positive: the shared discomfort of a particularly long and relentless climb, the allure and splendor of a vista on a sunny rock outcropping, spontaneous inclement weather, the kiss of mist off of a tumbling waterfall, blisters and sunburn and fatigued muscles and aching overused joints, a wildlife sighting or an unexpected wildflower or the presence of an interesting mushroom, a heavy pack, a light spirit. I have seen a casual walk in the woods break down perceived barriers to unite individuals from all walks of life around a common, simple shared experience.

Six years after our first experience with trail building, my wife and I embarked on a thru-hike (hiking a long-distance trail end to end) of the Appalachian Trail. When we crossed the Mason-Dixon Line and stepped into the Commonwealth of Pennsylvania, I was tired and ready to eat more food than I had in my pack, but I was also ecstatic. Pennsylvania might not have compared visually to the vast ridges and peaks of the Great Smoky Mountains in North Carolina and Tennessee, or to the abrupt granite rises and falls of the White Mountains in New Hampshire, or the Bigelow Preserve in Maine, but that did not matter. Viewpoints and expansive scenery, while always a joy to behold, had become somewhat commonplace in the weeks and months before. What mattered most to me in that moment was the trail immediately in front of me and the people immediately around me. I could not wait to share the state that I had called home for a decade with new friends, and to reconnect with family and old friends. I was equally as elated to visit places I had previously hiked to as I was to discover new parts of Pennsylvania. I was very much looking forward to reminiscing about the adventures I had already had in those woods, and I was thrilled to make new memories as well. When I passed close to Eckville and walked across the top of that minifridge-sized rock, and discovered that it still did not move six years after we had placed it, I felt profoundly happy. How many thousands of hikers had I unwittingly helped along the way, on whatever journey they might have found themselves on, however long or short?

I hope that the wild places in Pennsylvania come to mean as much to you as they do to me. This guide has been thrilling to research, taking me to amazing places I would never have visited otherwise, and entertaining me in ways I had not expected. My hope in writing this guide has been that you will find yourself in new places, in the company of new friends, enraptured by the natural beauty that occurs around all of us at all times, forming meaningful memories that will stick with you for years to come. These trails are an amazing resource for outdoor exploration, but they will only continue to exist as long as they are cared for and maintained. Please protect and respect these trails so that others may enjoy them as well, and, if you are able, consider volunteering with your local trail club. You will tend to find that the more time you spend outside, in any capacity, the more you will appreciate all it has to offer. Hike on!

MAP LEGEND

———	Described trail		≡≡≡	Interstate highway
– – – –	Important trail		═══	Secondary highway
◄———	Hike direction arrow		———	Minor highway, road, street
———	Perennial stream		– – – –	Unpaved road, trail
– – – –	Intermittent stream		⊢—⊢—⊢	Railroad
———	Major contour line		—··—	International border
———	Minor contour line		–·—··	State border
�	National/state park, wilderness		🅿	Parking area
	National/state forest, wildlife refuge		🚶	Trailhead
	Perennial body of water		•	City, town
	Intermittent body of water		⋐	Overlook, scenic view
	Swamp, marsh		Λ	Campground, campsite
	Wooded area		⋔	Shelter
			×	Mountain peak
			▪	Place of interest

Preparing for Your Hikes

There are few things you should take note of when using this guide. At the beginning of each entry, you will find a brief description and a breakdown of the statistics for the hike. The description provides a history of the area, the trail itself, or the persons associated with the trail, and it will hopefully enrich the hike with a bit of context. The statistical breakdown lists several pieces of information that will be useful to you on your journey.

The distance of each hike is measured to the nearest tenth of a mile, including any routes on the Mid State Trail, which traditionally is measured in kilometers. The hikes in this book have been broken down into four difficulty ratings: Easy, Moderate, Difficult, and Very Difficult. Next, an estimated hiking time will help you schedule your hike properly. This estimate is based on the length, elevation gain, and terrain of the hike, and it may vary based on how fast you like to walk and your physical fitness level. The hikes in this book are categorized either as out-and-back trips or as loops. Some loops have out-and-back portions, but as long as the described route forms a circuit somewhere along the way, it is classified as a loop. The last two lines in the breakdown deal with elevation. The total elevation gain is the summed quantity of all elevation gain throughout the hike. For example, if the trail goes over five separate hills that each climb 100 vertical feet, then the cumulative elevation gain is 5 x (100 feet) = 500 feet. Finally, the maximum elevation is the highest geographical point above sea level the route visits. This information can be useful when deciding where to hike, especially in the early spring, late fall, and winter, when the difference in weather between lower and higher elevations can be drastic.

This guide is by no means a comprehensive list of all the wonderful trails in the Keystone State. It is hoped that the hikes listed in this book will be jumping-off points for you to explore new places in Pennsylvania, both in your local wild spaces and in far off, distant forests.

WHAT TO BRING

Individuals new to hiking may have a difficult time figuring out what to bring with them into the woods. Many people have a tendency to either bring too much or too little. The truth is that both scenarios when taken to extremes can be either uncomfortable or flat-out dangerous. Seasoned outdoor enthusiasts will tell you that, as silly as it may seem, there is a learning curve when it comes to loading up your backpack for a trek into the wild. Indeed, the items necessary for a safe and enjoyable hike vary significantly based on a number of variables that include the length of the hike, the predicted weather conditions, the time of year, and personal preferences. Review the following for a basic breakdown of the gear that's needed for most hiking adventures.

Backpack: If you plan to walk for more than a mile, then you will need something to carry your gear. Almost any type of bag will do, but a sturdy, durable backpack is by far the most popular option. The volume of a backpack is measured either in liters or cubic inches. Daypacks range in volume anywhere from 15 liters (915 cubic inches) to 35 liters (2,135 cubic inches). Anything larger than that is usually intended for overnight trips into the woods. A wide variety of extra features are available on modern backpacks, including hydration bladder sleeves, water-resistant material, tear-resistant material, sternum straps, hip belts, and an abundance (or distinct lack) of pockets and compartments. Your preferences will ultimately dictate what you find necessary, but it is generally advisable to avoid drawstring-style backpacks. Their narrow shoulder strap cords do little to stabilize the load, and these packs can be very uncomfortable for more than a few minutes. In some cases, particularly on shorter hikes, a fanny pack or small messenger bag will do. Whatever option you choose, be sure to load everything into your pack before getting to the trailhead. This strategy is twofold in nature. First, it allows you to verify that everything fits inside your backpack. Second, it gives you a chance to make sure that the pack fits comfortably and does not hinder movement or negatively affect your balance.

Navigation: One of the most important things to remember when entering the wilderness is that it is your responsibility to know where you are located and where you are going. For this reason it is highly recommended that you carry a compass and procure a map for the area you will be visiting. This book features maps and detailed trail descriptions for each hike, so be sure to bring this guide along on your hike!

Electronic options exist, such as GPS devices and digital maps that can be downloaded to a phone. If you choose to carry these devices, make sure that they are charged and the maps are up-to-date, and always carry extra batteries. Additionally, if you plan to download a map to your phone, be sure to do so before leaving for the trailhead. Cell phone service in the woods is not reliable and is usually spotty at best. Most state parks offer free copies of the trail system within park boundaries, and many trailheads prominently display a map of the trail they mark. The maps that accompany each hike in this book are a quick and easy way to get started, but if you plan on altering the route, be sure to seek out a larger, more detailed map.

First Aid: It may be tempting to forgo carrying a first aid kit. You might think that it would never get used, and you may be right about that! But if an accident occurs, you will need to have the proper equipment to address the issue, at least temporarily. Most outfitters sell preassembled first aid kits, but you can easily make one at home out of items you probably already have in your medicine cabinet. A basic first aid kit should include adhesive bandages, gauze strips, adhesive medical tape (duct tape works in a pinch—and the tape could also be wrapped around a trekking pole or lighter if needed), antibiotic ointment, alcohol swabs, over-the-counter pain and allergy medication, tweezers, and nitrile gloves. Additionally, it is a good idea to bring along an extra dose of any prescription medications you take, just to be safe. All of these items should fit easily into a resealable plastic bag that can simply be stored in your backpack.

Headlamp or Flashlight: Almost

every avid hiker has a story of returning to the trailhead in the dark because they assumed they had enough time to finish before sunset. It is an easy mistake to make, and one that could potentially put you in serious danger. A reliable source of light can be a lifesaver when the sun begins to drop sooner than you expected, especially on uneven terrain or a sparsely marked trail. You probably already have a flashlight floating around your house that would easily fit into your backpack for just such an occasion. Another option is a headlamp, which can shine light on your surroundings without the use of your hands. In recent years, with the advent of LED technology, headlamps have become very affordable and compact, making them the most popular choice for those looking to explore the outdoors at night. Modern headlamps offer a number of features such as multiple light settings, low power warnings and battery indicators, USB charging, and red light filters, which can be used to keep from blinding your hiking partners. Whether you choose to carry a flashlight or a headlamp, make sure you carry extra batteries.

Knife: A knife can be useful for many things in the backcountry, and it should be a mainstay of your pack. A knife is useful for first aid purposes, meal preparation, impromptu gear repair, and making kindling. A simple folding-blade pocket knife will do in most cases, but you may want to consider a multi-tool or Swiss Army knife, which usually features a number of extra tools like a screwdriver, a bottle or can opener, a corkscrew, a small saw or file, and a pair of scissors or pliers.

Emergency Shelter: Another item that you will hopefully never have to use but should always carry is an emergency shelter. In the event that you get stranded or injured on the trail and cannot be rescued immediately, an emergency shelter will help protect you from the elements. This is especially important during shoulder seasons, when there is a wide fluctuation between high and low temperatures. An emergency shelter could be a bivy tent, a lightweight backpacking tarp, or an emergency Mylar space blanket. A space blanket is generally the most economical and lightweight option, because it folds down to the size of a deck of cards. Should you ever need to use it, your emergency shelter will help you retain body heat while protecting you from wind and precipitation.

Fire: Be sure your pack setup includes a lighter or waterproof matches stored in a plastic bag in case you need to start a fire. In an emergency, a fire can help keep you warm and dry, and can also be used to signal for help. You may want to carry some sort of kindling or firestarter to help get a fire going quickly as well. There is generally enough dry leaf litter in most places to start a fire, but commercial options exist as well. Common household items such as dryer lint, corn chips (a surprisingly flammable snack!), and cotton balls dipped in petroleum jelly can all be used to kick-start a fire. Even in damp conditions, birch bark and resinous pine cones work very well as fire starting implements. If you start a campfire, be sure that it is completely out before leaving the area. Douse the flames with water if possible (use dirt if water is scarce) and stir until the firepit is cool to the touch.

Sun Protection: Even on overcast days ultraviolet radiation from the sun can cause sunburn, and direct sunlight can cause sunburn in less than 15 minutes. The dense forest canopy does a great job of shading the vast majority of Pennsylvania's hiking trails during the summer, but protection from the sun is necessary at exposed overlooks or during the rest of the year when the leaves are off the trees. Consider using a sweat-resistant sunblock during the warmer months. When the weather is cooler, long pants, long sleeve shirts, a hat with a brim, and a bandanna draped over your neck all provide adequate protection from sunburn. Sunglasses are useful year-round, especially in the wintertime, when the reflected glare from the snow can be just as bright as the sun.

Clothes: Clothing choices vary widely from person to person, and they are usually based on personal preference. Some people get hot or cold quicker than others, and that can play a big part in what they choose to wear. Dressing in layers allows you to regulate your body temperature throughout the day, as the weather conditions and your body temperature change. In the summer a light shirt and shorts or a skirt are usually sufficient. In colder months consider wearing a base layer such as compression pants or long underwear, an insulating mid layer, and a jacket. You should also pack an extra coat and an additional layer or two in case you get cold. Weather can change quickly in the wilderness, so a rain jacket, windbreaker, or poncho should be carried year-round to protect you from precipitation and blustery winds. Synthetic or wool athletic clothing is usually preferred for outdoor activities. Both wool and synthetics help to

FAR-REACHING VIEWS AND ROCKY PENNSYLVANIA TREAD ON THE APPALACHIAN TRAIL

wick moisture away from the body. This keeps you cool and dry during the hike and comfortable and insulated during breaks. Wool socks are especially helpful in preventing blisters. Avoid cotton clothing, including denim, as much as possible because these materials do not insulate very well or dry very quickly.

Footwear: A wide variety of footwear can be worn on the trails of Pennsylvania. What you choose will largely be dictated by personal preference, but it is worth exploring the options that exist so that you can make the choice that best suits your needs. Trail-running shoes are usually lighter, more flexible, and faster-drying than traditional hiking boots, but generally they provide less cushioning and protection from pointy rocks and roots. High-top hiking boots provide the most ankle support and cushioning, and low-cut and mid-height hiking boots generally fall somewhere in between. Boots come in all types of materials, ranging from natural to synthetic, and they can be insulated and waterproof or extremely breathable. Lots of different rubber compounds are used to sole hiking boots, and each compound differs in its grip, flexibility, and durability. The easiest way to make a choice is to visit your local shoe store or outfitter and try on a few pairs of boots for yourself. Whichever option you choose, be aware that you will have to break in your boots before hiking in them to avoid getting hot spots and blisters. It is a good idea to wear your boots around for a few days before you hit the trail to get that process started.

Food: One of the best parts of a day spent walking in the woods is enjoying snacks. New hikers are sometimes surprised at how good food tastes outside in the fresh air after a long day of physical exertion. Pack foods that have a high calorie-to-weight ratio, such as nuts, dried fruit, jerky, granola and protein bars, peanut butter and jelly sandwiches, hard shelf-stable cheeses, hard-boiled eggs, and salami. Sugary candy like M&M's, Snickers, and Sour Patch Kids provide a quick boost of energy that are much needed on lazy afternoons. If you have a backpacking cookstove, you will be surprised at how good instant ramen noodles taste when paired with an outstanding view after a hard hike. A good rule of thumb is to carry two to three pounds of food for a full day of hiking. Whatever you choose to eat, bring a few extra snacks just in case your hike ends up taking longer than expected. When hiking in the winter, your body burns more calories warming the air you breathe, so err on the side of caution and carry a little more food than you are used to.

Water: Water will likely be the heaviest component of your pack, but it should not be overlooked. While everyone's hydration needs differ slightly, it is wise to budget roughly a liter of water for every two hours of hiking. On challenging hikes with lots of elevation gain, and during hot months, more water may be necessary. It is important to drink often, even when you do not feel thirsty, as it is very easy to become dehydrated while hiking. An easy way to cut down on pack weight is to carry water purification tablets or a small water filter like a Sawyer Squeeze or a Katadyn BeFree so that you can filter water as you need it. There is an abundance of streams running throughout Pennsylvania's wilderness, but you should always chemically treat or filter any water you drink from these refreshing sources. Untreated water, while tempting, has the potential to carry disease-causing pathogens. Drinking untreated water can make for a very unpleasant experience in a few days or weeks.

Miscellaneous: Many people like to bring a nonessential item or two along with them, depending on the length and intensity of the hike. Such items may include trekking poles or a walking stick to assist in water crossings and steep ascents and descents; a small paperback novel; a hammock or folding chair; a camera; binoculars; a notebook or journal; a small musical instrument like a harmonica, recorder, or kazoo; and a hip flask.

SAFETY

When on the trail, your safety and the safety of your hiking partners should be the highest priority. Stay on the trail, do not cross protective barriers, and keep away from the edge of steep drop-offs and waterfalls, especially in wet or slippery conditions. If you get lost, stay where you are. For the most part, staying safe in the wilderness is fairly straightforward. Here are a few tips for staying safe off trail, as it pertains to your hike.

• Plan ahead. Before driving to the trailhead look up the nearest town and hospital and write down any pertinent phone numbers. Cell phone service near many trailheads is unreliable, so this information is often difficult or impossible to look up on the go. On your way to the trailhead, make a note of nearby restaurants, grocery stores, and gas stations. Many trailheads in Pennsylvania are very remote, so make sure your vehicle is adequately fueled up.
• Establish a safety contact. Leave your plans with a friend or family member.

Be sure to give them a detailed overview of where you plan to hike, when you are leaving, what trails you will be on, and most important, when you plan to return, clearly communicating a cutoff time. Check in with your safety contact as soon as you are able to after you finish your hike. If you become incapacitated, lost, or stranded while on your hike and are unable to connect with your safety contact by the established cutoff time, this will alert them to contact the proper authorities.
• Bring your cell phone with you, but be mindful of the battery. Even if cell phone service is too weak to place a call, you may be able to shoot off a text message with your location requesting help. Be aware of your phone's charge though. Without a sufficient charge, your phone will be useless.

WILDLIFE

Pennsylvania is home to an amazing array of wildlife. With 66 native mammals, 39 native reptiles, 38 native amphibians, more than 400 wild bird species, and an abundance of fish, insects, arachnids, crustaceans, mollusks, and worms, the forests and streams of the Keystone State are teeming with life. Despite the plethora of creatures that reside in the woods, catching a glimpse of these forest dwellers is often easier said than done. The truth is that, in most instances, wildlife chooses not to interact with humans as a means of self-preservation. If, however, you remain patient, persistent, quiet, and still, the bolder of these creatures may choose to reveal themselves to you. Most of the woodland animals in Pennsylvania pose very little threat to humans, but there are a few things to keep in mind when you have an animal encounter.

- Black bears are the only bears that reside in Pennsylvania. Although their population is relatively dense throughout the state, seeing these omnivores is actually a fairly rare occurrence. Seeing a bear is always an exhilarating experience. Most of the time a bear will instinctively run away from humans, but occasionally a bear will act aggressive or unafraid of humans if they are trying to protect their young or have been fed by people in the past. Never feed a bear! Feeding a bear can condition it to equate humans with food. If you encounter a bear that does not seem afraid of you, do not run away. Bears may seem slow and clumsy, but these powerful animals can run up to 35 miles per hour and climb trees with ease. Running may trigger their predatory instinct. Instead, stand your ground and make loud noises. Yell at the bear, clack your trekking poles together, throw rocks and sticks at it, and slowly back away. Black bear attacks are extremely rare, but if the bear attacks, you should fight back with anything you may have.
- Of the 21 species of snakes that call Pennsylvania home, only 3 of them are venomous. The timber rattlesnake and the northern copperhead are most commonly encountered, having a wide distribution throughout the state. The massasauga rattlesnake is much more rare and is found only in the western part of the state, favoring wetlands and grassy fields. The timber rattlesnake and the northern copperhead are both fond of basking on rocky outcroppings and sunny sections of trail. Be mindful of where you step and sit. All snakes are docile unless provoked or startled, favoring to avoid humans than to be around them. If you encounter a snake, give it a wide berth and keep moving. Under no circumstances should you pick up a snake. Most snake bites occur when people try to handle these creatures. Furthermore, do not kill any snakes, as they play an important part in the control of rodents that spread disease and parasites.
- Ticks are one of the parasites that snakes help to keep in check. These tiny arachnids, some as small as a poppy seed, embed themselves into a host and feed on their blood. They can carry diseases such as Lyme disease and Rocky Mountain spotted fever, and cause other serious health problems. The best way to avoid these crawling pests is to check yourself often, both while hiking and after getting back to the trailhead. Stay on the trail as much as possible, and thoroughly check your shoes, socks, and pant legs if you must go off trail or walk through grassy areas. Tucking the bottom of your pants into your socks is a good way to keep ticks from crawling up your bare leg, and wearing light-colored clothing can make spotting crawling ticks easier. Ticks can use their hooklike legs to grab on to hair or fabrics, so wash your clothes and take a shower as soon as you get home, paying close attention to your hairline, armpits, crotch, and anywhere clothing fits snugly against your body, such as the top of your socks and your waistband. If you find a tick embedded in your skin, remove it with a pair of tweezers or a tick key as soon as possible.

Grab it by the head, or as close to the head as possible, and pull straight back. Do not twist the tick or pull it by the abdomen or apply petroleum jelly, dish soap, rubbing alcohol, or nail polish remover to it. And do not attempt to burn it off with a lighter or match. All of these latter methods have the potential to cause the tick to regurgitate into the bite and expose you to any pathogens it carries, or they could leave a piece of the tick behind in your skin. If you develop a fever or become sick after being bitten by a tick, visit your physician right away. Indications of Lyme disease include flu-like symptoms, joint pain, and sometimes a rash around the bite area that is often described as looking like a bull's-eye.

- If you encounter any animal that tries to approach you or seems aggressive, it is best to leave it alone and contact the authorities. While very rare, overly aggressive animals may be infected with rabies. Any mammal can carry rabies. Foxes, bobcats, raccoons, skunks, possums, bats, and coyotes are all common carriers. The likelihood of encountering a rabid animal is very low. Nonetheless, if you are bitten by a wild animal, visit the nearest hospital immediately.

DOGS

Most trail systems in Pennsylvania are very dog-friendly, as long as your dog can handle rocky terrain. If you choose to bring your four-legged friend with you on your hike, state law requires your dog to be attended and on a leash at all times. This is for the safety of your dog, other people, and the native wildlife. Additionally, it should be common sense to clean up after your dog. Many trailheads have trash cans where you can dispose of waste, but it is a good idea to keep a spare plastic bag in your pack or your car in the event none are available.

With the exception of the hike at Hawk Mountain Sanctuary, dogs are permitted on all the trails listed in this book.

WEATHER

The weather patterns in Pennsylvania are generally stable and consistent from season to season, but bear in mind that the weather can still change quickly. Check the weather forecast before you hit the trail and plan accordingly. Be prepared to turn around if you encounter inclement weather. As a rule of thumb, the temperature drops about 3 degrees for every 1,000 feet of elevation gain. The wind is often much stronger at higher elevations, which can exacerbate the drop in temperature. The Laurel Highlands and the Pocono and Allegheny Plateaus often receive much more snow in the winter, due to their elevation.

ETIQUETTE

The core of backcountry etiquette is centered on being thoughtful toward others. This means taking into consideration your impact on the trails and understanding that your actions can affect the experience of those visiting in the future. Be courteous to other hikers you meet on the trail. People are generally very friendly on the trail, and it is not uncommon to exchange a genial greeting or engage in conversation. Stay on the trail to avoid creating shortcuts and herd paths. Make yourself known and ask to pass slower hikers instead of going off trail to do so. On narrow trails, hikers going uphill have the right of way. Be aware of other trail users such as bicyclists and horse riders where applicable. Bicyclists should yield to hikers and horses, and hikers yield to horses. With the exception of emergencies, it is usually not appropriate to make phone calls in the forest, but if you must do so be courteous to anyone around and leave the area before answering the phone. Be sure to pack out any trash that you generate on the trail, such as candy and food wrappers. Consider carrying a plastic grocery bag in your backpack and using it to carry out any trash left by others. This practice requires very little effort but can dramatically transform a busy trail system, and it is a great habit to get into. Pack it in, pack it out!

WINTER

Hiking in the winter months can be an exhilarating experience. The lack of biting insects, less crowded trails, brisk air, and otherwise unseen views through the barren trees all make exploring the woods in winter an attractive prospect. The relative lack of high elevation in Pennsylvania lends itself to winter hiking, but extra care should be taken during the colder months to ensure your safety and well-being. Always make sure you have enough clothing for the weather conditions, including a warm hat and gloves. Hand and toe warmers can significantly improve your comfort level as well, as can a thermos of hot cocoa. Additionally, snowy and icy trail conditions can be difficult to traverse, and hiking might take longer than at other times of the year. Be aware of the time, as the sun sets much earlier in the winter months. Slip-on traction devices easily fit inside any pack and should be used when the conditions are icy. Snowshoes and hiking poles may be necessary during snowy winters as well. Many forest roads are not maintained in the wintertime, and getting to the trailhead may be impossible if there has been heavy snowfall recently. Consider sticking to previously hiked trails that you are already familiar with in the winter instead of exploring new areas.

LEAVE NO TRACE

The Leave No Trace Seven Principles were developed to ensure a sustainable, fulfilling, inclusive experience for all visitors to public lands. Many of the wild spaces cherished by outdoor enthusiasts throughout the nation reside on public lands. These places have intrinsic value, and they are often quite fragile, and they can very easily deteriorate from neglect and lack of respect. Therefore, these guidelines should be followed whenever possible for the safety of yourself and others, the continued preservation of native flora and fauna, and the reduction of negative impact on the land, such as spreading invasive species, erosion, and soil degradation. Remember, take nothing but photographs, leave nothing but footprints.

THE LEAVE NO TRACE SEVEN PRINCIPLES

1. Plan ahead and prepare
2. Travel and camp on durable surfaces
3. Dispose of waste properly
4. Leave what you find
5. Minimize campfire impacts
6. Respect wildlife
7. Be considerate of other visitors

I.

WESTERN PENNSYLVANIA

1

McConnells Mill State Park

DISTANCE: 7.1 miles

DIFFICULTY: Difficult

HIKING TIME: 3.5 hours

TYPE: Loop

TOTAL ELEVATION GAIN: 967'

MAXIMUM ELEVATION: 1,172'

The gristmill on Slippery Rock Creek was originally opened in 1852 by Daniel Kennedy, and it was later purchased by Thomas McConnell in 1875. McConnell made significant upgrades to the processing equipment that the mill used, replacing—among other things—the grindstones with roller mills, making it one of the first mills in the country to use the technology. For the next 50 years the mill processed corn, oats, and wheat. It ultimately closed down in 1928. In 1946 the mill was acquired by the Western Pennsylvania Conservancy, who worked to transfer the land to the Commonwealth of Pennsylvania. McConnells Mill State Park officially opened a little over a decade later in 1957, boasting a rich industrial and agricultural past that can still be experienced today; the mill is open to the public for limited hours throughout the year.

Aside from historical remnants, there is much to enjoy at McConnells Mill State Park. The park is a popular destination for paddlers, and it is common to see kayakers run the rapids that make up Slippery Rock Creek. The creek gorge also offers rock climbing and plenty of hiking on the steep canyon walls. The hike described here forms a narrow loop through the gorge, and it features a long out-and-back leg that visits picturesque Walnut Flats via the Slippery Rock Gorge Trail. The route passes many open rocky areas on both sides of Slippery Rock Creek, which make great waypoints, should you wish to stop and enjoy the sound of the rushing waters. It is worth noting that the Slippery Rock Gorge Trail is part of the North Country Trail, a National Scenic Trail that, when completed, will stretch more than 4,600 miles from Vermont to North Dakota.

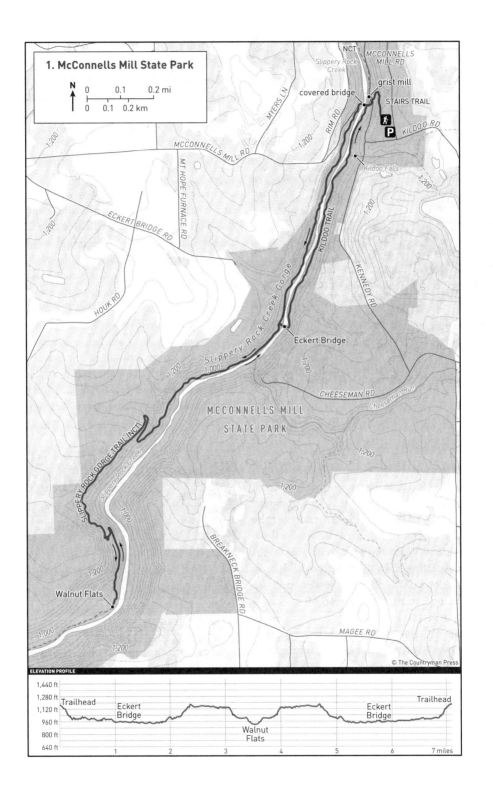

1. McConnells Mill State Park

THE COVERED BRIDGE AT McCONNELLS MILL STATE PARK

1.1 miles. The parking area will be on the right. Look for a gravel lot next to a large bathroom building and picnic tables.

GPS Shortcut: Search for "Kildoo Parking Lot" in Google Maps and your GPS will direct you to the trailhead.

THE HIKE

From the Kildoo parking area, head northwest past the restroom building and approach the edge of the canyon. Begin walking on the wide gravel tread of the Stairs Trail leading to the mill. The Stairs Trail heads steadily downhill, switchbacking on uniform stone steps and passing some rock ledges that protrude from the cliff side. The lively flow of Slippery Rock Creek lies at the bottom of the gorge, and along its eastern shore, just south of a dam spanning the creek, sits the old grist mill. Slippery Rock Creek powers the grist mill, which

GETTING THERE

The park is located north of Pittsburgh and about 20 miles south of I-80. From Pittsburgh, follow I-79 N and take exit 96 toward Portersville/Prospect. At the end of the ramp, turn left and follow PA 488 W for 0.5 mile, then turn right onto US 19 N. In 1.6 miles, turn left onto Kildoo Road. Follow Kildoo Road for 1.1 miles and turn right onto McConnells Mill Road. The parking area will be on the left immediately. Look for a large gravel lot with a bathroom building and picnic tables.

From the east, follow I-80 W and take exit 19A, merging onto I-79 S toward Pittsburgh. Follow I-79 for 17.7 miles and take exit 99 toward New Castle. Turn left at the end of the ramp and drive US 422 W for 1.8 miles. Turn left onto McConnells Mill Road, continuing for another

AN ANTIQUATED MILLSTONE ONCE USED BY THE GRIST MILL

THE GRIST MILL BESIDE SLIPPERY ROCK CREEK

still operates over the summer months. It is possible to tour the historic mill, but it is recommended that reservations be made in advance.

At the mill, turn to the left and follow a wide road grade, crossing Slippery Rock Creek on the covered bridge. The bridge, a National Historic Landmark, dates from 1874 and is one of two in Lawrence County. After crossing the bridge, walk up the road about 100 feet. Turn to the left to leave the road grade and begin following the blue and yellow blazes on the western half of the Kildoo Trail, part of the North Country Trail system. Follow the narrow riverside tread of these trails on varied rolling terrain, occasionally climbing short flights of rustic stone steps. As you continue downstream you will pass a large quantity of lichen-covered boulders as well as a few benches placed at random intervals. The trail is rocky and a bit cumbersome to navigate, but the surging waters of the creek with their rocky rapids and playful eddies are a pleasure to walk beside.

Arrive at a dilapidated road grade and concrete Eckert Bridge 1.5 miles after leaving the parking area. The Kildoo Trail turns to the left here and crosses Slippery Rock Creek on the bridge. If you wish to skip the visit to Walnut Flats, stay on the Kildoo Trail and follow it back to the grist mill. This will shorten the hike by a hefty 4.2 miles. To continue to Walnut Flats stay on the western side of the creek and continue following the blue and yellow blazes of the North Country Trail, which now shares its tread with the Slippery Rock Gorge Trail. This is the start of the out-and-back portion of the hike.

The Slippery Rock Gorge Trail continues along the creek, following terrain as rugged as the Kildoo Trail for another 0.4 mile. Cross a wooden footbridge over a small seasonal run at this point. After crossing the small bridge the terrain becomes slightly narrower, and the trail begins a long, moderately steep ascent for about 0.7 mile, crossing a few seasonal streams that drain from

ALONG THE KILDOO TRAIL

you can catch partial views of the other side of the canyon through the trees.

Begin descending toward the creek at mile 3.1, dropping aggressively on switchbacks and periodic log steps that give way to short rolling ups and downs as you reenter the gorge. You will arrive at a sign marking Walnut Flats a half mile later, shortly after the 3.6-mile marker. Walnut Flats is the lowest point in the Slippery Rock Creek Gorge, an alluvial floodplain located at a lazy bend in the creek. While not an attraction that draws large crowds, Walnut Flats is a great place to take a break, have a snack, watch the flowing water, and enjoy some solitude. A little exploration in this area will reveal subtle features to entertain and amuse amateur geologists. The

the canyon walls into Slippery Rock Creek below. When they are flowing, these water crossings are easily navigable thanks to some well-placed stepping stones.

At the 2.6-mile marker, after a steady climb and a few short switchbacks high above the creek, the North Country Trail mostly levels out. The trail here is nearer to the top of the gorge than the bottom, and follows a 0.5-mile-long stretch of easy, well-graded terrain that is almost entirely devoid of rocks and roots. Catch your breath along this segment of the hike and enjoy the beautiful scenery. This elevated course through the gorge is particularly dramatic in the fall, when the reds, yellows, and oranges of the changing foliage set the gorge on fire. When the leaves are mostly off the trees

WALNUT FLATS ON THE NORTH COUNTRY TRAIL

THE ROCKY BANK OF SLIPPERY ROCK CREEK

North Country Trail follows the Slippery Rock Gorge Trail toward Hells Hollow for another 4.1 miles before continuing farther westward. Because Hells Hollow is several miles from where you parked your vehicle, turn around when you are finished enjoying Walnut Flats and retrace your footsteps to head back to Eckert Bridge.

When you return to Eckert Bridge just after mile marker 5.7, turn right and follow the bridge across the creek. On the other side of the creek, turn left and rejoin the Kildoo Trail. You will immediately head up a short flight of wooden steps and enter the woods on the eastern side of the creek. Similar to the western side of Kildoo Trail, the terrain on the eastern side is rough and oftentimes uneven, featuring many rocky clearings along the water's edge and accentuated by the presence of massive boulders farther up the wooded canyon wall. Continue for 0.9 mile after crossing Slippery Rock Creek and approach a short footbridge. On the other side of the bridge you will arrive at Kildoo Falls, located on the right side of the trail. The small but scenic falls is a short distance off the trail and is well worth visiting, but it can be very slippery so be extremely careful.

After the boardwalk near the falls, the tread of the trail becomes slightly easier, shifting from rocks and roots to a lumpy, badly eroded asphalt path. In 0.2 mile you arrive at the covered bridge and grist mill. From here, turn left and head back up the Stairs Trail to reach the top of the gorge and return to your vehicle.

Frick Park
Falls Loop

DISTANCE: 2.4 miles	
DIFFICULTY: Easy	
HIKING TIME: 1.5 hours	
TYPE: Loop	
TOTAL ELEVATION GAIN: 370'	
MAXIMUM ELEVATION: 1,115'	

The largest of Pittsburgh's parks, Frick Park was a parting gift to the city by Henry Clay Frick. Frick was a successful businessman and a prominent figure in the coke and steel manufacturing industries. Upon his death in 1919, Frick bequeathed 155 acres of land to the city of Pittsburgh for use as a public park as well as setting up a trust fund to be used to maintain the land. Since then the park has grown in size significantly, spreading to a robust 644 acres. Frick Park's elaborate trail system provides a rustic getaway within the surrounding metropolis and is popular with hikers, runners, cyclists, and birdwatchers.

Described here is a short hike that follows an easy course through Frick Park. The trails pass through stately forest on well-defined footpaths, and they are just secluded enough that you may forget you are in the heart of the largest city in western Pennsylvania. The hike starts near the Frick Environmental Center, which houses classrooms and restroom facilities, and hosts a number of events throughout the year. Due to the sprawling trail system, there are many options to shorten or lengthen this hike. As such, picking up a trail map from the Frick Environmental Center is encouraged.

GETTING THERE

The hike begins near the Frick Environmental Center on Beechwood Boulevard, about 6 miles east of downtown Pittsburgh. From the west, follow I-376 E and take exit 74 toward Squirrel Hill/Homestead, merging onto Beechwood Boulevard at the end of the ramp. Continue for 0.2 mile, then turn left onto Monitor Street. In 0.4 mile turn left, once again joining Beechwood Boulevard. Follow Beechwood Boulevard for

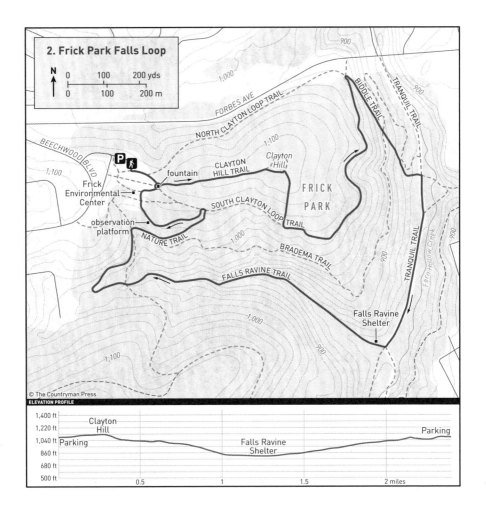

2. Frick Park Falls Loop

1.1 miles, to reach the park entrance on the right side of the road. Park in the small lot next to the Frick Environmental Center, under a large awning.

From the east, navigate toward Pittsburgh, then follow I-376 W and take exit 77 toward Edgewood/Swissvale. At the end of the ramp, turn right onto S Braddock Avenue, continuing for 0.9 mile. Turn left onto Forbes Avenue. Follow Forbes Avenue for 0.8 mile, then turn left onto S Dallas Avenue. Turn left again, immediately after turning onto S Dallas Avenue, to join Beechwood Boulevard. In 0.2 mile, you will reach Frick

Park on the left side of the road. Park in the small lot next to the Frick Environmental Center, under a large awning.

GPS Shortcut: In Google Maps set your destination as "Frick Park Beechwood Gate Entrance." The hike begins at the nearby parking lot.

THE HIKE

From the parking lot, head southsoutheast on the sidewalk, passing a service and utility barn with a large public bathroom on your left. Approach the fountain and at the end of the pavement

DESCENDING ON THE BIDDLE TRAIL

veer slightly to the left onto the Clayton Hill Trail, which is marked with old, faded orange blazes. The smooth, wide, very gradually ascending trail passes through a field area that is a great place to birdwatch. Leaving the field and entering the woods, you will notice a few cleared outdoor classroom areas on the left side of the trail, complete with wooden benches arranged in a circle. This, again, is another great place to stop and watch the many birds that make use of the park.

After roughly 0.3 mile, the Clayton Hill Trail splits and begins a short loop portion that circles the top of Clayton Hill. Turning left will put you on the loop clockwise and lengthens the hike a negligible amount. Follow the trail as it bends to the right and begin descending moderately on a gently winding singletrack. The narrow tread of this spur ends at the junction with the wide South Clayton Loop Trail. Turn left here and continue for 0.4 mile, descending around the mass of Clayton Hill on easy tread. Just before approaching the Forbes Avenue access area make a sharp right onto the Biddle Trail. The Biddle Trail continues to drop in elevation, gradually descending into Fern Hollow on a broad dirt pathway. As you make your way downhill, you will notice a few stone crib walls built into the hillside, and in 0.2 mile you pass the narrower Bradema Trail, which runs perpendicular to the Biddle Trail.

In another 0.1 mile the Biddle Trail intersects with the Tranquil Trail. Turn right, leaving the Biddle Trail, and begin following the flat dirt tread of the Tranquil Trail, which runs beside lazy Fern Hollow Creek, passing a few picnic tables, benches, and some strikingly large trees. In 0.3 mile, in an open grassy clearing, the Tranquil Trail meets with the Falls Ravine Trail. Turn right and

THE FALLS RAVINE TRAIL

begin heading uphill on the gravel tread of the Falls Ravine Trail, passing the crumbling remains of the Falls Ravine Shelter to the right.

As the name implies, the Falls Ravine Trail follows the curves of the gorge in between Clayton Hill to the north and Riverview Hill to the south. It ascends on a spacious gravel path, and a plethora of interesting rock outcroppings appear on either side of the trail amidst the maples and oaks that make up the forest. There is a small stream that runs in the ravine, fed by a wetland located near the Frick Environmental Center. At several points, a series of wooden footbridges crosses over the stream, whose meager flow softly tumbles downhill, forming diminutive cascading falls. Along with the footbridges, the trail features several fenced-in areas replete with benches for enjoying the deep ravine. The pleasant scenery and steep wooded hills on either side of the trail make this portion of the hike feel far more secluded than it actually is.

After 0.4 mile of climbing uphill through the ravine, you will reach a junction with the Riverview Extension Trail on the left. Continue straight to stay on the Falls Ravine Trail, turning to the right and heading more steeply uphill a short distance later. From the junction, a spur of the Falls Ravine Trail turns to the right and heads more directly uphill toward the Frick Environmental Center, so take whichever path you wish. In approximately 0.2 mile, you will come to a junction with the Nature Trail on the right side of the trail. Continuing on the Falls Ravine Trail will lead you back toward the parking area. If you want to keep going, turn to the right and follow the Nature Trail for 0.2 mile, passing by the Bradema Trail on the right and reconnecting with the South Clayton Loop Trail shortly thereafter.

Turn left on the South Clayton Loop Trail, then make another left onto the Woodland Trail almost immediately. Following the Woodland Trail for a short distance will lead you to a wooden observation platform among the trees. This is an excellent place to stop and enjoy the playful birds and the peaceful scenery, especially when the fall foliage is near its peak.

When you are finished, head toward the Frick Environmental Center and make your way past the fountain to arrive back at your vehicle.

Rachel Carson Trail Harrison Hills Loop

DISTANCE: 5.3 miles	
DIFFICULTY: Moderate	
HIKING TIME: 2.5 hours	
TYPE: Loop	
TOTAL ELEVATION GAIN: 715'	
MAXIMUM ELEVATION: 1,205'	

Rachel Carson was born in 1907 in the town of Springdale, northeast of Pittsburgh. In 1936, she became the second woman to be hired by the U.S. Bureau of Fisheries, working as an aquatic biologist for the next twelve years. Carson is best known, however, for her conservation work and nature writings, particularly her book *Silent Spring,* which was published in 1962. The book detailed the effect that synthetic pesticides had on the environment, and it played a large part in the banning of DDT and helped to ignite the environmental movement. Carson passed away in 1964, two years after *Silent Spring* was published, but she continues to be honored even now. Protected conservation areas have been named in her honor in Maine, Maryland, and South Carolina. In Pennsylvania, the Rachel Carson Trail celebrates her life and her work.

The Rachel Carson Trail is a point-to-point hiking trail north of Pittsburgh that stretches nearly 36 miles, from North Park to Harrison Hills Park. The trail passes through a variety of different environments and terrains, and it features many ascents and descents along the way. The Rachel Carson Trail is open only for day use pedestrian traffic. The hike detailed here utilizes a few trails in Harrison Hills Park and the Rachel Carson Trail to form a loop that passes through woodland, meadows, and swamps. The easternmost part of the circuit features drawn-out views of the Allegheny River from the top of a tall wooded bluff.

GETTING THERE

From the west, follow PA 28 N and take exit 16 toward Freeport/Millerstown. At the end of the ramp turn right onto Bakerstown Road. Drive for 0.6 mile. At

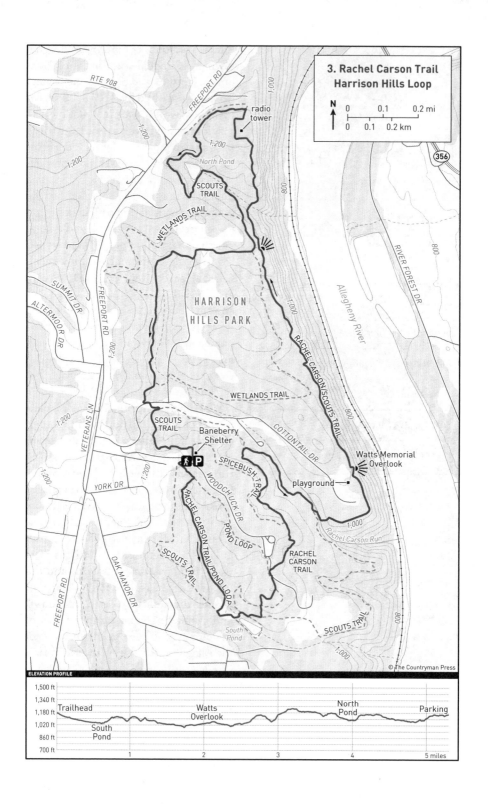

3. Rachel Carson Trail Harrison Hills Loop

RTE 908
FREEPORT RD
1,000
356
radio tower
1,200
North Pond
SCOUTS TRAIL
WETLANDS TRAIL
808
River Forest Dr
800
HARRISON HILLS PARK
SUMMIT DR
ALTERMOOR DR
FREEPORT RD
1,000
Allegheny River
RACHEL CARSON/SCOUTS TRAIL
800
WETLANDS TRAIL
1,200
VETERANS LN
SCOUTS TRAIL
Baneberry Shelter
COTTONTAIL DR
Watts Memorial Overlook
1,200
YORK DR
1,200
P
SPICEBUSH TRAIL
WOODCHUCK DR
POND LOOP
playground
1,000
OAK MANOR DR
FREEPORT RD
RACHEL CARSON TRAIL/POND LOOP
SCOUTS TRAIL
RACHEL CARSON TRAIL
Rachel Carson Run
South Pond
SCOUTS TRAIL
800
1,000
© The Countryman Press

ELEVATION PROFILE

1,500 ft
1,340 ft
1,180 ft
1,020 ft
860 ft
700 ft

Trailhead
South Pond
Watts Overlook
North Pond
Parking

1   2   3   4   5 miles

the light, turn right onto Freeport Road. In 0.9 mile, turn left and enter Harrison Hills Park on Sportsman Park Drive. The road splits shortly after entering the park. Stay right toward "South Attractions" at the split, and drive 0.3 mile to reach the parking area next to the Baneberry shelter, which has plentiful parking on either side of the road.

From the east, follow I-76 W and take exit 146 toward I-99. At the end of the ramp, turn left onto US 220 BUS N, then turn left in 0.3 mile, following signs for I-99 N. Drive I-99 N for 28.2 miles, then take exit 28 toward Ebensburg. Merge onto US 22 W and follow it for 15.9 miles. Take the Ebensburg/ Loretto exit and keep right at the end of the ramp to merge onto Rowena Drive. In 0.6 mile, Rowena Drive merges with E High Street. Follow the road for another 0.6 mile and veer right to merge onto US 422 W. Follow the route for 54.8 miles, then take the exit for PA 28 S toward Pittsburgh. Continue on PA 28 S for 13.3 miles, then take exit 16 toward Millerstown. Turn left at the end of the ramp and drive for 0.7 mile. At the light, turn right onto Freeport Road. In 0.9 mile, turn left and enter Harrison Hills Park on Sportsman Park Drive. The road splits shortly after entering the park. Stay right toward "South Attractions" at the split, and drive 0.3 mile to reach the parking area next to the Baneberry shelter, which has plentiful parking on either side of the road.

GPS Shortcut: Type "Baneberry Shelter, Harrison Hills Park" into Google Maps and your GPS will navigate you to the trailhead.

THE HIKE

From the parking area near Baneberry shelter, head into the woods on the

PEERING OVER THE EDGE OF THE ARCHING BRIDGE

red-blazed Scouts Trail. Immediately after entering the woods turn right and begin following the yellow blazes of the Rachel Carson Trail. In a short distance, the Rachel Carson Trail turns to the right, sharing tread with the orange-blazed Pond Loop as it skirts the edge of a grassy picnic and playground area. The trail meanders, generally trending downhill on terrain devoid of roots and rocks, passing by a swampy wetland area to the left. After 0.4 mile you momentarily emerge from the tree cover, entering a shrubby clearing that offers an excellent view of a small pond. The red-blazed Scouts Trail joins the Rachel Carson Trail, briefly sharing tread with the yellow and orange blazes here.

Follow the edge of the field, bending to the left to approach the pond

ON THE RACHEL CARSON TRAIL

for 0.5 mile, briefly sharing tread with the white-blazed Spicebush Trail. Pay attention to which way the blazes point; as the trail turns very often. At 1.3 miles, as the trail descends to a picnic area, the white blazes of the Spicebush Trail continue straight on and to the left, leaving the tread of the Rachel Carson Trail. Turn right at this point to stay on the Rachel Carson Trail as the footpath flattens and follows the flow of Rachel Carson Run to the left.

In 0.3 mile after leaving the Spicebush Trail, the Rachel Carson Trail crosses the run on an arching wooden footbridge and begins heading uphill to surmount a short hill, rejoining the Scouts Trail in the process. Continuing along this shared tread, you will skirt yet another picnic area. Follow the curve of the stream in the ravine below as the Allegheny River comes into view through the trees straight ahead. Turn to the left at the edge of the steep drop-off and follow the top of the bluff. Just before the 2-mile mark, you will approach a small playground. Veer right to continue behind it on a short paved path and along a chain link fence, arriving at the Watts Memorial Overlook, which offers an excellent view of the Allegheny River 400 feet below.

After enjoying the view, continue on the Rachel Carson and Scouts Trails, rambling along the cliff above the river on rolling terrain. From the wide tread on top of this bluff, another very pretty view can be seen, looking northward toward Freeport. In 0.5 mile, the trail begins a steady, moderate ascent. After climbing consistently for 0.2 mile, the trail briefly levels out before beginning a steep descent down the other side of the rounded shoulder, following a significantly narrower trail that is cut into

alongside the wetland. A short boardwalk leads over a portion of the marsh, featuring a bench should you wish to stop and enjoy the view, as well as a bird blind for wildlife viewing. After crossing the boardwalk, turn to the right and continue to follow the yellow blazes. A short distance later, the Rachel Carson Trail bends to the left and begins ascending moderately. The Pond Loop leaves the Rachel Carson Trail just after the boardwalk, and the Scouts Trail breaks away 0.1 mile after that. Continue to follow the yellow blazes of the Rachel Carson Trail.

In about 0.3 mile, cross a paved park road and enter the woods on the other side. The yellow blazes continue on short, abrupt ascents and descents that bend and curve through the hills

THE SWAMPY EDGE OF SOUTH POND

the side of the hill. Continue to follow the red- and yellow-blazed trails as they undulate above the Allegheny River.

After 3 miles of hiking, the Rachel Carson and Scouts Trails approach a fenced-off radio tower. Turn to the left and take the trail as it follows the fence clockwise all the way around the radio tower, eventually meeting with a gravel access road to the tower. Turn left and make your way down the access road. Just before a bend in the road, at mile marker 3.2, turn left off the road and follow the Scouts Trail, leaving the yellow-blazed Rachel Carson Trail behind.

Make your way along the winding Scouts Trail through shrubby forest for 0.9 mile, passing a small pond. Follow the flow of the stream it feeds before heading uphill very close to the tread of a sidehill stretch of the Rachel Carson Trail you had followed along the bluff earlier. From here, the green-blazed Wetlands Trail joins and follows the Scouts Trail for a short distance, separating less than 0.1 mile later. The Wetlands Trail continues straight on, while the Scouts Trail turns to the right. Follow the Scouts Trail, heading away from the edge of the cliff. The red blazes follow a dirt road through a field, passing a tall chimney swift birdhouse and entering the woods shortly thereafter.

At 4.5 miles, after crossing a handful

THE FOOTBRIDGE OVER RACHEL CARSON RUN

LOOKING NORTHEAST OVER THE ALLEGHENY RIVER

of small footbridges over swampy drainage runs, the Scouts Trail rejoins the Wetlands Trail and resumes its lazy, rolling course. The Wetlands Trail, again, leaves the Scouts Trail in 0.3 mile. Continue along the Scouts Trail, climbing steeply for a short distance. Cross a paved park road and resume the steady climb on the other side. The white-blazed Spicebush Trail rejoins the Scouts Trail after a sharp switchback and continues climbing for a short distance before leveling off significantly as the tread bends to the left.

In roughly 0.3 mile, the Spicebush Trail and the Scouts Trail approach the Baneberry shelter and picnic area and split once more. The Spicebush Trail turns to the left and the Scouts Trail bends to the right. Follow the Scouts Trail and head toward the pavilion to arrive back at your vehicle.

Oil Creek State Park

DISTANCE: 8 miles	
DIFFICULTY: Difficult	
HIKING TIME: 4 hours	
TYPE: Loop	
TOTAL ELEVATION GAIN: 1,090'	
MAXIMUM ELEVATION: 1,589'	

Located in northwestern Pennsylvania, Oil Creek State Park is a treasure trove of industrial history. The elongated park follows the serpentine north-to-south flow of Oil Creek in between Titusville and Oil City. The park sits beside what was once Drake Well, the first commercially successful oil well in the state of Pennsylvania. As such, the land the park now occupies is littered with remnants from its oil-drilling days, in the form of both dilapidated buildings and rusty metal refuse, as well as the physical scars that mar the land. The glory days of the oil industry in Pennsylvania were fairly short-lived, although a few energy companies still operate in the area. Oil Creek State Park was pieced together by the Civilian Conservation Corps in an effort to reclaim the forest and to allow it to bounce back from the harsh effects of industrial development.

The hike described here walks a circuit that meanders on both sides of Oil Creek. The majority of the hike follows Gerard Hiking Trail, a 36-mile loop that wanders the park. Two Adirondack-style shelters are located on the Gerard Hiking Trail, making it a great backpacking excursion for those seeking an overnight wilderness experience. (Contact the park office for more information on this loop.) On the eastern side of the creek, an optional stretch of trail leads to a pleasing, scenic viewpoint. Farther up the trail is a gushing waterfall that can be observed in a deep ravine. Featuring flourishing forest, rushing streams, and historical ruins, there is much to see and do in the woods along Oil Creek.

GETTING THERE

The parking lot is located north of Pittsburgh, near the western edge of Allegheny National Forest. From the

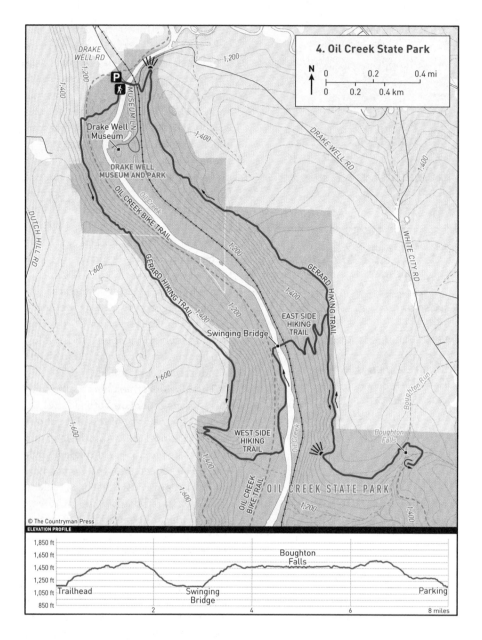

N

| 0 | 0.2 | 0.4 mi |
| 0 | 0.2 | 0.4 km |

Drake Well Museum

DRAKE WELL MUSEUM AND PARK

OIL CREEK BIKE TRAIL

GERARD HIKING TRAIL

GERARD HIKING TRAIL

EAST SIDE HIKING TRAIL

Swinging Bridge

WEST SIDE HIKING TRAIL

OIL CREEK BIKE TRAIL

OIL CREEK STATE PARK

Boughton Falls

DRAKE WELL RD

WHITE CITY RD

DUTCH HILL RD

© The Countryman Press

ELEVATION PROFILE

1,850 ft	
1,650 ft	Boughton Falls
1,450 ft	
1,250 ft	
1,050 ft	Trailhead · Swinging Bridge · Parking
850 ft	2 · 4 · 6 · 8 miles

west, drive I-79 N and take exit 116A to merge onto I-80 E, driving for 9.7 miles. Take exit 29. At the end of the ramp, turn left onto PA 8 N. Follow PA 8 N for 16.4 miles to Franklin, then turn right onto Liberty Street. In 0.2 mile, turn left onto US 322 W, cross the Allegheny River, then turn right onto PA 417 N. In 12.1 miles, turn left onto PA 8 N and continue for 6.8 miles. Turn right onto E Bloss Street. Over the next mile, E Bloss Street becomes Allen Street, then becomes Drake Well Road. Turn right into the Jersey Bridge Parking Lot just before the bridge crossing of Oil Creek. The hike starts from here.

From the east, drive I-80 W and take exit 78 toward Brookville/Sigel. At the end of the ramp, turn right and follow PA 36 N for 36.2 miles. In Tionesta, turn left and cross the Allegheny River, then turn right and continue on PA 36 N for another 9.6 miles. From here, continue straight on PA 27 W, driving for 5.2 miles to Titusville. Turn left onto Brown Street. Cross Oil Creek, then turn left onto Bank Street. Bank Street turns right and becomes Allen Street, and then it becomes Drake Well Road. Turn right into the Jersey Bridge Parking Lot just before the bridge crossing of Oil Creek. The hike starts from here.

GPS Shortcut: In Google Maps, run a search for "Jersey Bridge Parking Lot/Trailhead" near the city of Titusville. Your GPS will direct you to the parking lot where the trail starts.

THE HIKE

Head south from the parking lot, passing several picnic tables. Go under a gateway beside Oil Creek to pick up the yellow blazes of the Gerard Hiking Trail. Follow the flow of the creek downstream for a short distance on flat grassy tread, then bend to the right and head deeper into the woods. Approximately 0.2 mile after leaving the parking area, the trail reaches a trail register in a mailbox. The trail follows an extensive wooden walkway that navigates a wet marshy area then heads abruptly uphill on a series of steps to arrive at a paved bike path. Cross the bike path and head up another small set of stairs, then turn to the left and continue ascending on sidehill trail, albeit at a much more relaxed rate. The forest here is primarily composed of oaks and beeches, a common Pennsylvanian mix of hardwoods.

The terrain going uphill is fairly

THE SWINGING BRIDGE OVER OIL CREEK, AS SEEN FROM THE WEST SIDE HIKING TRAIL

smooth and wide, but as you come closer to the top of the gorge, the trail begins to level out somewhat and become rockier and strewn generously with protruding gnarled roots. Several areas on this elevated course may be wet and muddy, but all of them are easily navigated with a little help from some well-placed stepping stones. At the 1.1-mile mark, there is another trail register for Gerard Hiking Trail hikers. Immediately after the register, the Gerard Hiking Trail passes through a powerline swath and then continues down a short flight of stairs and some plank boardwalks before rejoining rocky terrain. As you progress through the area, you may be able to spot decaying remnants from the oil industry as they rust away in the woods off the

BOUGHTON FALLS

and eventually a swinging bridge and the East Side Hiking Trail.

As you continue to drop in elevation along the creek, you will notice that this trail is steeper, slightly rockier, and much less used than the Gerard Hiking Trail. In about 0.2 mile, at the 2.2-mile marker, the trail emerges from the tree cover into a circular clearing just west of the bike path. This is part of the Boughton historic site, where the third oil well was built along the creek. The ground here is covered with small pieces of shale and the smell of oil is often in the air. Continue through this clearing and cross the bike path, entering the woods on the other side to walk over another series of wooden boardwalks.

In 0.2 mile, the trail gently turns to the left and flattens significantly, roughly following the shoreline of Oil Creek from a distance heading upstream. This pleasant, grassy course continues for 0.5 mile before reaching a large suspension bridge that spans the creek. Follow the bridge across Oil Creek and begin heading uphill on the other side of the gorge, immediately passing a railroad and a small picnic area. From here the white-blazed connector trail ascends with a moderately steep grade, following wide switchbacks that zigzag up the sloping canyon wall past discarded pieces of machinery and a dilapidated building from the oil boom. At mile marker 3.5, the East Side Hiking Trail ends at the junction with the eastern side of the Gerard Hiking Trail. You have the option of turning either left or right. Turning left will eventually lead you back to the parking area, cutting the length of the hike by 2.8 miles and bypassing a scenic vista and Boughton Falls.

Turn right here and begin heading south on the Gerard Hiking Trail

trail. In 0.5 mile, the Gerard Hiking Trail begins to gradually trend downhill for 0.3 mile, then bends to the right and descends more aggressively on switchbacks for 0.1 mile to arrive at a small unnamed run that eventually empties into Oil Creek.

At the edge of this water flow, the Gerard Hiking Trail intersects with a white-blazed connector trail. West of Oil Creek it is known as the West Side Hiking Trail, and on the other side it is called the East Side Hiking Trail. Turn left here onto the West Side Hiking Trail and begin following the white blazes, descending toward Oil Creek

THE SWINGING BRIDGE FROM THE EAST SIDE HIKING TRAIL

toward Miller Farm. The tread of the yellow-blazed trail continues on wide, even terrain for a short distance before transitioning to narrow singletrack that meanders back and forth, following the curves of the canyon on rolling terrain. Arrive at a scenic vista approximately 0.7 mile after rejoining the Gerard Hiking Trail. A nicely framed view of Oil Creek can be seen through a clearing in the trees, looking northward. Take advantage of the bench there and enjoy a break, then continue heading south on the Gerard Hiking Trail. For the most part, the Gerard Hiking Trail is very well-marked, but the continuation from the viewpoint can be difficult to find. Just before you approach the vista, the trail turns to the left and heads away from the rounded rim at a right angle.

Continue on bumpy terrain for 0.3 mile, gently arcing to the east. The Gerard Hiking Trail enters a sprawling stand of large hemlock trees that populate this portion of the forest and, 0.2 mile later, crosses a few small seasonal streams and both branches of Boughton Run. Follow the trail past the water crossings, and descend on a wide, smooth, moderate grade through the hemlocks for a little more than 0.1 mile to reach a bench on the right side of the trail that offers a view overlooking the cascades of Boughton Falls in the ravine below. This shady perch is a great place to relax and enjoy the serene forest on a hot summer day. When you are ready, turn around and reverse your course up the Gerard Hiking Trail. Cross back over Boughton Run, pass the vista, and make your way back to the junction with the white-blazed connector trail.

INDUSTRIAL RUINS AT OIL CREEK STATE PARK

When you reach the East Side Hiking Trail, continue straight to stay on the Gerard Hiking Trail, heading north. The trail beyond the junction climbs moderately for 0.1 mile before largely leveling out, traversing the flat top of the plateau for another 0.5 mile. At mile 6.8 your route begins to descend gradually, dropping more aggressively as you advance, and in another 0.4 mile the trail crosses back over the powerline swath you navigated on the western side of Oil Creek. On the other side of the powerline swath, the grade of the trail relaxes and the descent becomes much more manageable. Continue heading down the trail on relatively easy terrain and pass down a short flight of steps at mile marker 7.7, just before the trail switches back. At the turn in the switchback, a short spur trail leads out to another view at another powerline clearing, the last scenic view to be had on this hike.

Make your way downhill for another 0.2 mile, switchbacking once more, and turn left to cross back over the train tracks you passed just after the swinging bridge. Veer to the right and cross Oil Creek on Drake Well Road and head down a flight of wooden stairs on the left side of the road to arrive back at the parking area.

Meadow Run Loop

DISTANCE: 2.1 miles	
DIFFICULTY: Moderate	
HIKING TIME: 1 hour	
TYPE: Loop	
TOTAL ELEVATION GAIN: 378'	
MAXIMUM ELEVATION: 1,590'	

Picture-perfect Meadow Run flows from south to north, emptying into the Youghiogheny River just south of the tiny borough of Ohiopyle. Meadow Run cascades over stone ledges and piled rock formations at several points on its way to the Youghiogheny and is breathtaking any time of year. Meadow Run is a popular fly-fishing stream as well. The stream winds partially through Ohiopyle State Park and can be accessed by walking a rustic footpath that meanders along the edge of the water. The trail is also used by rock climbers who recreate on two large cliff faces that are located on the path.

The hike described here follows a short, moderate loop through pleasant forest to reach three large cascade areas on Meadow Run. Coordinate your schedule to allow plenty of time to enjoy the shore of the run. On a hot sunny day, it is a wonderful place to relax and soak your feet. The trail also passes by two rock-climbing areas that are fun to explore even if you do not plan on scaling the cliff faces. Farther downstream, closer to the Youghiogheny River, Meadow Run spills through a smooth narrow channel in the rock creek bed to form natural waterslides. The busy waterslide area can be easily accessed from another parking lot on PA 381 near Ohiopyle Road or by continuing to follow Meadow Run downstream instead of looping back to your vehicle at the end of the hike. Be forewarned that when the water level is high the trail to the waterslides is impassable.

GETTING THERE

Ohiopyle State Park is located southeast of Pittsburgh. To get there from the west, follow I-76 E and take exit 91 for PA 31 toward Ligonier. At the end of the ramp,

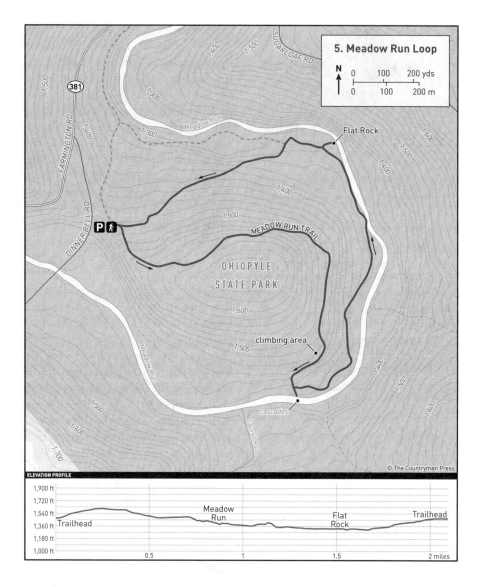

5. Meadow Run Loop

ELEVATION PROFILE

turn right onto PA 31 W, then turn left onto Hellein School Road. In 1.5 miles, keep straight across County Line Road and merge onto Melcroft Road, continuing for another 2.9 miles. Turn right onto PA 381 S and drive for 17.6 miles, passing through Ohiopyle. Turn left onto Dinner Bell Road and in 0.1 mile reach the parking lot on the left side of the road.

From the east, follow I-76 W and take exit 110 toward Johnstown/Somerset,

then turn right onto N Center Avenue. Drive for 0.5 mile, then turn right onto W Main Street and continue for 0.7 miles. Turn left onto Harrison Avenue, and in 0.1 mile turn right onto PA 281 S. Follow PA 281 S for 10.3 miles, then keep right and merge onto PA 653 W, continuing on this route for another 8.4 miles. Make a sharp left onto Clay Run Road and drive for 4.1 miles. Turn right onto Maple Summit Road. In another 4.1

miles turn left onto PA 381 S and follow it for 3 miles, passing through the town of Ohiopyle. Turn left onto Dinner Bell Road and in 0.1 mile reach the parking lot on the left side of the road.

GPS Shortcut: Type "Meadow Run Alternative Parking Area, Dinner Bell Road" into Google Maps and your GPS will navigate to the trailhead. There are a total of three parking areas for the Meadow Run Trail according to Google Maps. Be sure to park in the lot on Dinner Bell Road.

THE HIKE

Head to the eastern end of the parking area, toward a wooden sign marking the trail. The sign sits at the edge of the woods and points left toward Flat Rock and right toward the cascades and climbing area. Veer to the right and begin heading uphill on the yellow-blazed Meadow Run Trail. This narrow trail climbs a moderately steep grade through stands of rhododendrons and young beech trees, ascending a short, round knoll for roughly 0.2 mile. Near the top of the knoll, the trail widens and levels off briefly but significantly. For the time being, most of the rhododendrons dissipate and the forest opens up, providing an excellent opportunity to look around and take in the peaceful scenery on the wooded hilltop. When the leaves are off the trees, limited views of the surrounding ridges can be seen, dominating the skyline in all directions.

Begin descending through similarly dense, viny forest on a wide road-grade path. The yellow-blazed trail continues along the wide, well-graded path, trending downhill on rolling terrain for 0.4 mile. At this point, the Meadow Run Trail bends slightly to the left and leaves

ONE OF THE ROCK CLIMBING WALLS ON THE MEADOW RUN TRAIL

the road grade. A sign pointing toward the climbing area marks the turn. Immediately after leaving the wide road grade the trail narrows, dropping in elevation moderately, and very shortly arrives at the aforementioned climbing area. The climbing area is made up of two large separated cliffs. The Meadow Run Trail winds downhill in between both structures, passing near the top of the first area, a stand-alone buttress on the left side of the trail, then descends sharply toward the base of the second area, a massive sheer wall of rock on the right side of the trail with an ominous overhang near its top.

Continuing downhill past the

CASCADING WATERS ON MEADOW RUN

rock-climbing area, the forest begins to close in once more with dense stands of mountain laurel and rhododendron becoming much more prominent. You will likely be able to hear sounds of the Meadow Run cascades off in the distance, getting closer and closer with each step. Arrive at Meadow Run in 0.2 mile, where the main trail bends to the left and follows the flow of the run downstream. Before turning, however, take a short spur trail to the water's edge. From the rocky shore several lively cascades can be seen, the frothy water tumbling over thick stacks of exposed stone. This is a great place to stop and take a break, have a snack, read a book, or just sit back and enjoy the scenery.

When you are ready to continue, follow the main trail as it heads downstream. The terrain is fairly easy and the grade is flat and level. There are several other areas along this stretch of the trail where small spur trails lead to the shore of Meadow Run, offering a slightly different perspective than the first cascade area. The climbing area is visible from the run uphill and to the left when the leaves are off the trees. At the 1.1-mile mark, the Meadow Run Trail arrives at a faint junction. An old fly-fisherman path breaks off to the right, traveling a short distance toward a wide segment of the run. Bend to the left and briefly head away from the run, ascending a short uphill stretch on rocky terrain before again resuming the easy grade along the creek. After 1.5 miles of hiking, arrive at a wooden post denoting the Flat Rock attraction, which is a few feet off the main trail. This is perhaps the best area to enjoy Meadow Run; as the smooth, spacious face of a low sandstone ledge along the flowing water provides plenty of places to sit and relax.

Hike up the Meadow Run Trail for 0.2 mile to reach a trail junction marked by another wooden post. Continuing straight on will lead to the natural waterslides on Meadow Run in about 1 mile. This trail is not passable when the water level is high. Additionally, these waterslides can be reached from another parking area closer to the confluence with the Youghiogheny River. Instead, turn to the left to head uphill toward the parking area. While the ascent up from the run is the steepest, most sustained climb of the hike, it is still quite manageable. The terrain is easy and the wide, well-graded path climbs only moderately for 0.4 mile, arriving at the parking area after 2.1 miles of hiking.

6

Ferncliff Loop

DISTANCE: 2 miles	
DIFFICULTY: Easy	
HIKING TIME: 1 hour	
TYPE: Loop	
TOTAL ELEVATION GAIN: 167'	
MAXIMUM ELEVATION: 1,240'	

Located at the heart of Ohiopyle State Park, the Ferncliff Peninsula Natural Area is something of an oddity for Pennsylvania. It is flanked to the east, west, and south by the Youghiogheny River, which bends around the peninsula in a tight meander. Many plants grow on this small peninsula that are considered somewhat rare for the greater surrounding area, thanks to the warmer microclimate provided by the river. It is also geologically interesting, featuring rugged stone ledges on its eastern edge, right next to the flowing water. At certain points along these ledges prehistoric fossils of ancient plant life can be spotted. Because of these unique features, Ferncliff Peninsula Natural Area was declared a National Natural Landmark in 1973.

The hike described here follows a pleasant footpath that gently circumnavigates the peninsula, walking primarily along the edge of the Youghiogheny River through serene forest. The trail features splendid river views of rushing rapids and waterfalls. The area is very popular with kayakers, and it is common to see them running the rapids in the spring, summer, and fall. While short and certainly doable in a short amount of time, this trail is best experienced at a leisurely pace due to its distinctive characteristics. A few trails cross the peninsula, presenting options to shorten the excursion if desired. This is a great hike any time of year, although traction devices should be used in the winter, when ice buildup makes for slippery conditions along the riverside.

GETTING THERE

Ohiopyle State Park is located southeast of Pittsburgh. To get there from the west, follow I-76 E and take exit 91 for PA 31

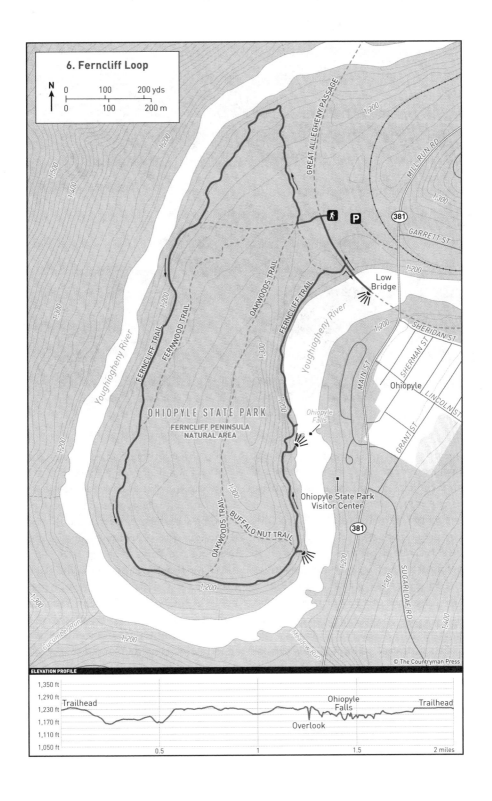

6. Ferncliff Loop

N
0   100   200 yds
0   100   200 m

GREAT ALLEGHENY PASSAGE

MILL RUN RD.

381

GARRETT ST

Low
Bridge

SHERIDAN ST.

OAKWOODS TRAIL

FERNCLIFF TRAIL

FERNCLIFF TRAIL

FERNWOOD TRAIL

Youghiogheny River

Youghiogheny River

SHERMAN ST.

MAIN ST.

Ohiopyle

LINCOLN ST.

Ohiopyle
Falls

GRANT ST.

OHIOPYLE STATE PARK
FERNCLIFF PENINSULA
NATURAL AREA

Ohiopyle State Park
Visitor Center

381

BUFFALO NUT TRAIL

OAKWOODS TRAIL

SUGARLOAF RD.

Cucumber Run

Meadow Run

© The Countryman Press

ELEVATION PROFILE

1,350 ft
1,290 ft
1,230 ft   Trailhead
1,170 ft
1,110 ft
1,050 ft

Ohiopyle
Falls

Trailhead

Overlook

0.5   1   1.5   2 miles

OHIOPYLE FALLS FROM FERNCLIFF PENINSULA NATURAL AREA

toward Ligonier. At the end of the ramp, turn right onto PA 31 W, then turn left onto Hellein School Road. In 1.5 miles, keep straight across County Line Road and merge onto Melcroft Road, continuing for another 2.9 miles. Turn right onto PA 381 S and drive for 16.5 miles. Just before crossing the Youghiogheny River and entering the town of Ohiopyle, turn right and park in a large gravel lot just north of the Great Allegheny Passage rail trail. The hike starts from here.

From the east, follow I-76 W and take exit 110 toward Johnstown/Somerset, then turn right onto N Center Avenue. Continue for 0.5 mile, then turn right onto W Main Street. Drive W Main Street for 0.7 miles. Turn left onto Harrison Avenue, and in 0.1 mile turn right onto PA 281 S. Follow PA 281 S for 10.3 miles, then keep right and merge onto

PA 653 W, continuing on this route for another 8.4 miles. Make a sharp left onto Clay Run Road and drive for 4.1 miles. Turn right onto Maple Summit Road. In another 4.1 miles, turn left onto PA 381 S and follow it for 1.8 miles. Just before crossing the Youghiogheny River and entering the town of Ohiopyle, turn right and park in a large gravel lot just north of the Great Allegheny Passage rail trail. The hike starts from here.

GPS Shortcut: Enter "Ferncliff Natural Area Parking" in Google Maps and your GPS will navigate to the trailhead.

THE HIKE

From the parking area, head west toward the small kiosk that marks the trailhead. Cross the gravel tread of the Great Allegheny Passage, a 150-mile rail trail that runs from Cumberland, Maryland, to Pittsburgh, Pennsylvania, and enter the Ferncliff Peninsula Natural Area. Continue heading into the woods on a short, well-established trail to arrive at a wooden post marking the Ferncliff Trail and a large stone bearing a bronze plaque honoring its National Natural Landmark status. The Ferncliff Trail runs to the left and the right, looping around the peninsula, and can be hiked in either direction. For the purposes of this hike, turn to the right and begin following the black blazes of the Ferncliff Trail to circumnavigate the peninsula in a counterclockwise fashion.

The trail descends gradually for approximately 0.2 mile, following a wide, mostly level trail. There are several spots where large, interwoven roots present a trip hazard, but for the most part walking the trail should be very

FOSSILS OF PREHISTORIC PLANT LIFE ON THE TRAIL

easy. Turn abruptly to the left just before reaching the edge of the Youghiogheny River and follow the trail as it parallels the flowing water, heading upstream.

BOULDERS AND RAPIDS ON THE YOUGHIOGHENY RIVER

Following the riverbank from a short distance, the meandering path is lined with a fair number of blocky boulders, and the surrounding forest is tall and shady, composed of a mix of deciduous and coniferous trees. Hemlocks, beeches, white pines, and oaks are all interspersed here. Through the trees to the right side of the trail, glimpses of surging rapids that churn the river can be seen. The tread of the trail advances through this pleasant forest scenery on rolling terrain that gradually trends uphill, while the ground to the right of the trail drops steeply to the river below.

In 0.5 mile, arrive at a trail intersection. The similarly named Fernwood Trail meets with the Ferncliff Trail from the left. Stay straight on the Ferncliff Trail and pass a small deer enclosure shortly after the junction. Continue to make your way along the lip of the peninsula, circling around the southern end of the landmass. In 0.3 mile, at mile marker 1.1, the Oakwoods Trail meets

with the Ferncliff Trail from the left. Go straight past this junction and follow the Ferncliff Trail for a little more than 0.1 mile to arrive at a flat stone outcropping that gazes out over the water to where Meadow Run empties into the bending Youghiogheny River. The Buffalo Nut Trail meets with the Ferncliff Trail here as well. The Buffalo Nut Trail heads uphill to the left and connects to the previously mentioned Oakwoods Trail. After enjoying the view, continue on the Ferncliff Trail as it bends around the tip of the peninsula and begin heading northward.

After leaving the viewpoint, enter into a thick stand of tall rhododendrons that narrows the trail significantly. The drop-off to the right here is very steep and treacherous. Segments of wooden fencing have been erected along this portion of the trail, so be safe and stay to the left of it. At the 1.4-mile marker, the Ferncliff Trail arrives at the Falls Overlook, another flat rock protruding

SURVEYING THE MAJESTY OF OHIOPYLE FALLS

TRAIL SIGN AND NATIONAL NATURAL LANDMARK DESIGNATION MARKER ON FERNCLIFF PENINSULA

from the peninsula that can be reached by following a short spur trail down a flight of rustic steps. From this slab of stone an impressive view of Ohiopyle Falls can be seen. The waterfall spans the entire width of the Youghiogheny River, and the turbulent water drops 20 feet before crashing into a foamy pool below and continuing to flow downstream. It is interesting and pertinent to note that the name *Ohiopyle* is derived from a phrase used by the Lenape natives, which loosely translates to "it turns very white," in reference to the raging, wild river as it flows over the falls. After taking in the view, head back up the steps and turn right. A short distance up the trail, Ohiopyle Falls can be experienced from a totally different perspective. This area is very close to the top of the falls and faces downstream. Use extreme caution here and stay a safe distance away from the edge of the quickly moving water. Take your time, enjoy the powerful river, and continue up the Ferncliff Trail when you are ready.

After leaving Ohiopyle Falls, the Ferncliff Trail follows the bank of the river for 0.5 mile, picking a course across the rocks that lie along the edge of the water. While the trail is fairly flat, the smooth, water-carved stone, pools of water, and continued river views will certainly force you to slow your pace. If you look carefully, closer to the edge of the forest, you may be able to spot fossils of prehistoric plant life embedded in the exposed rocks. At mile marker 1.9, a connector trail breaks off the Ferncliff Trail to the right, leading toward the Great Allegheny Passage. Turn onto this short spur toward a flight of wooden steps. The stairs emerge onto the gravel rail trail, just west of the Ohiopyle Low Bridge that spans the Youghiogheny River. The bridge is a great place to take another look at the Ohiopyle Valley from yet another vantage point.

After visiting the Ohiopyle Low Bridge, head back toward the staircase and continue on the Great Allegheny Passage for approximately 0.1 mile to arrive back at the parking area on the left side of the rail trail.

Bear Run Nature Reserve

DISTANCE: 5.2 miles	
DIFFICULTY: Moderate	
HIKING TIME: 2.5 hours	
TYPE: Loop	
TOTAL ELEVATION GAIN: 588'	
MAXIMUM ELEVATION: 1,938'	

South of Pittsburgh, the Bear Run Nature Reserve is owned and operated by the Western Pennsylvania Conservancy. The reserve sits adjacent to the northern end of Ohiopyle State Park. The reserve is open to the public and features over 20 miles of hiking through a variety of forest settings and terrains. The trails, which are marked with colored discs, form loops varying in length from 0.8 mile to 11.9 miles, with junctions regularly occurring. While the colored loop system forms a solid foundation for quick, easy-to-follow hiking excursions, the possibilities of piecing together customized hikes throughout this system are seemingly endless. Additionally, five group tenting campsites are located at various points throughout the trail system. These campsites provide an excellent opportunity for backpacking options, especially for those new to the activity. Campsites must be reserved online through the Western Pennsylvania Conservancy.

The route described in this entry follows the well-marked red loop throughout the Bear Run Nature Reserve. The trail passes through serene woodlands composed of various mixed mature hardwoods, and it passes a few tributaries of Bear Run (itself a tributary of the Youghiogheny River) and bouldery rock formations. Numerous options for shortening or lengthening the hike exist, as there are many trail intersections along the way. If you plan to alter the course detailed here, it is highly recommended that you acquire a trail map because the number of junctions can be overwhelming and slightly confusing.

GETTING THERE

Bear Run Nature Reserve is located southeast of Pittsburgh, just north of

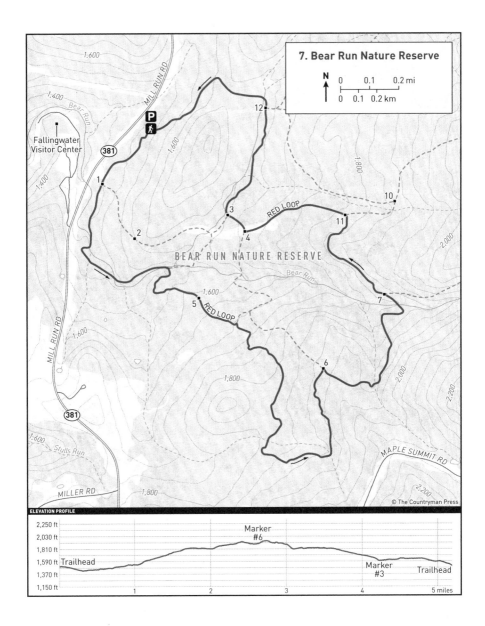

7. Bear Run Nature Reserve

N

| 0 | 0.1 | 0.2 mi |
| 0 | 0.1 | 0.2 km |

BEAR RUN NATURE RESERVE

RED LOOP

Fallingwater Visitor Center

MILL RUN RD

Bear Run

Stulls Run

MILLER RD

MAPLE SUMMIT RD

© The Countryman Press

ELEVATION PROFILE

2,250 ft			Marker #6		
2,030 ft					
1,810 ft					
1,590 ft Trailhead				Marker #3	
1,370 ft					Trailhead
1,150 ft	1	2	3	4	5 miles

the town of Ohiopyle. To get there from the west, follow I-76 E and take exit 91 for PA 31 toward Ligonier. At the end of the ramp, turn right onto PA 31 W, then turn left onto Hellein School Road. In 1.5 miles, keep straight across County Line Road and merge onto Melcroft Road, continuing for another 2.9 miles. Turn right onto PA 381 S and drive for 12.7 miles. The parking area will be on the left, behind a large renovated barn used for social gatherings.

From the east, follow I-76 W and take exit 110 toward Johnstown/Somerset, then turn right onto N Center Avenue. Continue for 0.5 mile, then turn right onto W Main Street. Drive W Main Street for 0.7 miles. Turn left onto

FOOTBRIDGE OVER BEAR RUN

Harrison Avenue, and in 0.1 mile turn right onto PA 281 S. Follow PA 281 S for 10.3 miles, then keep right and merge onto PA 653 W, continuing on this route for another 8.4 miles. Make a sharp left onto Clay Run Road and drive for 4.1 miles. Turn right onto Maple Summit Road. In another 4.1 miles, turn right onto PA 381 N and drive for 2 miles. The paved parking area will be on the right, behind a large wooden barn used for social gatherings.

GPS Shortcut: The trailhead is located behind The Barn at Fallingwater. Type "Bear Run Parking" into Google Maps and your GPS will direct you to the parking area.

THE HIKE

All the trails at Bear Run Nature Reserve are marked with colored metal discs, and many of the trails share tread with each other. It is not uncommon to see a trail marked with four or five different colors. For the duration of the hike detailed here you want to follow the red blazes. Additionally, numbered marker posts are found at many intersections, but not all of them are located at a junction.

From the parking area, head south and enter a stand of tall, stately white pine trees, meandering uphill slightly on the shared tread of the red, white, blue, and black loops. In 0.1 mile, as the tread dips downhill, the red loop leaves the stand of pine trees and enters a primarily deciduous forest, which feels comparatively more open and exposed. Just after leaving the pine stand, at marker post 1, the white and blue loops veer to the left and begin heading more steeply uphill. Stay straight to follow the red and black trail markers on well-graded, mostly level terrain. In another 0.3 mile, the red loop enters a sprawling grove

COLORFUL TRAIL MARKERS AT BEAR RUN NATURE RESERVE

of rhododendrons and crosses a small swampy area on a short boardwalk. The trail crosses Bear Run on a pretty little footbridge shortly after the boardwalk ends. On the other side of the run, bend to the left slightly and advance over several smaller seasonal streams on a string of stepping stones, then cross back over Bear Run on another footbridge. Nestled among the lush, green rhododendrons, the babbling flow of Bear Run is a tranquil sight, and the scenery along the run is certainly a highlight of the larger area.

After crossing the second footbridge the trail begins climbing up a few stone steps before continuing to meander through the forest roughly mirroring the stream. Arrive at a trail junction after hiking for 0.9 mile. A connector trail sparsely blazed with yellow Cs continues to the left and over the Bear

Run, while the red and black loops turn to the right and climb moderately, heading away from the run. Keep to the right to stay on the red and black loops. In a short distance, the trail circles around an area full of mossy boulders before bending back to the left and ascending through the ledges. In 0.4 mile, shortly after passing marker post 5, another yellow-blazed connector trail breaks off to the left. Stay straight to follow the red and black blazes, all the while climbing at a moderate angle on well-graded, occasionally rocky terrain. In another 0.4 mile, the trail levels out for a short distance, then turns to the left and begins trending downhill. Cross a seasonal water source on stepping stones in 0.2 mile and follow the wide footpath. Shortly thereafter, the trail turns to the left once more and starts heading back uphill. An old woods road continues straight on from here, blocked and barricaded by sticks and small logs to deter hikers from continuing onto it. The turn can be easy to miss, so keep an eye open for it.

After climbing moderately for approximately 0.5 mile, passing through a small hemlock stand next to a spring and a wet drainage area, arrive at marker post 6. At this point, the orange loop joins with the red and black loops. Turn to the left and ascend for a short distance, then crest the hill and begin heading downhill at a similar angle. Toward the bottom of the descent, the trail bends abruptly to the right and enters a mixed forest of oaks, hemlocks, and occasional rhododendrons. Cross a small stream, then bend back to the left and loosely follow the water flow, meandering along the edges of the ravine. In this area, the trail passes a plethora of boulders that decorate the woodland, many of them covered in moss, ferns, and lichen, displaying obtuse, angular bulges that protrude at odd angles. One particularly enchanting boulder is crowned with a massive hemlock, right around the 3-mile mark. The terrain along this stretch is very rough and rocky. The trail often winds around stacks of stone. It can be easy to lose the trail if you are not careful, so be mindful of which way the blazes point and take your time navigating this area.

THE GENTLE FLOW OF BEAR RUN

As you advance through the forest, the trail once more approaches Bear Run. Turn to the right and follow the run upstream on the elevated bank for a short distance, then turn to the left and cross the water on a wooden footbridge. In keeping with its picturesque nature, a few small cascades can be seen as you walk along Bear Run as well as from the footbridge over it. At the 3.3-mile mark, arrive at another trail junction in an open clearing as well as marker post 7. From here, the black loop turns sharply to the right, heading to the east. Stay straight and continue on the red and orange loops, entering another dense rhododendron stand at the end of the clearing. The trail follows the remains of an old woods road, descending moderately for 0.4 mile to arrive at marker post 11 and another trail intersection. The orange and blue loops turn to the right here, and head uphill. Turn to the left and follow the red and blue loops downhill.

In another 0.4 mile, at mile 4.1, the trail approaches marker post 4. Stay straight, briefly rejoining the orange loop, to continue along the red and blue loops. Less than 0.1 mile later, at marker post 3, the red loop turns to the right, leaving the orange and blue loops behind while simultaneously joining the yellow loop. Follow the red and yellow loops, heading northward beside a branch of Bear Run. The footpath features several plank boardwalks in this area, leading across marshy, muddy sections of trail.

HIKING IN THE PINES

After approximately 0.5 mile, reach marker post 12. Turn to the left, following the red, yellow, blue, and orange loops, and cross another footbridge shortly after the junction. The next 0.6 mile passes through another stand of tall white pines, following easy terrain around a small hill to arrive back at the parking area.

Minister Creek North Loop

DISTANCE: 6.6 miles	
DIFFICULTY: Very Difficult	
HIKING TIME: 3.5 hours	
TYPE: Loop	
TOTAL ELEVATION GAIN: 1,212'	
MAXIMUM ELEVATION: 1,742'	

The trail system at Minister Creek is located in the Allegheny National Forest, and it is certainly one of the finest trails in Pennsylvania. The system is made up of three overlapping loops around Minister Creek, with a spur trail leading down to the water's edge on the largest loop. The trails lead through forested countryside marked at fairly regular intervals by massive, lichen-covered boulders, some as large as houses. The northern portion of the trail system connects with the North Country Trail, creating a symbiotic relationship that benefits both trail systems. Currently about 3,100 miles of the North Country Trail are in place and open to the public. When completed, the North Country Trail will be the longest of eleven National Scenic Trails, and it will stretch from Vermont to North Dakota.

The hike detailed here follows the North Loop of the Minister Creek Trail, going clockwise through the circuitous trail system. Part of this hiking-only footpath follows disused railroad grades cut into the hillsides when the forest was logged in the late 1800s, although most of the trail follows narrow, winding singletrack. The enormous boulders strewn throughout the forest, a trademark feature of northwestern Pennsylvania, are especially scenic on this trail. Other highlights of this hike include a lovely view over the Minister Creek Valley, and a brief ramble through a deep gap in between towering cliff faces on the western side of the loop, a feature that emphasizes the natural beauty and value of Minister Creek.

GETTING THERE

From the west, follow I-80 E and take exit 60 for PA 66 N toward Shippenville. Follow PA 66 N for 32.7 miles, entering

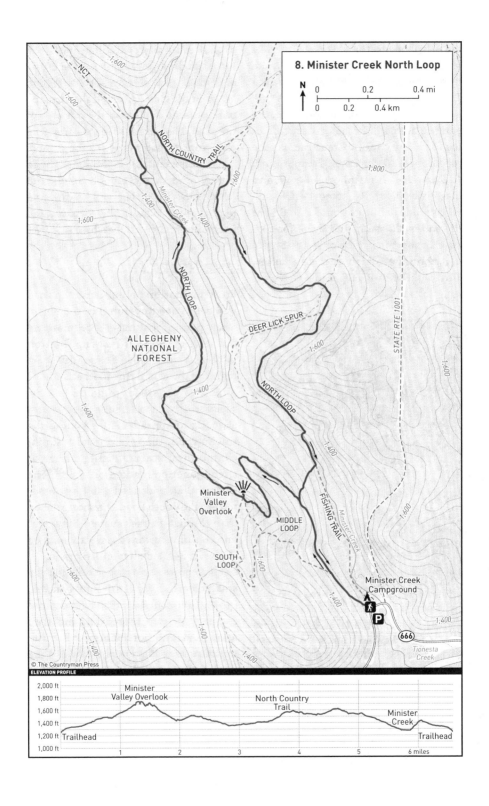

8. Minister Creek North Loop

N

| 0 | | 0.2 | | 0.4 mi |
| 0 | 0.2 | | 0.4 km | |

NCT

1,600

1,600

NORTH COUNTRY TRAIL

1,800

Minister Creek

1,600

1,400

NORTH LOOP

1,600

ALLEGHENY
NATIONAL
FOREST

DEER LICK SPUR

1,600

STATE RTE 1001

1,600

NORTH LOOP

1,400

1,400

1,600

1,600

Minister
Valley
Overlook

MIDDLE
LOOP

FISHING TRAIL

Minister Creek

SOUTH
LOOP

1,600

1,400

Minister Creek
Campground

1,600

1,400

666

Tionesta
Creek

1,400

1,400

© The Countryman Press

ELEVATION PROFILE

2,000 ft						
1,800 ft	Minister			North Country		
1,600 ft	Valley Overlook			Trail		
1,400 ft						Minister
1,200 ft	Trailhead					Creek
1,000 ft						Trailhead
	1	2	3	4	5	6 miles

the Allegheny National Forest. Turn left onto Blue Jay Creek Road, and continue for another 5.4 miles. Just after crossing Tionesta Creek, turn left onto PA 666 W. In 6 miles, just after a tight turn, the parking area will be on the left side of the road. The parking area is across the road from Minister Creek Campground.

From the east, follow I-80 W and take exit 78 for PA 36 toward Sigel/Brookville. Turn right onto PA 36 N at the end of the ramp and drive for 10.6 miles, then turn right onto PA 899 N and continue for another 10.8 miles. Turn right onto PA 66 N and drive for

6.8 miles. Turn left onto Blue Jay Creek Road and drive for 5.4 miles. After crossing Tionesta Creek, turn left onto PA 666 W. In 6 miles, just after a tight turn, the parking area will be on the left side of the road. The parking area is across the road from Minister Creek Campground.

GPS Shortcut: Type "Minister Creek Campground" into Google Maps and your GPS will direct you toward the parking area. The trailhead is located near Cherry Grove Township.

THE HIKE

From the parking area, cross the road and begin heading uphill to the northwest, passing behind a sign marking the start of the trail system. The trail is blazed with white diamonds. Upon entering the woods, the footpath climbs a moderately steep grade on a wide, rocky tread that in 0.1 mile merges with a woods road grade. After joining the woods road, the grade levels significantly. In another 0.1 mile, arrive at a trail junction marked by a sign. The branch that leads to the left advances toward the South Loop, the shortest loop in the Minister Creek system. Stay right and continue toward the North Loop on the wide, hemlock-lined road grade.

In 0.5 mile, the grassy road ends at a small clearing. Head straight, continuing on your course as the trail becomes rockier. Shortly thereafter, the trail arrives at another junction. Turning to the right leads downhill toward the flow of Minister Creek. Turn to the left instead, and begin ascending into a deciduous forest composed of oaks and beeches. The incline of the trail rises fairly quickly, advancing steadily uphill at an angle similar to the first portion of the hike. This area of the forest is littered with a large quantity of gigantic

IN THE ROCK RAVINE ON THE NORTH LOOP

THE VIEW FROM MINISTER VALLEY OVERLOOK

house-sized boulders, many of which are topped with a thick layer of lush green ferns, solitary saplings, and other resilient plant life. The boulders are a unique part of the Minister Creek trail system, and they will certainly occupy your mind while you ascend through the forest. In front of one of the largest boulders, the trail bends to the left on a lazy turn and continues uphill, switchbacking to the right in a short distance, just before approaching a stand of hemlock trees.

The footpath is greeted by several more huge boulders strewn throughout the forest and a sheer rock ledge on the left at the 1-mile mark. Shortly afterward, on the left side of the trail, a tree with an ornate, tentacle-like root system can be seen clinging to the rock face. Just after this oddity, the trail bends gently to the left and heads aggressively uphill

on rickety stone steps, passing through a weather-worn crack in the ledge. Two small alcoves on the left form shallow caves here, upheld by precariously jumbled rocks. Enter a dense cluster of mountain laurels and in 0.1 mile beyond the ledge pass arrive at a trail intersection. Portions of the South Loop, Middle Loop, and North Loop all converge here, near the Minister Valley Overlook. The vista is located to the right, on a flat stone platform that peeks out from over the treetops. The view looks to the northeast, surveying the Minister Creek Valley. Take in the scenery while you catch your breath, and when you are ready to continue, follow the North Loop. All the trails are marked with white diamonds here. The South Loop trails off along the top of the plateau, to the left of the vista, while the North Loop is located nearer the overlook. Its white diamond

FERN-COVERED BOULDER ALONG THE NORTH LOOP

Leave the ravine and follow the trail as it rambles along the base of the ledgy cliff wall for the next 0.2 mile, progressing along rolling ups and downs on narrow singletrack. Eventually the trail veers to the right and heads moderately downhill for 0.3 mile. Cross a tributary of Minister Creek on stepping stones, then head gradually uphill, passing through mountain laurels and immature birch trees. The terrain here is crisscrossed with roots and can be quite slippery when wet. Farther ahead, at mile 2.2, pass through a clearing punctuated with a multitude of dead trees. In the summer this portion of the trail may be somewhat overgrown, due to exposure to the open sky, which has allowed fast-growing shrubby undergrowth to flourish unchecked. On the other side of this 0.1-mile long clearing, the trail reenters the tree cover and begins to trend downhill at a relaxed rate.

At mile 2.8, the North Loop drops into the bottom of the valley and approaches the edge of Minister Creek. Turn to the left and follow the creek upstream through pretty, coniferous forest. The grade is fairly flat here, and the terrain beside the flow is even and pleasant. In 0.2 mile, the trail turns to the right and crosses another tributary, nearby to where it empties into Minister Creek. In the spring, and during periods of high rainfall, it may not be possible to cross this stream without getting wet. Follow the trail for 0.4 mile, passing through evergreen forest on continuing level terrain, and arrive at the junction with the North Country Trail. While you are following the North Country Trail, the blazes will be blue. Turn to the right and begin following the blue blazes, crossing a branch of the creek on a wooden footbridge. Right after the bridge, there is a backcountry tent site off to the left,

is emblazoned with a black N to differentiate it from the other trails.

Soon after leaving the vista, the trail descends on an abbreviated flight of stone steps to drop below the lip of the ledge, then it climbs back uphill toward the brim of the plateau, passing briefly through a deep ravine that unfolds from the canyon wall at the 1.4-mile mark. This passageway curves through a hall of stone approximately 10 feet wide and 50 feet deep, a rare and enchanting phenomenon for the state of Pennsylvania.

a few hundred feet behind an enormous birch tree. Very shortly after passing the birch tree, cross over another stream on another footbridge next to another campsite. The trail turns to the right here and begins to ascend moderately, getting progressively steeper, heading away from the creek through mixed forest and more scattered boulders.

At the trail junction at mile 3.9, the North Loop turns to the right, leaving the North Country Trail behind. After turning back onto the white-blazed North Loop, the trail dips down toward another miniscule branch of Minister Creek. Cross the small creek and head over a few long, conglomerate slabs of stone peppered with hundreds of white rounded pebbles. Follow undulating, rocky terrain that gently trends uphill, continuing to pass incredibly big boulders and a handful of seasonal runs for the next 1.1 miles.

At the 5-mile mark, arrive at a trail junction. To the right, a yellow-blazed spur trail descends into the gorge toward the Deer Lick tent sites before dead ending at Minister Creek. Unless you have a strong desire to visit the campsite, continue straight on the North Loop and begin a steady, 0.4-mile long sidehill descent. The trail bends to the left and levels out as it approaches the bottom of the valley, advancing along the hillside above Minister Creek for 0.3 mile. At mile 5.7, the North Loop drops the remaining elevation down to the creek and turns to the right to cross the water twice on a pair of footbridges.

Less than 0.1 mile after crossing the creek, the North Loop turns to the right and climbs very steeply uphill for 0.2 mile, arriving at the northernmost junction you passed at the start of the hike. Turn to the left and follow the white blazes downhill, retracing your footsteps for 0.5 mile to arrive back at the parking area. If you do not feel like ascending back to the junction, an unmarked fishing path continues along Minister Creek, arriving at the Minister Creek Campground across the street from the parking area. The difference in mileage between following the trail or the fishing path is negligible.

NARROW PASSAGE THROUGH CLEFT STONE

Hickory Creek Wilderness Trail

DISTANCE: 13.5 miles

DIFFICULTY: Difficult

HIKING TIME: 6.5 hours

TYPE: Loop

TOTAL ELEVATION GAIN: 1,378'

MAXIMUM ELEVATION: 1,901'

Located in Warren County, the Hickory Creek Wilderness is one of only two wilderness areas in Allegheny National Forest, the other being Allegheny Islands Wilderness. As a wilderness area, the land receives minimal attention in the way of grooming and maintenance. Instead the forces of nature largely dictate the way in which the land develops, with the help of the native flora and fauna. A hiking and backpacking trail that circles through the Hickory Creek Wilderness is the only human development the land has seen recently or will continue to see as long as it remains protected. The wilderness area designation also dictates the types of tools trail maintainers can use when clearing blowdown. As per federal guidelines, power tools such as chainsaws are not allowed to be used in wilderness areas. When trees topple over the trail, maintainers must hike out with hand saws and axes to clear the blowdown. The Hickory Creek Wilderness Trail is truly a labor of love.

The difficulty rating given to the Hickory Creek Wilderness Trail stems from its lengthy tread. The wilderness area features very little in terms of drastic elevation change, rising and falling only a little more than 100 feet per mile on average. The trail climbs moderately at most, and then not very consistently. Most of the terrain is really quite easy. Perhaps the toughest obstacle that hikers encounter comes from blown-over trees on the far end of the loop, although this is largely dependent on the time of year and the weather patterns. A few campsites along the trail at various points would make for a great short weekend backpacking trip. The Hickory Creek Wilderness Trail does not feature any vistas or waterfalls and, as a result, it is generally very quiet, making this

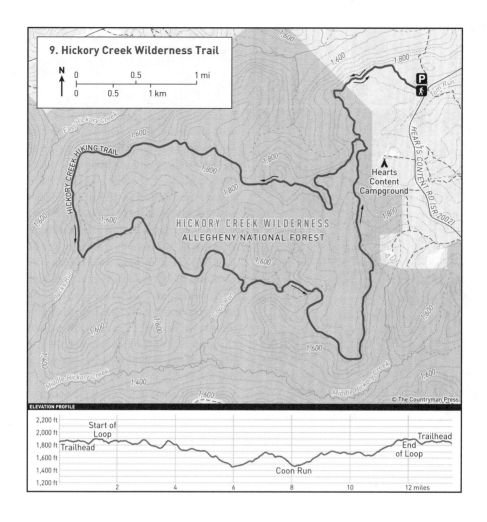

9. Hickory Creek Wilderness Trail

hike an excellent option for those seeking solitude.

GETTING THERE

From the west, follow I-80 E and take exit 29 for PA 8 toward Franklin/Oil City. At the end of the ramp turn left and follow PA 8 N for 16.4 miles. In the town of Franklin, turn right onto Liberty Street, then turn left in 0.7 mile and begin driving US 62 N. Follow US 62 N for 7.5 miles. Turn right onto Petroleum Street and cross the Allegheny River. In 0.3 mile, turn left onto W 1st Street and follow the road for 0.6 mile, as it turns into E Front Street, then E 2nd Street. Turn left to continue on US 62 N and follow the route for 26.9 miles. Turn right onto Kelly Hill Road and follow it for 3.9 miles. At this point, turn right onto Route 337 Road and drive for 7.7 miles. Turn right onto Hearts Content Road. In 3.2 miles, the gravel parking lot and trailhead will be on the right side of the road.

From the east, follow I-80 W and take exit 111 to merge onto PA 153 N.

ENTERING THE WILDERNESS AREA

trailhead, which is located near the borough of Tidioute.

THE HIKE

Enter the woods at the western side of the parking lot. A kiosk and trail register are located at the trailhead, so sign in before you begin your hike, especially if you plan to stay overnight. The Hickory Creek Wilderness Trail is marked with yellow blazes. It meanders along narrow singletrack and the terrain is well-graded and mostly free of rocks and roots. To start, the forest is mixed evenly between deciduous oaks and beeches, and coniferous evergreens such as the eastern hemlock and white pine. After you walk for 0.4 mile, the trail passes through a stand of very young white pine trees. Continue for another 0.4 mile to reach the edge of the Hickory Creek Wilderness, just after crossing a powerline swath. The perimeter of the wilderness is marked by a wooden sign, in the iconic shape and style used by the U.S. Forest Service to mark all nationally designated wilderness areas.

Continue on PA 153 N for 16.3 miles, then turn right onto US 219 N. Drive for 12.3 miles, passing through Ridgway. Turn right onto PA 948 N. Follow PA 948 N for 15.2 miles, then turn left to stay on the route as it merges with PA 66 S. In 2.7 miles, turn right to stay on PA 948 N, leaving PA 66 S behind. Continue on the route for 8.6 miles, then stay straight to merge with PA 666 E. In 2.3 miles, turn left onto Austin Hill Road. Follow Austin Hill Road for 7.1 miles, and continue straight as it turns into Hearts Content Road. In 6.6 miles, the parking area and trailhead will be on the left side of the road.

GPS Shortcut: Search for "Hickory Creek Wilderness Trail" in Google Maps and your GPS will navigate to the

Shortly after entering the wilderness area, the trail enters a grove of hemlock trees and passes in between a few flat boulders, and afterward it descends moderately. Continue following the trail across rolling elevation changes on occasionally rocky terrain for a total of 1.5 miles, winding through mixed forest of towering oak and hemlock as well as shrubby mountain laurel to reach the loop portion of the Hickory Creek Wilderness Trail. Turn to the right here and begin following the loop in a counterclockwise direction, advancing through a forest landscape very similar to what you just came through. As you walk, you will twist and turn through more rolling terrain, passing through shady, open evergreen groves and brighter, brushy deciduous tracts. The trail never climbs uphill for very long before the tread tips back downhill, and while these short, punctuated ascents and descents are fairly regular, they are never terribly difficult.

At mile marker 3.3, the Hickory Creek Wilderness Trail descends a short distance and becomes very twisty, winding back and forth several times in a short stretch. This convoluted section of the trail can be difficult to follow, as the frequent turns lend themselves to erroneously walking off-trail in the wrong direction. Pay close attention to which way the blazes point through this area. Also be mindful of your foot placement as there are numerous rocks in the trail, logs to clamber over, and small muddy pits to complicate matters. Approximately 0.2 mile after passing this serpentine segment, begin steadily climbing uphill over mossy rocks on a straight trajectory. This moderate climb, while not terribly strenuous, is certainly the most prolonged ascent yet in the trail system. At the top of this hill, the trail bends to the left and continues meandering through the forest. In 0.5 mile, while descending the side of this little hill, the Hickory Creek Wilderness Trail passes by another bouldery area, exhibiting many natural stacks of mossy rocks.

The forest opens up and brightens significantly after leaving the boulder area. This is due partially to the tall, spread-out trees that reside here, and their tendency to fall over if a very strong, sustained wind catches them at the right time of year. The open patches in the canopy allow more sunlight to reach the forest floor, both illuminating the forest, and letting other plant life take off on a race for sunlight and survival. The trail is congested with a lot of blowdown here, complicated further by the smaller, brushier plants that thrive in the surplus of sunlight. Continue following the yellow blazes as they progress through the wilderness along the top of a rounded hilltop ridge, heading south.

At the 5.4-mile mark, the trail bends to the left and begins descending moderately into a shallow gulch in between two hills. In 0.5 mile, the slope of the hillside begins to slacken, approaching the bank of a branch of Jacks Run. Toward the bottom of the hill there are many small, wet, muddy areas that may be cumbersome to navigate before you arrive at the edge of the water in a grassy clearing. It appears as though the trail could head several directions here. You want to turn to the left to follow the blazes, and begin walking alongside the creek, crossing it a few times and passing a few suitable campsite areas on the way. The terrain beside Jacks Run is well-graded and easy to walk, and the forest is composed of thick brush and cheery hemlocks.

Continue for 0.7 mile, then cross the creek once more, passing another small campsite on the right. Beyond the flow of Jacks Run, the Hickory Creek Wilderness Trail gradually ascends a broad, stunted hill for 0.8 mile through several densely packed patches of beech saplings before curving to the left and descending a moderately steep grade down very narrow sidehill tread. Shortly after the 8.1-mile mark, approach the edge of Coon Run, crossing it 0.1 mile later on a series of stepping stones under a very large hemlock tree. Approximately 100 feet after crossing the stream, the trail turns sharply to the left and ascends very gradually, mirroring another branch of Coon Run for 0.4

TRAILHEAD SIGNAGE AT THE HICKORY CREEK TRAIL

for 0.4 mile, crossing primarily deciduous forest. As you continue, the ascent gains the top of the plateau and levels out while isolated hemlocks begin to appear here and there, dotting the forest with their dark green foliage. The trail passes through another patch of twiggy beech saplings, then descends a short distance and bends to the left, emerging onto an old woods road grade at mile marker 9.7. Follow the wide road that goes gradually up and over a small corner of the plateau for 1.2 miles, descending toward a branch of Middle Hickory Creek. Ascend along the creek, pass through a particularly rocky area, and then cross over the flowing water. After crossing Middle Hickory Creek, the trail tips uphill at a steady, mellow angle, continuing through the forest, alternating between deciduous and coniferous trees. While fairly easy, this leg of the hike will most likely feel a bit drawn-out.

Hike while gradually trending uphill for 1.1 miles, completing the loop and arriving back at the trail junction at the 12-mile mark. Turn right here and follow your previous course out of the wilderness area, reaching the parking area in 1.5 miles.

mile. This part of the hike follows wide, level tread and can be very soggy during rainy months, as water must flow across the trail to drain into Coon Run. Turn to the left and cross the stream once more.

Follow the sparse yellow blazes uphill

10

Hearts Content National Scenic Area

DISTANCE: 1.1 miles	
DIFFICULTY: Easy	
HIKING TIME: 1 hour	
TYPE: Loop	
TOTAL ELEVATION GAIN: 124'	
MAXIMUM ELEVATION: 1,906'	

Hearts Content National Scenic Area is a 120-acre wooded area located in Allegheny National Forest. The land features a campground and day use area with picnic tables and cross-country ski trails as well as an easily accessible nature trail. The nature trail meanders through about 20 acres of forest, showcasing a magnificent example of old-growth forest. This forest is one of the only old-growth forests left in the northeast that still contain white pines. These ancient trees are somewhere between 300 and 400 years old, and they were initially spared from clear-cutting in the late 19th century. The Wheeler and Dusenbury Lumber Company, which owned the land then, sold it to the U.S. Forest Service in 1922. This land was designated as a National Scenic Area in 1934, and registered as a National Natural Landmark in 1973.

The interpretive loop trail through the venerable trees is very easy and quite enjoyable. The diminutive trail system is composed of two stacked loops, a short loop and a long loop. It is a great option for families with children, and it will almost certainly be enjoyed by every age group. The hiking at Hearts Content National Scenic Area can be done as a relaxing standalone hike, or it can be done to add a few extra miles onto a longer day of hiking. (Both Minister Creek and Hickory Creek Wilderness are close by.) However you choose to enjoy the trail, be sure to give yourself plenty of time to experience the magnitude of the trees, and to contemplate just how long these silent giants have been standing.

GETTING THERE

From the west, follow I-80 E and take exit 29 for PA 8 toward Franklin/Oil City. At

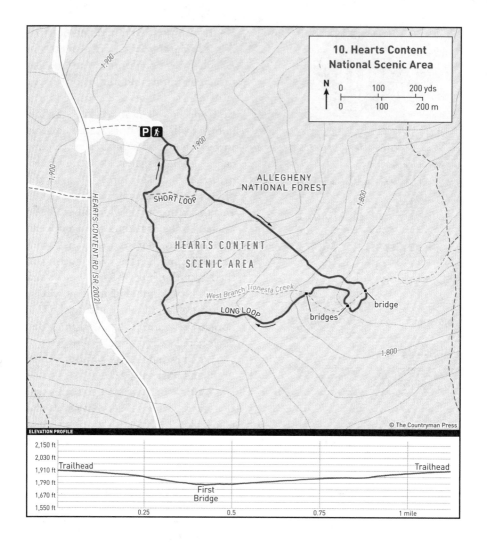

the end of the ramp turn left and follow PA 8 N for 16.4 miles. In the town of Franklin, turn right onto Liberty Street, then turn left in 0.7 mile and begin driving on US 62 N. Follow US 62 N for 7.5 miles. Turn right onto Petroleum Street and cross the Allegheny River. In 0.3 mile, turn left onto W 1st Street and follow the road for 0.6 mile, as it turns into E Front Street, then E 2nd Street. Turn left to continue on US 62 N and follow the route for 26.9 miles. Turn right onto Kelly Hill Road and follow it for

3.9 miles. At this point, turn right onto Route 337 Road and drive for 7.7 miles. Turn right onto Hearts Content Road. In 3.7 miles, the parking lot and trailhead will be on the left side of the road.

From the east, follow I-80 W and take exit 111 to merge onto PA 153 N. Continue on PA 153 N for 16.3 miles, then turn right onto US 219 N. Drive for 12.3 miles, passing through Ridgway. Turn right onto PA 948 N. Follow PA 948 N for 15.2 miles, then turn left to stay on the route as it merges with PA 66 S. In

THE HAZARDS OF HIKING IN OLD-GROWTH FOREST

loop going clockwise. Its course initially passes several signs that delve into the composition of the forest as well as identifying a few different tree species including hemlock, maple, and beech. Also of note is a stone bearing a bronze plaque, commemorating the National Natural Landmark status.

Roughly 0.1 mile in, you reach a trail junction. The short loop turns to the right here, breaking off the long loop. Keep left and continue on the long loop. The trail meanders gently downhill on well-graded gravel tread cushioned with pine needles. The terrain is very easy, with an overall absence of trip hazards, which lends itself well to keeping your eyes on your surroundings, as opposed to on the trail. There are a number of fallen trees littering the

2.7 miles, turn right to stay on PA 948 N, leaving PA 66 S behind. Continue on the route for 8.6 miles, then stay straight to merge with PA 666 E. In 2.3 miles, turn left onto Austin Hill Road. Follow Austin Hill Road for 7.1 miles, and continue straight as it turns into Hearts Content Road. In 6.1 miles, the parking area and trailhead will be on the right side of the road.

GPS Shortcut: Type "Hearts Content Recreation Site" into Google maps and your GPS will navigate to the trailhead.

THE HIKE

Enter the woods at the eastern end of the parking lot, picking up the interpretive trail, which is marked by a wooden sign. The tread of the interpretive trail is very easily discernible, although it is not marked with any blazes. Keep to the left; the trail splits almost immediately after entering the tree cover, and follow the

NATIONAL NATURAL LANDMARK PLAQUE AT HEARTS CONTENT

GAZING UPWARD AT THE MASSIVE TREES

the ground on either side of the trail. In the spring and summer, the peachy, floral aroma of the lush ferns mingles with the scent of pine and hemlock in the fresh air.

After hiking for 0.5 mile, the trail bends to the right in a horseshoe curve and begins sending hikers back uphill at a very mellow angle. As you advance, the interpretive trail crosses over a handful of narrow seasonal runs on plank bridges. This meager flow is the West Branch Tionesta Creek. You will notice that the trees will get progressively larger as you continue, nourished through the years no doubt by the trickling flow of these small streams. The quantity of these massive trees is staggering, a special treat for amateur dendrologists. These towering evergreen giants, in many instances, can be challenging to identify at a glance due to their sheer size. Rarely are white pines and hemlocks with such an expansive circumference encountered.

Continue uphill for another 0.5 mile, passing through the virgin forest and navigating a few muddy trail sections to arrive at a split in the trail. An unsigned herd path veers to the left, leading out to the grassy field that borders the parking area. To complete the loop and finish the hike, you can either head through the field back to your vehicle, or you can keep right and continue under the shade of the trees for a short distance to arrive back at the start of the loop.

forest floor here, the enormous mossy trunks slowly decaying in the shade of the thick canopy. These logs are a great place to stop and listen to the variety of birds that take refuge in the ancient woods. A large population of ferns grow here in the spring and summer, covering

Roaring Run Natural Area

DISTANCE: 8.5 miles	
DIFFICULTY: Difficult	
HIKING TIME: 4 hours	
TYPE: Loop	
TOTAL ELEVATION GAIN: 1,434'	
MAXIMUM ELEVATION: 2,791'	

In the Laurel Highlands region of Pennsylvania lies Roaring Run Natural Area. This area, which is part of Forbes State Forest, is made up of more than 3,500 acres of land. The land was timbered in the early 20th century, then again in the 1960s before being sold to the Western Pennsylvania Conservancy, eventually passing into the hands of the Commonwealth of Pennsylvania. The result of the extensive logging and subsequent protection is a woodland in varying stages of regrowth. Adolescent and mature trees mingle here, and in certain places cleared fields can be observed as they are reclaimed by the forest. A mountain stream, the namesake of the natural area, runs through the woods. It is fed by a number of springs and is home to native brook trout. The natural area also features more than 15 miles of foot trails.

This hike through Roaring Run Natural Area climbs the northern slope of the deep Roaring Run watershed, passing the craggy boulders that form Painter Rock. From there, the trail descends to the run and follows the water downstream to close up the loop. This hike can be enjoyed any time of year, but in the summertime long pants are recommended due to the thorny brush on the northern slope. Roaring Run is also an excellent place to cool off in the summer months. The creekside portion of the hike crosses the stream more than two dozen times, all without the benefit of a constructed footbridge. During periods of high rainfall it may be impossible to cross without getting wet, so plan accordingly and keep an extra change of shoes and socks in your car.

GETTING THERE

From the west, follow I-76 E and take exit 91 toward Ligonier. At the end of the

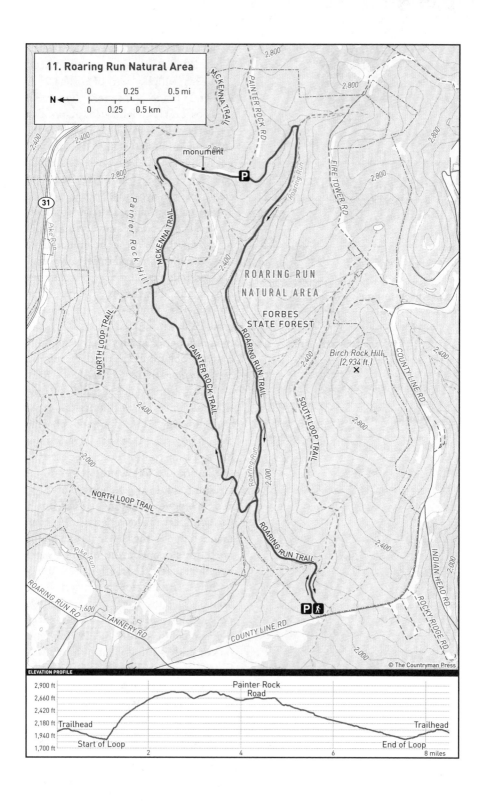

11. Roaring Run Natural Area

N ←

| 0 | 0.25 | 0.5 mi |
| 0 | 0.25 | 0.5 km |

31

monument

MCKENNA TRAIL

PAINTER ROCK RD

Roaring Run

FIRE TOWER RD

Painter Rock Hill

MCKENNA TRAIL

ROARING RUN
NATURAL AREA

FORBES
STATE FOREST

NORTH LOOP TRAIL

PAINTER ROCK TRAIL

ROARING RUN TRAIL

Birch Rock Hill
(2,934 ft.)
✕

COUNTY LINE RD

SOUTH LOOP TRAIL

Roaring Run

NORTH LOOP TRAIL

Pike Run

Roaring Run

ROARING RUN TRAIL

ROARING RUN RD

TANNERY RD

COUNTY LINE RD

INDIAN HEAD RD

ROCKY RIDGE RD

© The Countryman Press

ELEVATION PROFILE

	Painter Rock
2,900 ft	Road
2,660 ft	
2,420 ft	
2,180 ft Trailhead	Trailhead
1,940 ft	
1,700 ft	Start of Loop	End of Loop

2   4   6
8 miles

ramp, turn left onto PA 31 E. Drive for 2.2 miles, then turn right onto PA 381 S/PA 711 S. Continue for 1.3 miles, then turn left onto County Line Road. In 1.3 miles, the trailhead, a small gravel parking lot, will be on the left side of the road. It is marked by a wooden sign.

From the east, follow I-76 W and take exit 91 toward Ligonier. Turn left onto PA 31 E at the end of the ramp and drive for 2.2 miles. Turn right onto PA 381 S/ PA 711 S and drive for 1.3 miles. Turn left onto County Line Road. In 1.3 miles, reach a small gravel parking lot on the left side of the road, marked by a wooden sign. The hike starts from here.

GPS Shortcut: Enter "Roaring Run Natural Area County Line Road Parking" into Google Maps and your GPS will direct you to the trailhead near the borough of Champion.

THE HIKE

Enter the woods on the yellow-blazed Roaring Run Trail at the south end of the parking lot. The trail climbs gradually but steadily for 0.2 mile right from the start, following old, rocky road before dipping and heading downhill at a similar angle. Just after beginning the mellow descent, arrive at a trail junction. The South Loop Trail, which is blazed blue and yellow, breaks off to the right and heads uphill. Instead, keep to the left to stay on the Roaring Run Trail, which continues to gradually descend. In 0.5 mile, Roaring Run itself will come into view off in the distance through the trees to the left, and in another 0.2 mile, arrive at an intersection with the Painter Rock Trail. Turn left onto the Painter Rock Trail, which is also marked with yellow blazes.

The Painter Rock Trail is immediately much narrower than the Roaring

SOMBER STONE MARKER AT THE NORTHERN END OF THE ROARING RUN LOOP

Run Trail, passing among some mossy boulders that are randomly strewn throughout the forest. The Painter Rock Trail crosses Roaring Run a short distance from the intersection. Be aware that unless the water level is low, it may be impossible to cross the creek without getting your feet wet. On the other side of Roaring Run, the Painter Rock Trail passes through a short stretch of extremely rocky terrain, then makes an abrupt turn, cutting back sharply to the right and beginning a steep ascent up rocky, rooty sidehill terrain. This portion of the trail can sometimes be overgrown with thick, thorny underbrush in the summer months, a common side effect of a rebounding forest. Normally the leaves of the trees soak up almost

TRANQUIL VALLEY SCENERY ON THE PATH TO ROARING RUN

all the sunlight, keeping the shorter, shrubbier brush in check. In a younger, immature forest—especially one on the

ON THE ROARING RUN TRAIL

mend from clear-cutting—the canopy is scant and spotty because the trees are spread out and their crowns are small. The overabundance of nourishing sunlight allows the underbrush to take off, with certain plant species spreading very quickly. Because of the potential for thorny plant life on the trail, it is best to wear long pants or tall socks through here.

After 0.3 mile of steep, occasionally winding climbing, the Painter Rock Trail reaches the crest of Laurel Ridge, continuing more directly up the spine of the ridge. To the left, the gently sloping north edge of the mountain continues downhill, and to the right, the forest drops away at a steep angle, falling nearly 1,000 feet down to Roaring Run. At the 1.9 mile marker, a sign on the left side of the trail indicates the connector trail to the North Loop Trail. Head straight past this junction to stay on the Painter Rock Trail. Arrive at the cracked and crumbling cliff ledges of Painter Rock very shortly after passing the North Loop Trail connector. When the leaves are off the trees, a partially obscured view can be seen to the south. Even if the leaves block the view, the craggy formation is certainly interesting and there are plenty of crevices to explore along the foot of the rocks.

Continue following the Painter Rock Trail past the rock outcropping when you are ready, continuing to ascend along the edge of the ridge for another 0.3 mile, passing a few more unique rock formations. At this point the trail levels out slightly and bends to the left, heading away from the steep drop-off on grassy terrain that is significantly less brushy. At the 2.7 mile mark, arrive at another junction with the North Loop Trail. Keep right and head downhill, picking up the tread of the McKenna Trail. The McKenna Trail is blazed blue and yellow, and its tread is wide and well-graded. In 0.2 mile, a leg of the Roaring Run Trail breaks off the McKenna Trail to the right. Continue straight on the McKenna Trail to stay up near the top of Laurel Ridge for now. Beyond this junction, the McKenna Trail gently trends uphill, passing several very large oak trees in the process. Reach another leg of the Roaring Run Trail in 0.4 mile. Turn right here, leaving the McKenna Trail behind, and begin heading downhill on a moderately steep slope on the narrow, bumpy tread of the Roaring Run Trail.

Follow the uneven, winding sidehill tread of this portion of the Roaring Run Trail for 0.5 mile, passing through a few wet spots where rainfall drains into the Roaring Run basin. The trail meets with the dirt road grade of Nedro Road beyond these drainage flats. Turn left onto the old road, and follow it gradually uphill, following alternating red and yellow blazes. After 0.2 mile, on the left side

of the trail, a stone monument stands, memorializing three children who were killed by a falling tree in 1896 while riding their sleigh home from church. The monument is a unique highlight of the hike, albeit one that is quite macabre. Continue on the road for another 0.2 mile past the monument to arrive at a large parking area. The road grade turns left here and becomes Painter Rock Road, which heads uphill on very bumpy terrain. Walk through the parking area

ONE OF MANY SMALL CASCADES ALONG ROARING RUN

SNOWY SIDEHILL TREAD DROPPING INTO THE VALLEY

more prominent farther on. As the trail progresses, its tread drops in elevation moderately and becomes much rockier. The trail switchbacks sharply to the right at one point, descends in a small ravine to cross two trickling streams, and at mile marker 4.8 arrives at the main tread of the Roaring Run Trail. For the next 2.7 miles, the Roaring Run Trail follows the flow downstream, crossing the run at many points, all without the aid of footbridges. It is possible to pick your way across the water on stepping stones at most of these crossings, but if the water level is high, it may be impossible to cross without getting your feet wet. In the summertime, this portion of the hike is a great way to relax and cool down, especially since the scenery surrounding Roaring Run is some of the prettiest in Pennsylvania. The gradually descending trail along the creek is extremely picturesque, featuring large blocky boulders and lush green vegetation that perfectly complement the babbling brook and its miniature cascades and eddys.

At the 7.5 mile mark, the Roaring Run Trail arrives back at the junction with the Painter Rock Trail. Head uphill away from the stream, continuing on the Roaring Run Trail to arrive back at the parking area and your vehicle in approximately 1 mile.

and pick up the continuation of the Roaring Run Trail.

After leaving the road grade, the yellow-blazed trail meanders through deciduous forest composed of cherry and beech trees, with oaks becoming

Wolf Rocks Loop

DISTANCE: 4.5 miles	
DIFFICULTY: Moderate	
HIKING TIME: 2 hours	
TYPE: Loop	
TOTAL ELEVATION GAIN: 309'	
MAXIMUM ELEVATION: 2,734'	

One of the finest hikes in the Forbes State Forest, the walk to Wolf Rocks is considered by some to be one of the easiest. The trail wanders through the woods on relaxed, rolling ups and downs and generously rewards hikers with a magnificent view that does not quite match the relatively small amount of physical effort required to reach the vista. By no means does this discrepancy in effort-to-payoff cheapen the experience. It does, however, mean that the viewpoint can be busy on pleasant, sunny, summer weekends. Thankfully the rocky vista is large enough to accommodate a good number of visitors at one time.

The Wolf Rocks Trail heads northwest from the parking lot in Laurel Summit State Park and meanders gently through the Forbes State Forest to reach the vista on the rocks. The excursion, which is suitable for hikers of all ages and skill levels, starts and ends at the picnic area in the state park. If you have the time and energy after completing the loop, consider tacking the hike to nearby Beam Rocks onto your day. While both hikes are excellent on their own, the combination of the two makes a great pairing for individuals exploring the Laurel Highlands region.

GETTING THERE

From the west, follow I-76 E and take exit 91 toward Ligonier. At the end of the ramp, turn right onto PA 31 E and drive for 0.6 mile. Take the first right and pass over the highway, continuing onto Main Street. In 0.2 mile, turn left onto PA 711/Ligonier Street and drive for 12.2 miles. Turn right onto US 30 E and continue for 7.5 miles. Turn right onto Laurel Summit Road and drive for 5.6 miles. Turn right onto Linn Run Road. In 0.1 mile, turn right to enter Laurel Summit State

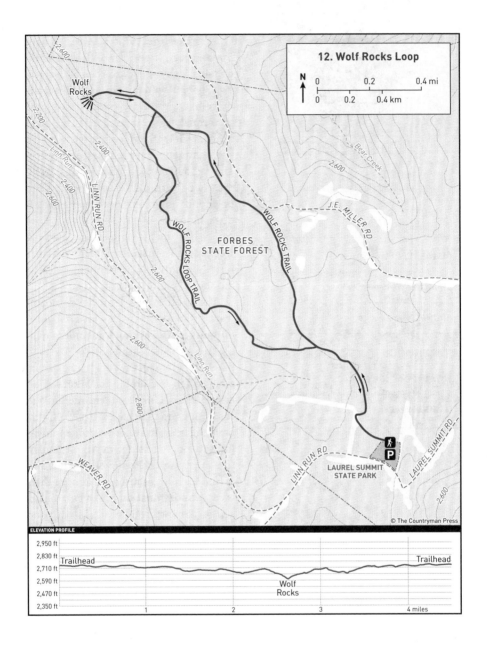

12. Wolf Rocks Loop

ELEVATION PROFILE

Park. The Wolf Rocks Trail starts to the left of the pit toilets, which are located at the large gravel parking lot.

From the east, follow I-76 W and take exit 146 toward US 220/I-99. At the end of the ramp, merge onto US 220 BUS S, and drive for 0.3 mile. Turn right onto Weber Lane. In one mile, turn left onto Country Ridge Road and follow it for 0.3 mile. Turn right onto US 30 W and continue to follow it for 36.6 miles. Turn left onto Laurel Summit Road. In 5.6 miles, Laurel Summit Road turns to the right and becomes Linn Run Road. Turn right

ENJOYING THE WOLF ROCKS VISTA

into Laurel Summit State Park. The Wolf Rocks Trail starts to the left of the pit toilets, which are located at the large gravel parking lot.

GPS Shortcut: Type "Wolf Rocks Trail Trailhead" into Google Maps and your GPS will navigate you to the trailhead which is located near the Laurel Mountain Ski Resort.

THE HIKE

Enter the woods on the Wolf Rocks Trail at the northwest end of the parking area. The trail is marked with blue blazes and is wide, gravelly, and fairly flat right from the start, with a few roots and rocks here and there to keep the hike interesting. Thick patches of mountain laurel, rhododendrons, hemlock, and white pines grow on either side of the pathway, hedging in the trail with their fleshy, aromatic evergreen leaves and needles. After 0.1 mile, an old grassy road grade runs across the trail. Continue straight to stay on the Wolf Rocks Trail, which becomes a bit rockier as the forest opens up in 0.4 mile. You will need to pay more attention to where you step at this point, but

AT THE START OF THE WOLF ROCKS TRAIL

faintly discernible herd path on the right side of the trail leads to the dirt tread of J. E. Miller Road. Stay on the Wolf Rocks Trail, curving through the forest past this short spur to the road. The forest in this area is mostly deciduous, with many stately oak trees populating the top of Laurel Ridge. In the summer, a multitude of ferns grow here, dancing in the sunlight to give the landscape a subtle hint of movement.

After hiking for 1.8 miles on the wide, rocky trail, the Wolf Rocks Trail arrives at another intersection. To the left is the other end of the Wolf Rocks Loop Trail, which leads back to the first intersection. Continue straight, descending slightly to stay on the Wolf Rocks Trail. About 100 feet past the intersection, the Bobcat Trail breaks off to the right. Again, stay straight, continuing to descend gradually, and arrive at the vista on Wolf Rocks in a little more than 0.2 mile, just after entering a dense stand of mountain laurel and rhododendrons. This magnificent vista looks to the northwest, over a fairly narrow gorge. At the bottom of the gorge lies Linn Run, 500 feet below and out of sight. As its name suggests, the viewpoint is a rocky ledge with a few outcroppings that jut out from the chaotic collection of stones, allowing for dramatic photos as well as providing numerous places to sit and enjoy the scenery. This viewpoint is a popular place to take in the sunset on balmy summer nights.

When you are finished at the vista, head back to the intersection on the Wolf Rocks Trail, passing the Bobcat Trail on the way. At the intersection, veer to the right and begin following the Wolf Rocks Loop Trail. The red-blazed Wolf Rocks Loop Trail drops down about 100 feet, paralleling the tread of the Wolf Rocks Trail off the ridgetop. The equally wide footpath gently bends

you will be able to enjoy a view deeper into the forest here.

Very shortly after the change in terrain, the Wolf Rocks Trail arrives at an intersection. Two trails break away to the left, the Hobblebush Trail and the Wolf Rocks Loop Trail, while the Spruce Flats Trail leads to the right. You will eventually return to this point on the Wolf Rocks Loop Trail, but for now stay straight through this busy intersection and continue to follow the blue blazes of the Wolf Rocks Trail. Beyond the junction, the trail meanders through the Forbes State Forest, following very mellow terrain. At the 1.1-mile mark, a

GAZING OUT OVER THE LINN RUN GORGE

quite often as it follows rolling terrain, occasionally crossing a few small seasonal sources of flowing water on stepping stones and buried culverts. While the elevation change on this leg of the hike is very manageable, it is certainly the most climbing you will have encountered thus far. In addition to the ups and downs, the terrain on the Wolf Rocks Loop Trail is much rockier than the tread of the blue-blazed trail. If you are hiking when the leaves are off the trees, there is the potential for continued, partially obstructed views of the Linn Run gorge off to the right.

In approximately 1.7 miles, the Wolf Rocks Loop Trail arrives at the first trail junction you encountered, emerging into the intersection clearing to the left of the Hobblebush Trail. From this point, turn right and rejoin the blue-blazed Wolf Rocks Trail. Retrace your previous course along this trail and arrive back at the parking area in 0.5 mile.

Beam Rocks

DISTANCE: 0.9 mile

DIFFICULTY: Easy

HIKING TIME: 1 hour

TYPE: Out and Back

TOTAL ELEVATION GAIN: 109'

MAXIMUM ELEVATION: 2,721'

In Forbes State Forest, just north of Laurel Summit State Park, is the Beam Rocks Trail. This easy hike leads to a broad, natural stone platform that surveys the surrounding forest. The hike, which can be done by hikers of all skill levels at any time of year, is very popular on its own or as an addendum to the nearby Wolf Rocks Loop. Rock climbers also enjoy the formation, and they may be seen scaling the rocks from time to time.

The short hike to Beam Rocks follows a wide gravel footpath down gently descending terrain. From the oddly sculpted stone outcropping, one can experience excellent views looking westward. Just before reaching the vista, a spur of the Beam Rocks Trail connects with the Laurel Highlands Hiking Trail, a 70-mile backpacking trail that follows Laurel Ridge on its slanting northward course. As always, please use caution on the rocks as the sheer drop-off from the vista is close to 80 feet. It is possible to descend to the base of Beam Rocks by following either a leg of the Beam Rocks Trail or a number of unmarked paths. The unmarked paths require scrambling down steep stone faces, and the descending spur of the Beam Rocks Trail requires a short bushwhack to reach the bottom of the rocks. Both options should only be attempted at your own risk.

GETTING THERE

From the west, follow I-76 E and take exit 91 toward Ligonier. At the end of the ramp, turn right onto PA 31 E and drive for 0.6 mile. Take the first right and pass over the highway, continuing onto Main Street. In 0.2 mile, turn left onto PA 711/ Ligonier Street and drive for 12.2 miles. Turn right onto US 30 E and continue for

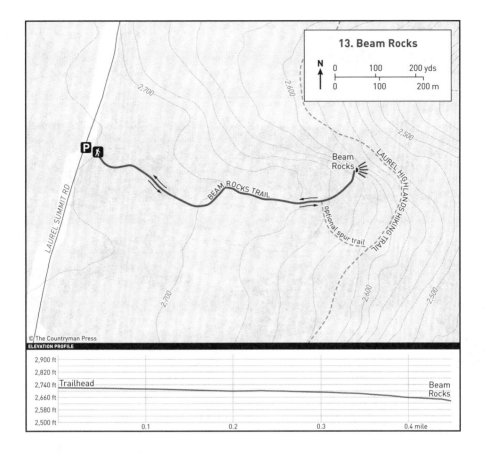

© The Countryman Press

7.5 miles. Turn right onto Laurel Summit Road. Follow Laurel Summit Road for 4.2 miles to reach the Beam Rock parking area on the right side of the road.

From the east, follow I-76 W and take exit 146 toward US 220/I-99. At the end of the ramp, merge onto US 220 BUS S, and drive for 0.3 mile. Turn right onto Weber Lane. In one mile, turn left onto Country Ridge Road and follow it for 0.3 mile. Turn right onto US 30 W and continue to follow it for 36.6 miles. Turn left onto Laurel Summit Road. In 4.2 miles, the parking area, a gravel pull off, will be on the left side of the road.

GPS Shortcut: Type "Beam Rock Parking" into Google Maps and your GPS will navigate you to the trailhead

located near the Laurel Mountain Ski Resort.

THE HIKE

Head into the woods on the east side of the road, next to a metal sign at the parking area that marks the start of the short, pleasant, and popular Beam Rocks Trail. The trail is marked with red blazes, and it follows wide gravel tread that gently trends uphill. The terrain is easy and the forest is fairly open, allowing you to gaze deep into the trees. The majority of the trees at the start of the trail are deciduous, mostly oaks and beeches, which is a common Pennsylvanian mix. After 0.2 mile, the deciduous forest gives way to

THE LOOKOUT AT BEAM ROCKS

a patch of nice hemlocks and the ubiquitous mountain laurels that darken the woods of the Keystone State. Continue hiking through the hemlocks along the wide, easy trail.

A short distance after entering the evergreen trees, the trail bends to the left and begins descending just as gradually as the ascent. Follow the path as it passes beside a small collection of boulders covered with ferns and moss, skirting the foot of their prominent protrusion. In another 0.1 mile, the red blazes of the Beam Rocks Trail split, with one leg of the trail leading to the right, descending off the ridgetop and connecting with the Laurel Highlands Hiking Trail. The Laurel Highlands Hiking Trail runs through the forest below the overlook at Beam Rocks, but it does not lead directly underneath the craggy cliff. If you wish to explore the bottom of the rock formation but want to avoid the steep scramble down the side of the rocks, you can turn right here and follow the path down toward the Laurel Highlands Hiking Trail and turn left onto the yellow-blazed trail, but you will have to bushwhack a short distance to reach the base of Beam Rocks. To head toward the vista on top of the rocks, keep left and continue descending gradually.

Arrive at the summit of Beam Rocks roughly 0.1 mile after the trail splits. The vista looks to the east from a wide, flat rock platform that peeks out 90 feet above the forest below. The wavy texture of the rock can be slippery in wet, snowy, or icy conditions, so use caution, especially near the edge. This is a great place to take a break and enjoy the scenery. In the fall, the foliage puts on an impressive show from the vista, especially at sunrise. If you wish to explore the bottom of the rocks, follow an unmarked herd path to the left just before stepping onto the broad platform. This steeply descending route requires the use of both hands and feet and can be very challenging, even for experienced hikers. Be smart, and do not continue farther downhill if you feel unsafe or unsure.

To return to the parking area, turn around and retrace your footsteps, heading back up the Beam Rocks Trail.

BEAM ROCKS AS SEEN FROM BELOW

Mount Davis High Point

DISTANCE: 6 miles	
DIFFICULTY: Difficult	
HIKING TIME: 3 hours	
TYPE: Loop	
TOTAL ELEVATION GAIN: 860'	
MAXIMUM ELEVATION: 3,213'	

Rising to the height of 3,213 feet above sea level, the high point on Mount Davis is the tallest naturally occurring point in the state of Pennsylvania. The elevation and accompanying weather conditions have hindered the growth of many of the trees and allowed hardier vegetation that is usually found farther north to grow in the area. The mountain was named after John Nelson Davis who was, among other things, a surveyor and naturalist who was fascinated by the mountain. After Davis's death in 1913, the Commonwealth of Pennsylvania began purchasing the land around the high point, and in 1974 the newly named Mount Davis Natural Area was established. Since then, the mountain has been a popular tourist destination, due not only to its status as the highest point in the state but also because of the trail network both in Mount Davis Natural Area and in the tract of Forbes State Forest that surrounds it.

The hike described here follows high-clearance forest roads, shared-use trail, and hiking-only footpaths that ramble around the mountaintop. Scenic views can be had at a few points throughout the hike, especially when the leaves are off the trees. Other highlights include a peaceful walk along a tributary of Laurel Run known as Tub Mill Run, unique rock formations, historical markers, and an observation tower. While the wooded summit does not offer any sort of view naturally, the metal observation tower provides an excellent 360-degree view of the surrounding forest, gazing over the stunted trees that inhabit the high point. A relief map at the top of the tower makes it easy to identify nearby natural features and colors the view with a touch of context.

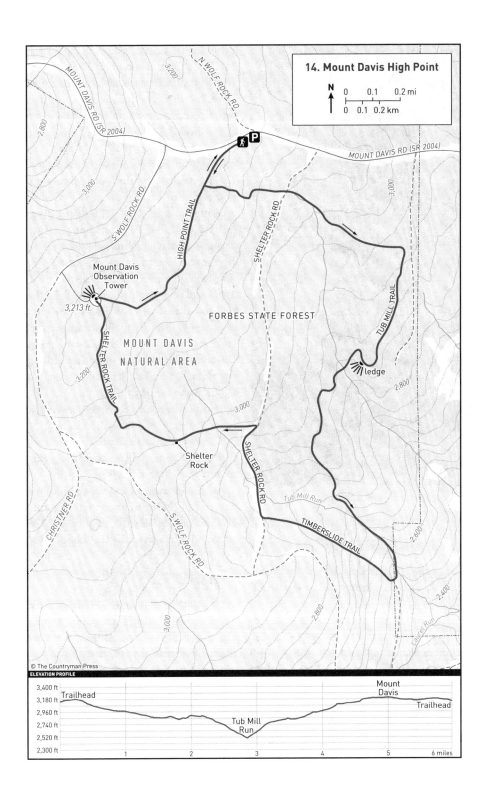

14. Mount Davis High Point

N

0   0.1   0.2 mi
0 0.1 0.2 km

MOUNT DAVIS RD (SR 2004)

N WOLF ROCK RD

3,200

3,000

MOUNT DAVIS RD (SR 2004)

P

S WOLF ROCK RD

SHELTER ROCK RD

HIGH POINT TRAIL

Mount Davis
Observation
Tower

3,213 ft.

FORBES STATE FOREST

TUB MILL TRAIL

ledge

2,800

MOUNT DAVIS
NATURAL AREA

SHELTER ROCK TRAIL

3,200

3,000

Shelter
Rock

SHELTER ROCK RD

Tub Mill Run

2,600

CHRISTNER RD

S WOLF ROCK RD

TIMBERSLIDE TRAIL

2,400

Laurel Run

2,800

3,000

© The Countryman Press

ELEVATION PROFILE

3,400 ft
3,180 ft   Trailhead
2,960 ft
2,740 ft
2,520 ft
2,300 ft

Tub Mill
Run

Mount
Davis

Trailhead

1   2   3   4   5   6 miles

THE OBSERVATION TOWER ON TOP OF MOUNT DAVIS

GETTING THERE

From the west, follow I-76 E and take exit 91 toward Ligonier. At the end of the ramp, turn left and follow PA 31 E for 11.7 miles, then turn right onto Trent Road and continue for 3.7 miles. Make a left onto Countyline Road and continue to follow the road for 6 miles, passing through New Centerville and Rockwood. The road becomes Rockdale Road in Rockwood just before crossing Casselman River. Continue for 4.2 miles on Rockdale Road, then turn right onto Old Mule Trail Road and follow it for 4.4 miles. Turn right onto Matlick Road,

drive for 1.6 miles, then turn right onto Mt Davis Road. Make a right in 0.8 mile to stay on Mt Davis Road, and 2.5 miles later arrive at the parking area on the left side of the road, in front of a large picnic area.

From the east, take I-76 W and take exit 110 toward Somerset/Johnstown. After exiting, loop under the interstate and continue straight across N Center Avenue and follow N Pleasant Avenue for 0.7 mile. Turn left onto E Main Street and drive 0.3 mile. Make a slight right onto Plank Road and continue for 2 miles. Turn right and merge onto US 219 S and follow it for 10 miles. Take the exit toward US 219 S BUS and turn left at the end of the ramp. In 2.1 miles, turn right onto Broadway Street and cross Casselman River. On the other side of the river, Broadway Street becomes Mt Davis Road. Follow Mt Davis Road for 4.2 miles, then turn right to stay on the road. In 1.6 miles, make another right to continue on Mt Davis Road. In 2.5 miles, the parking area will be on the left side of the road, in front of a large picnic area.

GPS Shortcut: In Google Maps search for "Mount Davis Pennsylvania Highpoint Trailhead" and your GPS will navigate you to the trailhead.

THE HIKE

Walk southwest from the parking area, heading mildly uphill through the picnic area, roughly paralleling the nearby road. Enter the woods, turning to the left onto a wide grassy path behind a metal gate. This is the High Point Trail, a yellow-blazed footpath that occupies the remains of an old forest road grade. Continue up this easy, mountain laurel-lined trail for 0.1 mile to reach a signed intersection. Going straight and staying on the High Point Trail will lead you to the observation tower on the summit. For now, turn to the left and begin following the Tub Mill Trail. The Tub Mill Trail is also marked with yellow blazes at this point and rambles through Mount Davis Natural Area, heading moderately downhill. The tread of this route starts as a wide, mossy footpath, similar to the terrain before the intersection, but it becomes rockier and rootier the farther it travels from the High Point Trail, eventually tapering to a narrow singletrack.

Approximately 0.5 mile after beginning the hike, the Tub Mill Trail is intersected by Shelter Rock Road, a gravel access road that forms the boundary of Mount Davis Natural Area. If you wanted to bypass the rest of the Tub Mill Trail, you could turn right onto Shelter Rock Road, following it for just under 1 mile to meet with the Shelter Rock Trail, which leads up toward the observation tower. For the purposes of this hike, turn left onto the road and cross a culvert. Immediately after crossing the culvert, turn right and reenter the woods, continuing on the Tub Mill Trail. You will notice that the trail, now outside of Mount Davis Natural Area, is now marked with red blazes. The terrain on this stretch of the trail is much more rugged, advancing through the pretty, spacious forest on bands of pointy jagged rocks, occasionally alternating with short lengths of smooth mossy tread.

At the 1.1-mile mark, in the midst of a young, spindly patch of trees, the Tub Mill Trail turns to the right just before reaching another gravel access road. Follow the red blazes as they mirror the tread of the road for 0.4 mile along relatively easy, gradually descending terrain. At the 1.5-mile mark, the trail briefly bends to the right around a large rock formation, emerging onto the top of a wooded 20-foot-tall ledge. While the view from the ledge is not particularly far-reaching, surveying the densely treed hollow below, it is nonetheless a very pleasant, tranquil sight to behold. Continue along the mossy edge of this short precipice for a short distance, then turn to the left and descend through a crack in the ledge, and begin making your way through the hollow. In 0.3 mile, cross the bed of a seasonal watercourse, which, when running, empties into Tub Mill Run farther downstream. On the other side of this tributary, begin heading through an area of Forbes State Forest that was recently clear-cut. The stumps of felled trees litter the forest floor in the thick brush on either side

HISTORICAL MARKER ADORNING THE SUMMIT

HEADING UPHILL ON THE TIMBERSLIDE TRAIL

the creek, which is shaded in tall hemlock trees. Continue to follow picturesque Tub Mill Run downhill for 0.2 mile, often passing small cascades that spill over stepped rocks into tuneful pools below. There are plenty of comfortable places to stop and rest along the edge of the stream, should you wish to do so.

At the 2.7-mile mark, the Tub Mill Trail crosses the run and advances through the forest for 0.1 mile to meet with the Timberslide Trail. Turn right and begin ascending the sparsely red-blazed Timberslide Trail. This is the steepest, longest sustained climb of the entire hike, heading uphill on rocky tread that gets progressively steeper as you gain elevation, navigating through rhododendrons and mountain laurels. Near the top, the grade begins to ease, and after 0.6 mile the Timberslide Trail meets with the broad, grassy tread of Shelter Rock Road. Turn right and follow Shelter Rock Road, trending uphill at a much easier angle of ascent. Shelter Rock Road passes Wildcat Spring on the right, then crosses over a bridge spanning Tub Mill Run. Continue following the road grade gradually uphill.

In 0.4 mile, arrive at the junction of the Shelter Rock Trail. Turn left onto the Shelter Rock Trail and follow its yellow blazes, continuing to ascend moderately for approximately 0.3 mile to reach the namesake of this trail off to the left. Shelter Rock is a tall, rounded rock formation with a small overhanging portion that would certainly provide a welcome reprieve from the elements in a pinch. Follow the trail past Shelter Rock as it bends to the right and resume a mild climb, rambling over blocky boulders at random intervals. Roughly 0.5 mile after passing Shelter Rock, the trail climbs up one more short, moderate section before leveling out entirely. From this point on,

of the trail here, and to the left through the clearing a scenic view looks to the southeast. After crossing the clear-cut area, the grade of the Tub Mill Trail levels off and traverses the edge of the clearing for a short distance, continuing to offer limited views of the surrounding valleys and ridges, especially in the fall and winter months.

At the 2.2-mile mark, the trail resumes through more densely wooded forest. Pass another cluster of boulders before beginning to descend over lumpy, moss-covered rocks, getting progressively closer to the flow of Tub Mill Run. In 0.3 mile, the descending path reaches the edge of the Shelter Rock Trail follows the flat top of the mountain on a fairly straight trajectory amidst short, gnarled trees that have been stunted by exposure to the intense weather conditions that exist at this elevation.

At mile 4.8, the Mount Davis Trail breaks off the Shelter Rock Trail to the right. This very short connector trail bypasses the observation tower and connects to the High Point Trail. Stay on the Shelter Rock Trail and arrive at an old, circular asphalt road shortly after the junction. This is the summit of Mount Davis, the highest point in the state of Pennsylvania. In the center of the circle lies the observation tower, which offers a 360-degree view of the area. A brass relief map at the top of the tower aids in identifying natural landmarks. Looking south from the tower on a clear day, one can see well into Maryland. At the foot of the tower, there are several brass plaques mounted on stones to provide a bit of geological and historical context to the mountain.

When you are finished enjoying the observation tower, pick up the High Point Trail at the eastern edge of the paved circle. Pass the junction with the Mount Davis Trail a short distance after resuming the hike on the High Point Trail. The High Point Trail follows easy terrain on wide, grassy tread for 0.9 mile, very gradually descending to arrive once more at the junction with the Tub Mill Trail. From here, stay straight on the High Point Trail and follow it to where it ends near Mount Davis Road. Turn right after you emerge from the woods and make your way through the picnic area to return to your vehicle.

Cook Forest Ancient Forest Loop

DISTANCE: 2.9 miles	
DIFFICULTY: Moderate	
HIKING TIME: 1.5 hours	
TYPE: Loop	
TOTAL ELEVATION GAIN: 536'	
MAXIMUM ELEVATION: 1,541'	

In the center of Cook Forest State Park lies the Forest Cathedral Natural Area. This portion of the park sits to the east of Toms Run and features old-growth white pines and hemlock trees that were spared from clear-cutting during the logging boom. The natural area supports a system of footpaths that explore the deep mossy folds of the land, winding through fern-covered understory beneath the giant trees. Walking through the shady forest, a feeling of peace, tranquility, and reverence is almost physically palpable. Some of the trees here are nearly 200 feet tall and have been standing for over 350 years. Given the rich ecological history and the profound feeling of awe the forest instills in its visitors, it comes as no surprise that this tract of land was preserved.

The moderate hike described here follows a number of trails through the Forest Cathedral Natural Area, including a stretch on the North Country Trail, the only trail in the park that is blazed blue instead of yellow. The North Country Trail also shares tread with the Baker Trail through the park. The Baker Trail is a 132-mile hiking and backpacking trail, starting near Freeport in the south and ending in the Allegheny National Forest in the north. From the parking area, the trail follows along Toms Run and crosses the water on a swinging bridge before delving into the heart of the old-growth forest. The terrain is relatively smooth and easy to follow for the majority of the hike, and the elevation changes only moderately. This hike is one that can be enjoyed by hikers of all ages and skill levels. On its own the Ancient Forest Loop is a relaxing afternoon jaunt, but it can also be combined with a number of other trails for a longer, customized,

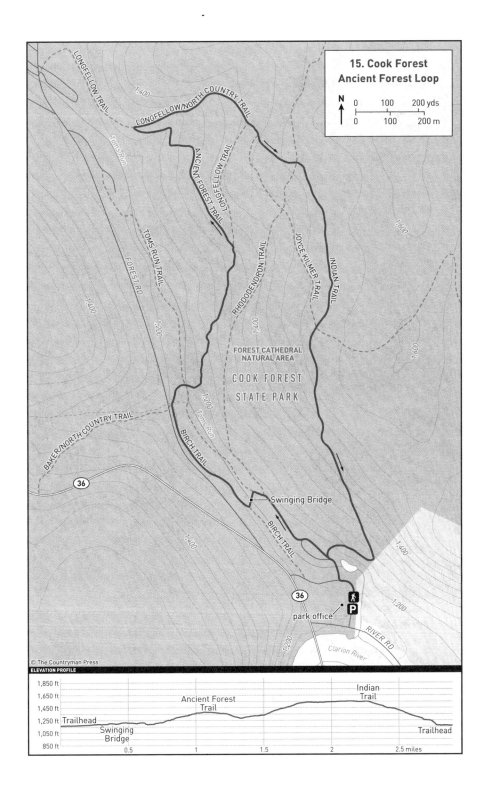

HIKERS ON THE SWINGING BRIDGE OVER TOMS RUN

more demanding walk through the woods.

GETTING THERE

From the west, follow I-80 E and take exit 62 toward Clarion. At the end of the ramp, turn left onto PA 68 E and continue straight for 3.1 miles, passing through the borough of Clarion. After crossing the Clarion River, the road becomes Miola Road. Follow Miola Road for 10.5 miles, then turn right onto PA 36 E. Follow the road for 3.2 miles, then turn left onto State Route 2002, just before crossing the Clarion River again. The parking area will be on the left in 200 feet, in front of a state park building.

From the east, follow I-80 W and take exit 78 toward Brookville/Sigel. At the end of the ramp, turn right onto PA 36 N. Follow PA 36 N for 15.6 miles, passing through Sigel. Cross the Clarion River and immediately turn right onto State Route 2002. The parking area will be on the left in 200 feet, in front of a state park building.

GPS Shortcut: Enter "Cook Forest State Park Indian Cabin Office" into Google Maps and your GPS will direct you to the parking area.

THE HIKE

From the parking area, head north on the gravel road that roughly follows Toms Run, crossing the water on a footbridge to the left of a children's fishing pond. Make your way through a circle of state park cabins and enter the woods on the Rhododendron Trail. Follow the wide, shady tread of the Rhododendron Trail, mirroring the run upstream for a scant 0.1 mile, then turn to the left and cross Toms Run on the swinging bridge, a narrow cable suspension bridge that

spans the water. On the other side of the run, turn right and resume hiking upstream along Toms Run on the Birch Trail on rolling terrain that ascends and descends gradually to moderately on similarly wide, easy terrain.

After hiking for 0.5 mile, your course begins to bend farther away from Toms Run, leading more closely to Forest Road to the left of the trail. Continue through the shade of the hemlocks for another 0.1 mile to arrive at an intersection with the Longfellow Trail, just after a small gravel parking area. The Birch Trail continues north along the road, while the Longfellow Trail bends to the right, descending back toward the stream. The Longfellow Trail is part of the Baker Trail and the North Country Trail, and as such is marked with blue and yellow blazes, in contrast to the solely yellow

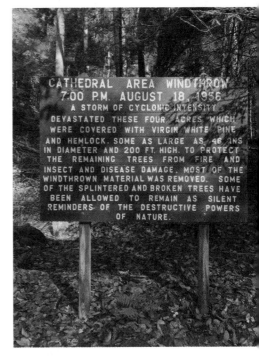

WOODEN SIGN MARKING THE CATHEDRAL AREA WINDTHROW

PEACEFUL SCENERY ON THE NORTH COUNTRY TRAIL

current trajectory. Turn to the right to stay on the Longfellow, Baker, and North Country Trails, which continue to share tread with each other. The trail climbs more aggressively after meeting with the Red Eft Trail, ascending for 0.2 mile to meet the Ancient Forest Trail at the 1-mile mark. Turn left onto the Ancient Forest Trail, leaving the blue-blazed trails for the time being, and continue on wide, easy sidehill tread through majestic old-growth forest. A multitude of white pine and hemlock trees populate the hillside here, their dense canopies reaching straight up toward the sky, towering above the fern-covered understory. On cool, misty mornings, a smattering of scattered sunlight occasionally penetrates the considerable cover of the treetops, made visible to the naked eye by the moisture hanging in the air. This awe-inspiring phenomenon invokes a feeling of beautiful stillness, making it absolutely clear why this area came to be known as the Forest Cathedral. Continue at a relaxed pace on gently rolling hills to thoroughly enjoy the greatest population of old-growth white pines in the northeastern United States. At a few places on the Ancient Forest Trail, rustic benches have been cut into the massive trunks of fallen trees to encourage hikers to take a break and more intimately enjoy this special place.

The Ancient Forest Trail ends in 0.3 mile, shortly after crossing a small seasonal stream on a plank footbridge and ascending a short folded hillside, meeting once again with the Longfellow, Baker, and North Country Trails on a wide, gravel tread. Turn right and follow the blue-blazes uphill moderately for 0.2 mile. The trails bend to the right, leveling out significantly through a windthrow area. A large wooden sign marks the start of this area, giving a brief

blazes that denote every other footpath in the park. Turn right onto the Longfellow Trail and head down a short set of wooden steps. At the bottom of the staircase, use the small footbridge to cross a stream that empties into Toms Run. After crossing this footbridge, arrive at a junction with the Toms Run Trail, which continues upstream to the left. Turn right here again and walk on another footbridge to cross back over Toms Run. The blue-blazed trail turns sharply to the left after crossing this second bridge and heads uphill at a relaxed pace on bumpy, rooty terrain.

Ascend gradually for approximately 0.1 mile to arrive at another trail junction, this time with the Red Eft Trail that continues straight ahead on your

MASSIVE MOSSY BOULDERS ON THE INDIAN TRAIL

description of the destruction caused by an intense storm that occurred on August 18th, 1956. Continue through the windthrow area, passing a cacophony of broken and uprooted trees to arrive at the northern end of the Indian Trail in 0.1 mile.

Turn left onto the Indian Trail, once more leaving the blue-blazed trail. Head gradually uphill, crossing the tread of the Rhododendron Trail in 0.2 mile. Continue to follow the Indian Trail through the old-growth trees and a scattered collection of large boulders. For the next 0.6 mile, the trail is well-graded albeit quite rooty as it begins to trend downhill very slowly. At mile marker 2.6, the Indian Trail approaches the boundary of Cook Forest State Park. Make an abrupt turn to the right to avoid the private property and begin heading downhill aggressively at the southern end of the rounded Forest Cathedral ridge. This quick, direct descent leads 0.1 mile to the cabin area near the start of the hike.

From the cabin area, turn left and head back over Toms Run, making your way down the gravel road toward the Clarion River to arrive back at your vehicle.

II.

CENTRAL PENNSYLVANIA

16

Teaberry and Lincoln Loops

DISTANCE: 5.4 miles	
DIFFICULTY: Difficult	
HIKING TIME: 2 hours	
TYPE: Loop	
TOTAL ELEVATION GAIN: 597'	
MAXIMUM ELEVATION: 2,041'	

Home to many elk, bears, deer, and other wildlife, the sprawling 48,186-acre Quehanna Wild Area is a part of both the Elk and Moshannon State Forests, and it is the largest designated wild area in the state. The state acquired the land in the 1970s after a long and somewhat tumultuous industrial history; very rarely is nuclear radiation contamination mentioned when discussing a wild area. Thankfully for hikers, hunters, anglers, and wildlife alike, the low level radiation dump sites on this land have been found to be harmless.

The Quehanna Trail, a 75-mile hiking trail, circles through Quehanna Wild Area and Moshannon State Forest to the west. Part of the rugged and lonely Quehanna Trail system, the Teaberry Loop and Lincoln Loop Trails are actually two separate loops that can be linked together easily and hiked in an afternoon. While these trails do not actually share tread with the Quehanna Trail itself, a portion of the hike follows the Quehanna Trail Eastern Cross Connector (Q.T.E.C.C.) which, along with the Quehanna Trail Western Cross Connector (Q.T.W.C.C.), bisect the main loop and collectively add an additional 30 miles of trail to the Quehanna Trail system. When considering the plethora of other trails like the Teaberry Loop and Lincoln Loop Trails, intertwined throughout this wild area, the opportunities for exploration begin to feel boundless. The hike described here is an excellent introduction to the Quehanna Wild Area, and it features three striking vistas and a very picturesque stream.

GETTING THERE

From the west, follow I-80 E and take exit 101 toward Dubois/Penfield. At the

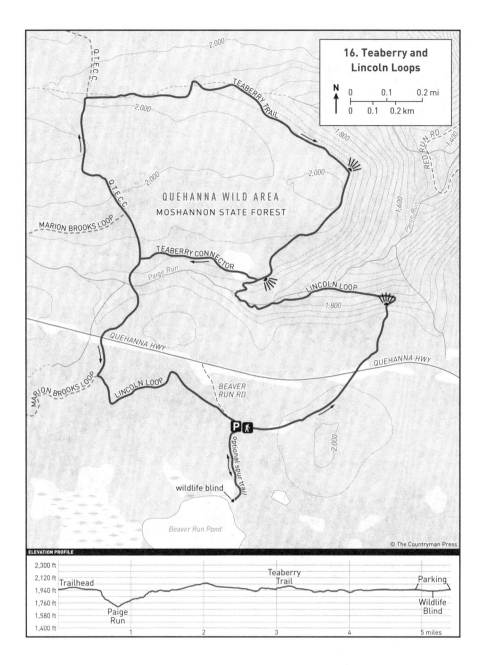

16. Teaberry and Lincoln Loops

ELEVATION PROFILE

end of the ramp, turn left and follow PA 255 N toward Penfield. Continue to follow PA 255 N for 16.2 miles, then make a slight right onto PA 555 E. Follow PA 555 E for 6.7 miles. Turn right onto the Quehanna Highway, following it for 10 miles. Keep an eye out for elk along this stretch of road! Turn right onto Beaver Run Road. The parking area will be on the right in 0.2 mile.

From the east, take I-80 W to exit 147 heading toward Snow Shoe. Merge onto Beech Creek Road at the end of the ramp, and follow it to the junction of PA

THE CASCADING FLOW OF PAIGE RUN

144 N. Turn left and follow PA 144 N for 5 miles. Turn left onto PA 897 W. After 9.7 miles, make a slight right onto the Quehanna Highway. Follow the Quehanna Highway for 13.3 miles, being careful to watch for elk, then turn left onto Beaver Run Road. In 0.2 mile, the parking area will be on the right.

GPS Shortcut: Search Google Maps for "Beaver Run Pond Wildlife Viewing Area Parking" and set it as your destination. Your GPS will lead you to the parking area near the town of Benezette.

THE HIKE

Head into the woods at the eastern end of the parking lot on an overgrown dirt road and begin to follow yellow blazes. This is the start of the Lincoln Loop, which follows the wide tread of the old dirt road, passes through a small open meadow, and in 0.4 mile arrives at the Quehanna Highway. Cross the highway and resume your walk on the disused dirt road, passing through areas peppered with white pine. Shortly after crossing the Quehanna Highway, the trail turns to the left and leaves the road grade behind. Descend moderately through an open meadow as the trail narrows. Afterward, the trail approaches a striking vista that looks to the north from a stone ledge. From here, make a sharp left and descend through dense rhododendrons to the foot of the ledge on short sketchy switchbacks, moving through a cleared area littered with the trunks of cut trees farther downhill. The trail again turns to the left by a chunky rock and begins to drop into a small hollow among young beech trees and more rhododendrons. The slope of the descent at this point is fairly mellow, but the terrain is quite challenging, forcing you to clamber over protruding rocks and roots on tightly constricted trail.

After 0.8 mile of hiking, the trail bends to the left immediately after passing an enormous boulder and begins a moderate ascent alongside the shadowy and scenic Paige Run. As before, the rough terrain makes this portion of the trail very difficult. Paige Run is extremely picturesque, however, featuring many small cascades and tuneful, burbling pools that provide a pleasing distraction from the arduous climb. Follow Paige Run upstream for 0.5 mile, passing through rhododendrons, hemlocks, and birches. From here you will turn to the right, crossing the stream on a series of wide stepping-stones, and continue to climb, heading away from

CLIMBING UPWARD THROUGH RHODODENDRON TUNNELS ON THE TEABERRY TRAIL

LAYERS OF SLOPING SHOULDERS AT QUEHANNA WILD AREA

the run. Your course zigzags uphill on steep, rugged, somewhat exposed trail and arrives at a post marking a junction with the Teaberry Loop Trail and the Teaberry Connector Trail 0.1 mile later. Heading west toward the Quehanna Trail East Cross Connector or Q.T.E.C.C., The Teaberry Connector Trail is marked on the signpost with an "L.L." as it is still considered part of the Lincoln Loop.

Turn left and begin walking the Teaberry Connector Trail, continuing to follow yellow blazes. The terrain of the connector is much more easygoing than that of the Lincoln Loop, as it passes through cheery mountain laurels before giving way to a scrub field. The open space here dramatically presents itself in stark contrast to the enclosed walk along Paige Run, but it is nonetheless equally beautiful. As you approach the end of the connector, the brush begins to fill out with white pines and assorted maples. The Teaberry Connector Trail ends at the Q.T.E.C.C., which trails off to the left and right. Turn right and begin following the trail north. About 0.1 mile later, the Marion Brooks Loop turns off to the left. If followed, this trail would eventually lead you out of the Quehanna Wild Area and to neighboring Marion Brooks Natural Area, which contains one of the largest stands of white birch trees in Pennsylvania. You want to continue straight, however, staying on the Q.T.E.C.C., and advance through tranquil Quehanna forest. As you proceed, the trail winds through a maze of dense mountain laurels that is especially captivating in the spring when their cuplike white and pink flowers are in bloom.

After approximately 2.1 total miles of hiking, turn right off the Q.T.E.C.C. onto the Teaberry Loop Trail, which is also marked with yellow blazes. Follow the Teaberry Loop Trail, skirting the edge of a narrow marsh, alternating between open areas similar to the Teaberry Connector Trail and the cover of white pines and oaks as well as more mountain laurels. The trail descends gradually, passing mossy rocks, following the flow of a small stream that drains from the marsh. As this drainage continues downhill and develops into a more substantial flow, rhododendrons begin to become more prominent. At mile 2.7 the trail turns to the left and begins a short climb up to the top of the hillside, passing through a stretch of intermittent rhododendron tunnels. Emerge at a small viewpoint on the left side of the trail at the 3-mile mark. This view looks to the northeast and may be somewhat obstructed by foliage depending on the time of year. Keep following the Teaberry Loop Trail, advancing on the sidehill trail, and

THE LEDGE VIEWPOINT ABOVE PAIGE RUN

ascending up and over a gentle bump to reach a larger, more exposed vista 0.5 mile later. From the top of a wide lumpy rock, one can enjoy the muffled roar of Paige Run in the ravine below as well as a good view looking southeast. This is a great place to sprawl out on a sunny day to eat a snack and take a break.

Continuing on, you will reach the junction with the Lincoln Loop and the Teaberry Connector Trail less than 0.1 mile after leaving the viewpoint. Turn right and follow the Teaberry Connector Trail to the Q.T.E.C.C., passing through the brushy field once more. When you reach the Q.T.E.C.C. this time, turn to the left and descend a short distance to Paige Run, which you will cross on a wooden footbridge. Afterward, the trail ascends gradually through red and white pine and crosses back over the Quehanna Highway at 4.25 miles. A short distance after reentering the woods on the other side of the road, the Lincoln Loop makes a sharp left,

while the Q.T.E.C.C. continues straight on. Turn to the left and follow the Lincoln Loop for 0.5 mile to reach the road you followed to reach the parking area. From here, veer right and follow the road for 0.1 mile to arrive back at your vehicle.

A short optional spur trail leads from the parking lot to the wildlife viewing area, which looks out over marshy Beaver Run Pond. It is an excellent place to see waterfowl and songbirds from behind a wooden bird blind. To reach the wildlife viewing area, enter the woods on a wide footpath behind the information kiosk at the southwestern end of the parking lot. This easy trail alternates between soft grass and crushed gravel, passing through mixed forest. After 0.25 mile, the trail ends at the bird blind, which is a relaxing place to unwind after your hike. When you are finished, head back the way you came to return to your vehicle. Visiting the wildlife viewing area will add 0.5 mile to your hike.

Fred Woods Trail

DISTANCE: 5 miles

DIFFICULTY: Easy

HIKING TIME: 2 hours

TYPE: Loop

TOTAL ELEVATION GAIN: 428'

MAXIMUM ELEVATION: 1,994'

Located in Elk State Forest, the pleasant Fred Woods Trail attracts hikers of all skill levels due to its easy tread and impressive features. Built from 1980 to 1981 by the Camp Quehanna Young Adult Conservation Corps, the trail is dedicated to the memory of a Bureau of Forestry foreman who died working on state forest land in 1975. While information on the life and work of the late Fred Woods is fairly scarce, his profound impact on Elk State Forest is still felt decades later. Very few individuals have public trails named in memory of their efforts, especially trail systems that feature such beautiful natural features as the Fred Woods Trail.

The trail system includes two scenic overlooks, a number of large boulders, and a short optional spur trail that passes through a narrow stone corridor. Those seeking a relaxing hike to exciting viewpoints will appreciate that the trailhead sits on top of the mountain. The drive to the trailhead follows PA 555, part of Pennsylvania's Scenic Elk Drive, and ends on a dirt road that, while bumpy and steep, is sure to be less strenuous than climbing to the top on foot. When following PA 555, be on the lookout for elk, which were reintroduced in Pennsylvania starting in 1913. Please note that the dirt road is not maintained in winter, meaning this hike is only accessible when there is no snow on the ground.

GETTING THERE

From the west, follow I-80 E and take exit 101 toward Dubois/Penfield. At the end of the ramp, turn left and follow PA 255 N toward Penfield. Continue to follow PA 255 for 16.2 miles, then make a slight right onto PA 555 E. Follow PA 555 E for 25.5 miles. Shortly before reaching

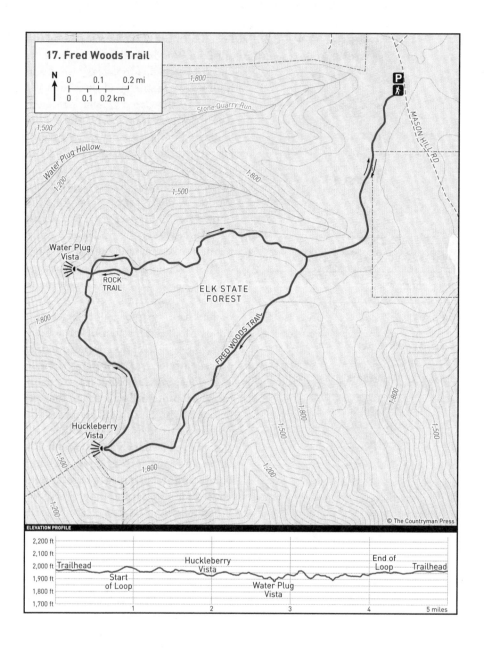

17. Fred Woods Trail

ELK STATE FOREST

Water Plug Vista

ROCK TRAIL

Huckleberry Vista

FRED WOODS TRAIL

Stone Quarry Run

Water Plug Hollow

MASON HILL RD

© The Countryman Press

ELEVATION PROFILE

Trailhead — Start of Loop — Huckleberry Vista — Water Plug Vista — End of Loop — Trailhead

the town of Driftwood, turn left onto Mason Hill Road and follow it for 3.7 miles. The trailhead will be on the left side of the road.

From the east, take PA 120 W heading west from Lock Haven and drive to the small town of Driftwood. From Driftwood, turn left onto Chestnut Street, which turns to the left and becomes PA 555 W. Follow PA 555 W for 0.7 mile and turn right onto Mason Hill Road. Follow Mason Hill Road for 3.7 miles to reach the trailhead on the left side of the road.

Mason Hill Road is not maintained in the winter months.

GPS Shortcut: Type "Fred Woods

Trail" into Google Maps and your GPS will navigate you to the trailhead.

THE HIKE

From the parking area enter the woods to the southwest next to a small information kiosk. The yellow blazes of the Fred Woods Trail follow the remains of a wide woods road, passing by a large stand of hemlocks immediately. After a short distance, the trail bends to the left and begins meandering through serene forest composed of both deciduous and coniferous trees. There may be muddy sections on this portion of the trail during periods of high rainfall or snowmelt, but these are easily traversable on well-placed stepping-stones and primitive log bridges. After 0.4 mile of easy hiking, the trail meets an old stone fence and briefly follows it before ascending a short gradual uphill section.

After 0.75 mile, the trail splits at the start of the loop portion of the Fred Woods Trail, which is marked by a large wooden sign. You have the option to go either direction from this point. For the purpose of this hike, turn to the left and continue to follow the yellow blazes. The terrain will become rockier than the old road grade you walked previously but should still be easy to navigate. In another 0.75 mile, pass through an area dotted with large blocky boulders on either side of the trail and begin a gradual ascent on the wooded lip of the mountain shortly thereafter. From here the ground drops off to the left of the trail down a very steep slope. When the leaves are off the trees, you can catch limited views of the Bennett Branch of the Sinnemahoning Creek flowing in the valley below. The trail levels off a short distance beyond this point and continues to follow the edge of

ENTERING THE CORRIDOR ON THE ROCK TRAIL

the mountaintop as it bends to the west and becomes significantly less rocky. After 1.9 miles of hiking, you will reach the Huckleberry Vista that looks out to the west from beneath a few weathered pine trees, peering out over the winding valley below. There are several good sitting rocks at this viewpoint, making it an excellent place to take a break, should you wish to do so.

After enjoying the vista, continue to follow the Fred Woods Trail as it wanders the mountaintop, heading north on rugged terrain. The trail narrows a short distance later as you meander through a section of huckleberry bushes and mountain laurels. You exit this shrubby corridor by passing through a large split rock formation. After hiking for

EXPANSIVE SCENERY AT THE HUCKLEBERRY VISTA

2.6 miles, you will reach the western end of the Rock Trail, which breaks off the Fred Woods Trail and continues uphill through a grove of hemlocks. If you turn to the right and take the Rock Trail, you will reconnect with the Fred Woods Trail 0.2 mile later, but you will miss seeing several house-sized boulders, the second vista, and will only save yourself 0.2 mile of walking. Turn to the left and follow the Fred Woods Trail on a gradual downhill grade to reach the Water Plug Vista less than 0.1 mile later on a wide flat rock. The Water Plug Vista looks out to the west over Water Plug Hollow below.

Continue on the Fred Woods Trail as it turns sharply to the east from the Water Plug Vista. As you progress you will pass several massive boulders resting on either side of the trail, and after 2.8 miles of hiking, you will reach the opposite end of the yellow-blazed Rock Trail. If you want to skip the Rock Trail, veer to the left, otherwise turn right here and begin to thread your way through a curious stone corridor. The sheer walls of this crevice are carpeted in delicate green moss. Toward the end of this short corridor, the trail passes under a tall rock overhang and then squeezes between a large flat stone slab leaning against the wall of the corridor. Upon exiting the corridor, the trail makes a quick U-turn to climb to the top of the crevice, which gives you the unique perspective of looking into the corridor you just passed through. Use caution near the edge of the crevice since it is not fenced off. Continue to follow the narrow Rock Trail as it winds downhill through dark hemlocks and mountain laurels, passing smaller split-rock rooms on the way. After following the Rock Trail for 0.2 mile, you will arrive back at the Fred Woods Trail just before Water Plug Vista. Turn right and follow the trail past the vista, retracing your footsteps to the junction with the eastern end of the Rock Trail, which you will reach after 3.2 total miles of hiking.

Continue past the turnoff for the Rock Trail this time, veering to the left to resume hiking on the tread of the Fred Woods Trail. The trail gradually descends a short distance from here, and it continues to snake through large boulders strewn about on either side of the trail. At 3.5 miles in, cross a wooden footbridge over the flow of a seasonal stream and enter a small grove of juvenile hemlocks. Pay close attention to the blazes and which direction the trail goes, as it regularly twists and turns at this point, oftentimes snaking around for no reason other than to lead you to, through, or nearby interesting rock formations.

THE WATER PLUG VISTA ALONG THE FRED WOODS TRAIL

After 4.25 miles of hiking, the trail reconnects you with the approach trail at the wooden sign you passed earlier. Turn left here and retrace your footsteps back down the old road grade to arrive back at your vehicle 0.75 mile later.

Little Juniata Natural Area

DISTANCE: 3.3 miles

DIFFICULTY: Difficult

HIKING TIME: 2.5 hours

TYPE: Out and Back

TOTAL ELEVATION GAIN: 1,341'

MAXIMUM ELEVATION: 2,039'

By definition, Pennsylvania's natural areas are protected from development to preserve unique plants, important animal populations, or interesting geographic features. Natural areas see very little "help" from human hands, and they are primarily allowed to evolve organically in their natural, wild state, maintained only by the delicate balance of a working ecosystem. As a result, these areas tend to be more rugged than state parks or game lands. The Mid State Trail through Little Juniata Natural Area, for example, climbs steeply up the southern tip of Tussey Mountain, following stretches of very difficult terrain to reach an exposed slope of white Tuscarora sandstone talus, or rock debris. While other trails may be smoothed out or rerouted to easier, more accessible terrain, the trails in a natural area embrace the existing conditions and allow outdoor enthusiasts to experience their surroundings through the lens nature intended.

The hike described here starts on the northern banks of the Little Juniata River in the Barree Gorge, and it ascends to the expansive ridge of Tussey Mountain on the Mid State Trail. The course follows disused road grade and rocky tread to a majestic viewpoint on the top of the ridge. Along the way, you will pass towering cliff faces and get a few limited views of the surrounding valley. The last leg of this hike follows extremely rough, rocky terrain that is challenging even when the weather conditions are excellent. If, however, you are willing to endure the rugged terrain, you will be rewarded with one of Pennsylvania's best views.

The Mid State Trail is the only trail system in Pennsylvania whose governing body uses the metric system to measure distance and elevation. For the sake

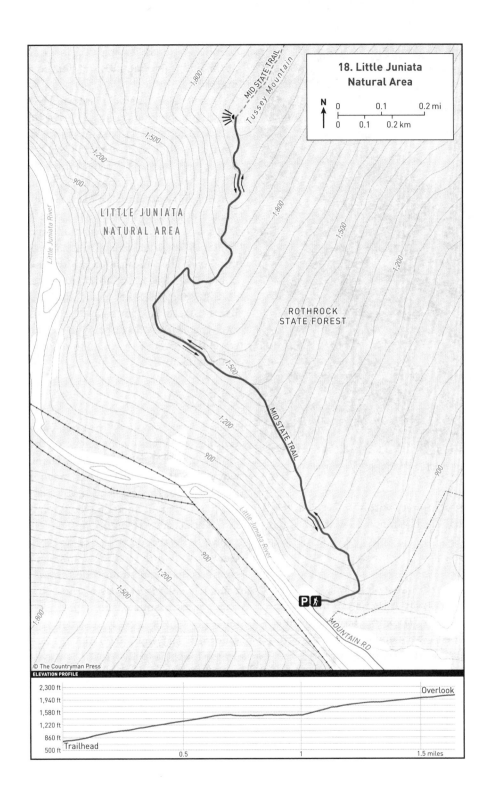

18. Little Juniata Natural Area

N

| 0 | 0.1 | 0.2 mi |

| 0 | 0.1 | 0.2 km |

1,800

MID STATE TRAIL

Tussey Mountain

1,500

1,200

900

Little Juniata River

LITTLE JUNIATA
NATURAL AREA

1,800

1,500

1,200

ROTHROCK
STATE FOREST

1,500

1,200

MID STATE TRAIL

900

900

Little Juniata River

1,200

900

1,500

1,800

1,200

P 🚶

MOUNTAIN RD

© The Countryman Press

ELEVATION PROFILE

2,300 ft	Overlook
1,940 ft	
1,580 ft	
1,220 ft	
860 ft	
500 ft	Trailhead

0.5   1   1.5 miles

STONE LOOKOUT ON TOP OF TUSSEY MOUNTAIN

Mountain Road. The parking area is at the end of Mountain Road, next to a metal gate.

From the east, navigate toward Lewistown and pick up US 522 S. Drive US 522 S for 41 miles, passing through Huntingdon. Turn right onto Bridge Street and follow it for 0.5 mile into Alexandria. Turn left onto Main Street. In 0.6 mile, turn right onto Barree Road, following it for 2.1 miles. Turn left onto Black Oak Road. Cross over the Little Juniata River, then turn left onto Mountain Road. The parking area is at the end of Mountain Road, next to a metal gate.

GPS Shortcut: Enter "Mid State Trail Barree Trailhead" into Google Maps and your GPS will direct you to the trailhead, located on Mountain Road outside the town of Barree.

THE HIKE

Head into the woods at the southeastern side of the parking lot, following the orange-blazed Mid State Trail. A wooden sign points the way up this trail, toward Spruce Knob. The trail leads away from the parking area, immediately ascending a moderately steep grade. The terrain quickly becomes rocky as well. Gently bend to the left in 0.1 mile and continue up the mountainside through primarily oak forest, passing over purplish sandstone inlaid with bright green moss. The rocks briefly dissipate 0.3 mile in, giving way to tread that is more grassy than it is rocky. When the leaves are off the trees, there are decent, partially obstructed views from here that look out across the gorge to the left. In another 0.2 mile, as the rocks become more prevalent in the terrain, you will begin to enter a forest marked with evergreen trees. There are a few small white pines and mountain laurels along

of continuity within this guide, the US standard system is used in this entry.

GETTING THERE

From the west, follow US 22 E heading toward Altoona. Merge onto I-99 N and take exit 32 toward Franktown Road. At the end of the ramp, turn left. Follow Franktown Road for 3.7 miles, then turn left and rejoin US 22 E. Follow the road for 17.7 miles. Turn left onto Bridge Street and follow it for 0.5 mile into Alexandria. Turn left onto Main Street. In 0.6 mile, turn right onto Barree Road, following it for 2.1 miles. Turn left on Black Oak Road. Cross over the Little Juniata River, then turn left onto the trail, and a large quantity of Virginia pines are off to the left on the edge of the ridge.

The farther you ascend on this moderately sloping stretch of trail, the rougher the trail becomes, passing at several points through bands of sparkling rock with fingers that stretch across the narrow tread. After 0.7 mile of hiking, the Mid State Trail turns to the left, intersecting with an old road grade. Turn left and follow the grassy path, descending slightly as you begin to work your way around the head of Tussey Mountain. For the next 0.2 mile, you will continue to follow this easy terrain, advancing through more and more Virginia pines. The slope of the mountain drops off steeply to the left. You will pass two areas on the right side of the trail featuring tall cliff faces that reveal a cross section of the mountain's geology. There is a good view looking through a window of trees just before the trail bends to the right and goes along the side of the ridge. From this modest framed viewpoint you can see the head of Short Mountain, which sits south of Tussey Mountain, on the other side of Little Juniata River.

At the 1-mile mark, the trail veers to the right and leaves the road grade, ascending very steeply on sidehill tread. Make your way uphill for 0.1 mile, then turn abruptly to the right, crossing above a small patch of boulders on level tread. When the leaves are off the trees, there is a good view here looking to the northwest. After crossing the top of this short boulder field, the trail ascends one more steep bank before curving to the left and approaching the crest of the ridgetop. From this point on, the terrain is extremely rocky, forcing you to focus on your step as you progress over large, sharp boulders. While you will still gain elevation, the rate of ascent is much more mellow here, which should make the tough terrain a little more manageable.

Continue up the ridge of Tussey

FOLLOWING MOSSY TREAD ON THE MID STATE TRAIL

VIEW OF BRUSH MOUNTAIN FROM THE SUMMIT OF TUSSEY MOUNTAIN

Mountain, winding through the woods on the rocky spine. In 0.6 mile, just before reaching the 1.7-mile mark, you will come to a large exposed area that is strewn with light-colored boulders. The Mid State Trail veers to the right here, continuing along the ridgetop, and it reenters the shade of the forest next to a wooden sign. However, a faintly discernible herd path leads to the left, into the open boulder area. Following this herd path a short distance will lead you to a stone pulpit, obviously made by some very industrious and driven individuals. The elevated platform is surrounded by a short wall, and it features high-backed chairs that provide an excellent place to rest and take in the panoramic view. Looking out over the countryside below, you can make out several farms in the valley. The presence of Brush Mountain dominates the view to the west. This viewpoint may be one of the best in Pennsylvania, due at least partly to the rough terrain one needs to traverse to reach the rocky perch.

When you are finished enjoying the view, head back to the Mid State Trail and descend the ridge the way you came. Arrive back at your vehicle on the shore of Little Juniata River in just over 1.6 miles.

19

Thousand Steps

DISTANCE: 2.8 miles

DIFFICULTY: Very Difficult

HIKING TIME: 2.5 hours

TYPE: Out and Back

TOTAL ELEVATION GAIN: 1,057'

MAXIMUM ELEVATION: 1,552'

At the beginning of the 20th century, the Harbison-Walker Company established quarries on Jacks Mountain, near the town of Mount Union. The long mountain was rich in Tuscarora sandstone, which was used to make silica bricks. These heat-resistant bricks were a key component in the production of glass, iron, and steel, and were therefore in high demand. The Harbison-Walker Company laid miles of railroad on Jacks Mountain, terracing the steep slope to more easily retrieve the valuable stone. In 1936, the employees of Harbison-Walker built the path known as Thousand Steps, using stone from the mountainside that they dug into the tough ground. This demanding route—incredibly enough—was originally used by the workers to reach the top of the ridge, where they began a long, arduous workday.

Climbing strenuously up Jacks Mountain, the Thousand Steps is now a very popular segment of the Standing Stone Trail that can be quite busy when the weather is nice. The Standing Stone Trail is an 80-mile footpath that connects the Mid State Trail and the Tuscarora Trail. The Standing Stone Trail is also a part of the Great Eastern Trail system, a linear trail that runs from Alabama to New York. After ascending the steps, the trail visits two scenic vistas as well as an old brick building that was once used to store railcars, a remnant of a time when the area was quarried. There are actually slightly more than one thousand steps leading up the mountainside. Ambitious hikers may try to count the exact number of steps in an effort to take their mind off the grueling climb. For those too preoccupied with trying to imagine this brutal staircase as their morning commute, the exact number of steps is listed at the end of this entry.

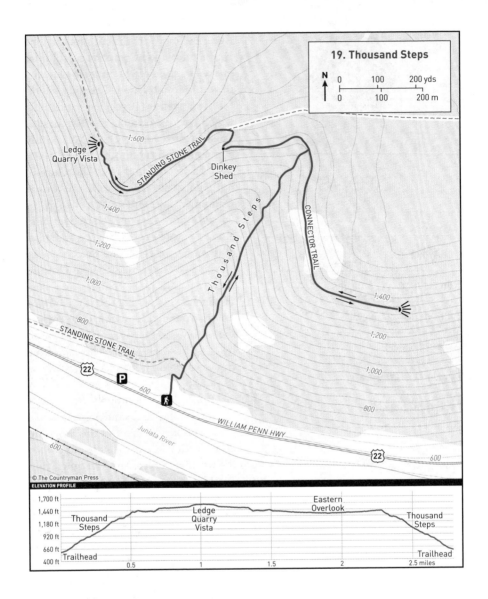

GETTING THERE

From the west, follow US 22 E heading toward Altoona. Merge onto I-99 N and take exit 32 toward Franktown Road. At the end of the ramp, turn left. Follow Franktown Road for 3.7 miles, then turn left and rejoin US 22 E. Follow the road for 34.4 miles to reach the parking area, a long gravel pull off, on the left side of the road.

From the east, navigate toward Lewistown and pick up US 522 S. Drive US 522 S for 28 miles to reach the parking area. The parking lot is a long gravel area on the right side of the road, just past Mount Union.

GPS Shortcut: Search Google Maps for "Thousand Steps section of the Standing Stone Trail" and your GPS will navigate to the parking area, a long gravel pull off alongside US 22.

THE DINKEY SHED

trail ends here, and this sign signals the start of the Thousand Steps portion of the trail.

From this point, continue straight and follow the orange blazes of the Standing Stone Trail as you climb on exquisite stone steps. The stairs ascend incredibly steeply most of the time, occasionally coming upon brief intervals of flat, disused rail grade that will certainly be a welcome break from the relentless climb. Each time the trail reaches one of these rail grades, follow the trail as it turns to the left, and then resume climbing stone steps a short distance later. After 0.25 mile of climbing, the stairs pass through a small scree field. By turning around here on the broad flat stones near the top of the field, you can catch a good view of the landscape to the west, a subtle reminder of how far

THE HIKE

Head east from the parking lot, following the shoulder of the road for about 200 feet to reach a wooden sign marking the Thousand Steps, the Standing Stone Trail, and the Great Eastern Trail. Turn left here and enter the woods. This is a blue-blazed connector trail that will lead you to the Standing Stone Trail. Climb moderately on wide dirt tread along a stream that flows downhill on the left side of the trail. After another 200 feet, you will come to a spring area where there are several decaying building foundations. Turn to the right and continue ascending at a quicker rate on rocky terrain. About 0.1 mile after leaving the road, you will arrive at the Standing Stone Trail and an information board that features a brief history of the area. The blue-blazed connector

ASCENDING JACKS MOUNTAIN ON THOUSAND STEPS

PANORAMIC VIEW OF THE JUNIATA RIVER VALLEY

you have already ascended—and of how much farther you have yet to go.

Continue to ascend the stone steps, climbing through evergreen forest composed of Virginia pine, hemlock, and the occasional mountain laurel. The stairs are incredibly well built, and they are all sturdy, stable, and level despite the heavy use they receive. Some of the rocks feature colorful orange and red and purple bursts of oxide streaking, while others display bizarre textures that include crisscrossing veins, dappled pock marks, and wavy stripes. Shortly after the 0.5-mile mark, the Thousand Steps section of the trail ends at a junction with another railroad grade that is cut into the side of the mountain.

Turn to the left and continue to follow the Standing Stone Trail, passing the foot of several blocky rock outcroppings and sections of an old stone crib wall. The terrain on this disused railroad grade is extremely easy and the tread is wide, giving you an opportunity to recover from the grueling climb while

you take in your surroundings. Follow the trail for 0.2 mile to reach the dinkey shed, a stone building used to store and service the locomotives that operated when the quarry was active.

Turn to the right in front of the dinkey shed and ascend a small section of stone steps. The Standing Stone Trail turns to the left less than 0.1 mile later and continues along easy rail grade tread. Follow the trail as it passes through a small stand of silver birch trees, and then reenter the dark cover of the fragrant pines, whose needles carpet the broad trail. The trail bends to the right, circling around the edge of the mountaintop and ascending gently to the Ledge Quarry vista, which you will reach just past the 1-mile marker. From this westward-facing viewpoint, the winding Juniata River and the borough of Mill Creek are visible. The vista has one large sitting boulder and a few more good seats along the edge of the drop-off, on an old rusty railroad track that protrudes from the ground.

When you are ready to continue, turn around and head back down the Standing Stone Trail, past the dinkey shed, to return to the top of the Thousand Steps. Continue straight past the steps on a blue-blazed spur trail. This short trail ends in 0.3 mile, leading to another vista that looks to the east. The first 0.2 mile of this spur are extremely rocky, because you're passing along the top of an extended talus slope. The top of this rocky field is open and exposed, though it periodically passes underneath the bending boughs of a pine tree. Turning around at this point will give you excellent views of the area you just visited. The dinkey shed is visible through the trees, and, looking at the wooded ridge-top above the shed, it becomes clear how much of the mountain was hauled away when the quarry was open.

The pointy rocks hindering progress on the first leg of the spur trail largely disappear for the last 0.1-mile stretch. The trail leads past more antiquated stone walling as white pine begins to come into prominence. At the end of the blue-blazed spur, the forest opens to a round, flat platform with a vista that

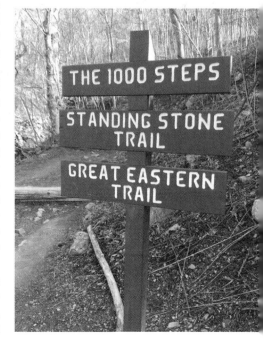

WOODEN SIGN ALONG THE TRAIL

GAZING WEST FROM THE LEDGE QUARRY VISTA

faces the east. The view from here lacks the definition and obvious focal point that the Ledge Quarry vista possesses, but on a hazy day the ridges that layer and fade into the horizon offer hikers a moody, contemplative sight.

When you are finished here, retrace your steps along the spur trail. When you reach the junction with the Standing Stone Trail, turn left and carefully descend back to the parking area. Depending on your perspective, going down the Thousand Steps may be harder than going up them, so be sure to take your time and have fun.

There are 1,037 steps in total.

Ralph's Views

DISTANCE: 6.9 miles	
DIFFICULTY: Moderate	
HIKING TIME: 3 hours	
TYPE: Out and Back	
TOTAL ELEVATION GAIN: 1,049'	
MAXIMUM ELEVATION: 2,229'	

In 1995, seasoned Pennsylvania outdoorsman Ralph Seeley undertook something of a reconnaissance mission. Working with Moshannon district forester Ken Barnes, the two began investigating a potential route for a sizable hiking trail. The idea was to create a trail that would circle all the way around Black Moshannon State Park. Seeley was no stranger to trail building, having worked to rebuild the Quehanna Wild Area trail system in the wake of a tornado that flattened a large band of forest in 1985. By 1996, construction of this footpath was underway by Seeley, the Moshannon State Forest District, the Keystone Trails Association, and a handful of local trail clubs. A few years later, after long, sweaty days of hard, dirty work, the 42-mile Allegheny Front Trail was open for hikers to enjoy.

The hike described here follows a section of the Allegheny Front Trail to the southeastern edge of the Allegheny Plateau. Walking a short section along the rocky perimeter of the elevation will lead you to no less than two viewpoints named in honor of Ralph Seeley for his tireless work on the trails in Pennsylvania.

GETTING THERE

Coming from the west, follow I-99 N from Altoona and take exit 61 toward Philipsburg/Port Matilda. At the end of the ramp, turn right and follow US 220 ALT N for 0.5 mile, then turn left, continuing to follow US 220 ALT N. After 4.1 miles, turn left onto Steele Hollow Road and follow it for 4.4 miles. Make a sharp left onto Beaver Road, following it for 1.7 miles to reach Shirks Road. Turn left onto Shirks Road. The parking lot will be immediately on the left.

From the east, follow US 322 W to

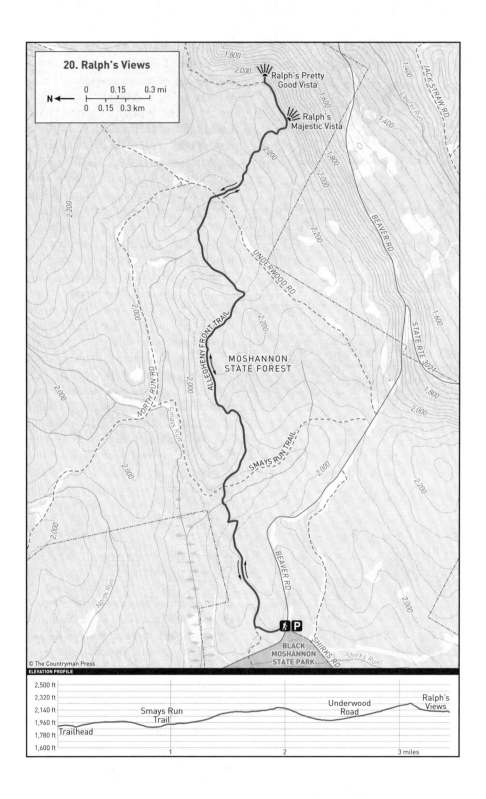

20. Ralph's Views

N ← | 0   0.15   0.3 mi
0   0.15 0.3 km

Ralph's Pretty
Good Vista

Ralph's
Majestic Vista

1,800
2,000
2,200
2,200
2,000
2,200
2,200
1,600
1,800
2,000
1,400
1,400
2,000
1,600
1,800
2,000

JACK STRAW RD.

Laurel Run

BEAVER RD.

STATE RTE 3023

UNDERWOOD RD.

ALLEGHENY FRONT TRAIL

MOSHANNON
STATE FOREST

NORTH RUN RD.

Smays Run

SMAYS RUN TRAIL

North Run

BEAVER RD.

SHIRKS RD.

Shirk's Run

BLACK
MOSHANNON
STATE PARK

© The Countryman Press

ELEVATION PROFILE

2,500 ft				Ralph's
2,320 ft			Underwood	Views
2,140 ft	Smays Run		Road	
1,960 ft	Trail			
1,780 ft	Trailhead			
1,600 ft		1	2	3 miles

where it merges with I-99 S north of State College. After 3.5 miles, take exit 68 toward Gray Woods Waddle. Continue to follow signs toward PA 550 and merge onto Twenty-Eighth Division Highway/N Atherton Street. After 4.4 miles, veer to the right and merge onto US 220 ALT N, following it for 1.3 miles. Turn left and follow Steele Hollow Road for 4.4 miles. Make a sharp left onto Beaver Road, following it for 1.7 miles to reach Shirks Road. Turn left onto Shirks Road. The parking lot will be immediately on the left.

GPS Shortcut: Enter "Allegheny Front Trail/Moss-Hanne Shirks Road Access Point" into Google Maps and your GPS will direct you to the trailhead.

THE HIKE

From the parking area on Shirks Road, pick up the access trail for the Allegheny Front and Moss-Hanne Trails. Follow the yellow and red blazes northeast. The trail passes through a narrow strip of trees and crosses Beaver Road, climbing a short bank on the other side before reentering the woods. This short, shady connector trail passes through white pine and hemlock stands, and in roughly 0.2 mile it arrives at a post marking the junction with the Allegheny Front and Moss-Hanne Trails. Turn to the right here and begin to follow the Allegheny Front Trail (A.F.T.) on gently rolling terrain. After leaving the connector trail, the A.F.T. enters a sparsely treed area awash with sweet-smelling ferns. It continues through this scant forest for 0.6 mile, eventually beginning a gradual descent that curves down a short hillside to enter into the relative shade of the evergreens yet again. From here the trail crosses over the southernmost

SPUR TRAIL TO RALPH'S PRETTY GOOD VIEW

branch of Smays Run on a very nice wooden footbridge and passes by a campsite area immediately afterward. You arrive at the wide, gravel tread of Smays Run Trail 0.9 mile after leaving the parking area.

Cross Smays Run Trail and continue on the A.F.T. up a brief gradual ascent, after which the trail largely levels. This portion of the trail passes through a broad, shallow cleft between hilltops to your left and right, advancing through young, brushy forest on easy terrain. Follow the trail as it bends to the left 1.3 miles in and begin another gradual ascent, winding lazily uphill. Turn to the right as you approach the top of this shrub-covered slope and continue on a trajectory similar to the course followed in the shallow depression you just left. Pass through a grassy expanse and enjoy limited views to the north, crossing the remains of a forest road shortly before reaching the 2-mile mark.

After crossing this disused road, the trail turns to the left and descends moderately on rough, rocky terrain before progressing through a flat tract of dense forest. After 0.4 mile, the trail turns to the right and follows the tread of another antiquated woods road heading east. About 0.2 mile later, the A.F.T. intersects with Underwood Road. Cross this dirt road and follow the narrowing trail into the woods on the other side. From here the trail climbs moderately on increasingly rocky terrain, zigzagging through the thick mountain laurels that hedge in the trail on either side. At mile marker 3.1 you will reach the rocky

RALPH'S MAJESTIC VISTA ON THE ALLEGHENY FRONT TRAIL

A MOODY MORNING FROM RALPH'S PRETTY GOOD VIEW

crest of the Allegheny Front. Descend down the other side of the wooded crest, weaving through a few tilting split rock formations to reach Ralph's Majestic Vista 0.1 mile later. This point is marked by a wooden sign and looks out over the valley to the south toward Bald Eagle State Forest.

Continue on the A.F.T. as it follows the tree-covered edge of the plateau. About 0.2 mile later, just after the 3.4-mile marker, you will reach another wooden sign denoting the second of Ralph's vistas. Follow a short spur trail downhill beyond this sign to reach Ralph's Pretty Good View, a playfully named point that gazes over the valley in a similar direction to the view you already enjoyed. Both vista areas have comfortable places to sit and take a break while you contemplate the scenery. Despite Ralph's designations it is ultimately up to you to decide which vista presents a more dramatic view.

When you are finished at Ralph's Pretty Good View, follow the spur trail to return to the Allegheny Front Trail. Turn left to head back the way you came. When you reach the connector trail, turn left and follow it to return to your vehicle.

Chimney Rocks Loop

DISTANCE: 5.3 miles

DIFFICULTY: Difficult

HIKING TIME: 2.5 hours

TYPE: Loop

TOTAL ELEVATION GAIN: 1,048'

MAXIMUM ELEVATION: 1,940'

For many Appalachian Trail (A.T.) thru-hikers, the mention of Pennsylvania elicits strong, mixed feelings. It is the seventh state for those hiking northbound from Georgia to Maine. Crossing through the state, thru-hikers pass the halfway mark of their protracted journey and begin to see fewer miles left to go than they have already come. And yet, by the time these stalwart, stinky individuals reach Pennsylvania they will have already come to know it by a different name: Rocksylvania. Horror stories of unbelievably rocky tread that devours shoes and twists ankles run rampant long before thru hikers cross the Mason-Dixon Line and pass from Maryland into the Keystone State. The stories go that the A.T. in Pennsylvania is more like a narrow path of angular rocks, all set on edge, pointing straight up, slowing progress and trying the patience of even the most placid souls. Worst of all, they say there are no views in Pennsylvania! Many thru-hikers arrive in Pennsylvania expecting the worst, only to be surprised to find that the rumors are extremely exaggerated— at least at the start.

The hike to Chimney Rocks follows the Appalachian Trail north through Michaux State Forest up Buzzard Peak, one of the first challenging climbs the state has to offer. The beautiful rock formation at the top rewards hikers with a marvelous view and plenty of niches and crevices to explore. Looping back on other lesser traveled trails, you will walk beside peaceful Tumbling Run. Along the way you will pass through sections of trail that are littered with rocks, but instead of being a deterrent, you may find that they flavor the hike with a bit of intrigue and a dash of variety.

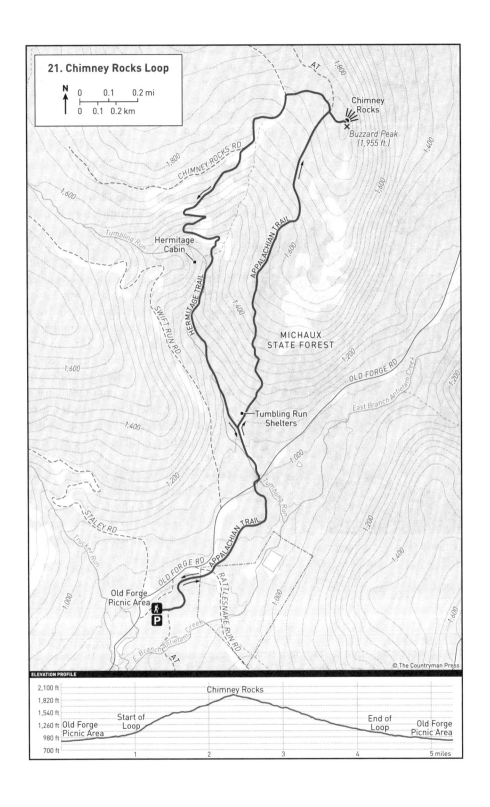

21. Chimney Rocks Loop

N
0   0.1   0.2 mi
0   0.1   0.2 km

Chimney Rocks

Buzzard Peak
(1,955 ft.)

AT

1,800

1,800

1,600

1,400

1,600

1,400

CHIMNEY ROCKS RD

Tumbling Run

Hermitage
Cabin

HERMITAGE TRAIL

APPALACHIAN TRAIL

SWIFT RUN RD

1,400

1,600

1,400

1,200

MICHAUX
STATE FOREST

1,200

OLD FORGE RD

East Branch Antietam Creek

1,200

Tumbling Run
Shelters

1,000

1,200

1,400

1,600

Tumbling Run

1,200

1,000

STALEY RD

Trucker Run

1,000

OLD FORGE RD

APPALACHIAN TRAIL

RATTLESNAKE RUN RD

Old Forge
Picnic Area

P

E. Branch Antietam Creek

AT

© The Countryman Press

ELEVATION PROFILE

2,100 ft	Chimney Rocks
1,820 ft	
1,540 ft	Start of
1,260 ft	Old Forge Loop End of Old Forge
980 ft	Picnic Area Loop Picnic Area
700 ft	1 2 3 4 5 miles

EXPLORING THE CRACKS AND CREVICES BELOW THE VISTA

GETTING THERE

From the west, follow I-76 E toward Harrisburg and take exit 161 toward Breezewood/Baltimore. Stay on I-70 E for 1.3 miles, then turn right onto US 30 E toward Chambersburg/Gettysburg. Drive US 30 E for 24.9 miles and turn right onto PA 75 S. In 2.1 miles, turn left onto Lemar Road and follow it for 7.6 miles. Then turn left onto PA 16, continuing on this road for 15.4 miles. Finally, turn left onto Old Forge Road and drive

for 4.9 miles to reach the parking area at the Old Forge Picnic Area on the left.

Coming from the east, pick up I-76 W traveling toward Harrisburg. Take exit 236 toward Gettysburg and follow US 15 S for 28.9 miles. Take the exit for PA 116 toward Hanover, turning right at the end of the ramp to join PA 116 W. Follow this road for 11.1 miles, then keep right and merge onto Jacks Mountain Road. Drive for 2.8 miles and turn right onto PA 16 W. In 5.5 miles, turn right onto Bear Mountain Road, then 200 feet later turn left onto Mentzer Gap Road. Stay on Mentzer Gap Road for 1.2 miles before turning right onto Old Forge Road. Arrive at the parking area at Old Forge Picnic Area on the right in 3.2 miles.

From the north, follow I-81 S to exit 14. Turn left at the end of the ramp and follow PA 316 S for 12.2 miles. In Waynesboro, turn left onto Main Street and follow PA 16 E. After 2.6 miles, turn left onto Old Forge Road. In 4.9 miles on the right, you will reach the parking area at Old Forge Picnic Area. The hike starts from here.

GPS Shortcut: Enter "Old Forge Picnic Area" into Google Maps and your GPS will direct you to the parking area, located near the town of Waynesboro.

THE HIKE

Head downhill from the parking area, passing a gate and crossing a grassy field, toward a springhouse at the eastern perimeter of the picnic grounds. Turn left just past the springhouse (which offers "pure drinking water year round") and begin following the white blazes of the Appalachian Trail. Follow this historic tread, heading through pleasant white pine and small spruce trees. The trail skirts private property about 0.25 mile in, passes under a power

THE VIEW NORTHEAST FROM CHIMNEY ROCKS

line, and crosses Rattlesnake Run Road a few hundred feet up trail. As you reenter the woods on the other side of the road, the terrain grows more rugged. A fair amount of rocks and roots will keep you glancing at your foot placement to keep from stumbling as the trail begins to trend uphill at a gradual rate.

Arrive at Old Forge Road after 0.7 mile of hiking. Turn to the right and follow the roadside to cross Tumbling Run. Enter the woods on the opposite side of the road a short distance from where the trail meets with the road and continue to ascend slowly, more or less paralleling the run to your left. In 0.2 mile, you will come to a fork in the trail. The Appalachian Trail bends to the right while the blue-blazed Hermitage Trail continues to follow Tumbling Run upstream. Turn right here to stay on the Appalachian Trail. The trail immediately passes by the Tumbling Run Shelters, an immaculately maintained backpacking camp featuring two Adirondack shelters (one

"snoring" shelter and one "non-snoring" shelter), several small tent sites, a larger group tenting area, a pavilion-covered picnic table, and a very clean privy.

Beyond the shelter area you will begin a steep and steady 0.6-mile ascent, as the trail climbs up and over several chunky stone steps placed on top of each other to form a rudimentary staircase. For 0.2 mile after this persistent climb, the trail grade levels off significantly and the terrain becomes more even before continuing to ascend at a moderate rate, crossing over large slabs of stone and crumbling ledges. Around mile marker 2.2, amid a high concentration of boulders, the Appalachian Trail meets with a blue-blazed trail, which branches off to the right, providing access to Chimney Rocks. Turn right and follow the blue-blazed trail uphill for just under 0.1 mile to reach the crest of the ridge as well as the lookout at Chimney Rocks. A large collection of jumbled boulders creates a modest network of narrow crevices to explore, and from the top, hikers are rewarded with an excellent view looking northeast.

Return back to the junction with the Appalachian Trail when you are finished at the viewpoint and turn right. Approximately 20 feet up the Appalachian Trail, the blue-blazed Chimney Rocks Trail continues, turning to the left and heading downhill. Follow the Chimney Rocks Trail downhill to descend gradually through the rocky forest and arrive at grassy Chimney Rocks Road, nearly 0.2 mile after leaving the ridgetop. Turn left onto this well-used woods road and descend farther, following sparse blue blazes. The road eventually bends back and forth as you advance downhill, and at mile marker 3.6, after descending a short flight of stone steps leading away from the road grade, arrive at a trail junction.

A short spur trail heading off to the right travels over Tumbling Run on a wooden footbridge to the Hermitage Cabin, which is owned and maintained by the Potomac Appalachian Trail Club. A much smaller stream flows from your left, eventually feeding into Tumbling Run. Veer to the left, crossing this small feeder stream, and follow the Hermitage Trail. This trail descends moderately, creeping along the base of a short, blocky ledge, eventually giving way to a more gradual descent on rough, very rocky terrain by the edge of Tumbling Run. After 0.5 mile of hiking, the Hermitage Trail connects back to the Appalachian Trail near the Tumbling Run Shelters at mile marker 4.3. From here, head downhill, cross Old Forge Road and Rattlesnake Run Road, and continue to follow the white blazes back to your vehicle at the picnic area.

PEERING OUT OVER MICHAUX STATE FOREST FROM CHIMNEY ROCKS

Sunset Rocks Loop

DISTANCE: 8.2 miles

DIFFICULTY: Difficult

HIKING TIME: 4 hours

TYPE: Loop

TOTAL ELEVATION GAIN: 1,201'

MAXIMUM ELEVATION: 1,434'

Although the Appalachian Trail (A.T.) through Pennsylvania is rarely, if ever, listed as a favorite section of trail by thru-hikers, it is notable for several reasons. As mentioned in the Chimney Rocks Loop entry, the Pennsylvania portion of the A.T. has a reputation for being extremely rocky. The vast majority of thru-hikers, individuals attempting to walk the entire 2,000-mile stretch of the Appalachian Trail from Georgia to Maine, are quick to bring up this fact. Perhaps the next noteworthy detail about the Appalachian Trail in Pennsylvania is that the official halfway mark lies in the Keystone State. While the length of the A.T. varies slightly from year to year as the trail is rerouted or modified in accordance with landowner agreements, thru-hikers must walk more than 1,000 miles only to be halfway to the northern terminus at Mount Katahdin in Maine. Since the 1980s, it has been the tradition among thru-hikers to celebrate the monumental achievement of reaching the halfway mark by eating a half gallon of ice cream in Pine Grove Furnace State Park, an entirely different monumental feat that has become known as the Half Gallon Challenge.

This hike starts in Pine Grove Furnace State Park and follows the Appalachian Trail southbound to Toms Run Shelter, looping back on the Sunset Rocks Trail. This challenging stretch of trail requires hikers to scramble up and down rock outcroppings, but the effort is rewarded with a scenic vista. The trail also passes by an antiquated Appalachian Trail halfway monument from 2011, when the total distance of the A.T. was 2,181 miles. In the summer months, the general store in Pine Grove Furnace State Park is a great place to relax and cool down after your hike. It is, however, not advisable to eat a half gallon of ice cream.

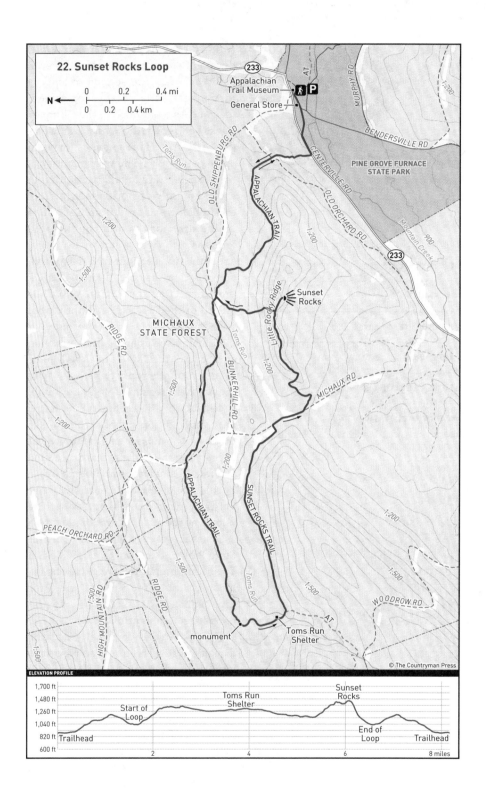

22. Sunset Rocks Loop

N ←

| 0 | 0.2 | 0.4 mi |
| 0 | 0.2 | 0.4 km |

Appalachian Trail Museum

General Store

PINE GROVE FURNACE STATE PARK

MICHAUX STATE FOREST

Sunset Rocks

Little Rocky Ridge

Toms Run

APPALACHIAN TRAIL

OLD SHIPPENBURG RD

CENTERVILLE RD

OLD ORCHARD RD

Mountain Creek

MURPHY RD

BENDERSVILLE RD

RIDGE RD

BUNKERHILL RD

MICHAUX RD

PEACH ORCHARD RD

RIDGE RD

HIGH MOUNTAIN RD

APPALACHIAN TRAIL

SUNSET ROCKS TRAIL

WOODROW RD

AT

monument

Toms Run Shelter

Toms Run

© The Countryman Press

ELEVATION PROFILE

1,700 ft				
1,480 ft				
1,260 ft				
1,040 ft				
820 ft				
600 ft				

Start of Loop

Toms Run Shelter

Sunset Rocks

End of Loop

Trailhead

Trailhead

2   4   6   8 miles

GETTING THERE

From the west, drive I-76 E toward Harrisburg and take exit 201 toward Shippensburg/Chambersburg. At the end of the ramp, turn left onto PA 997 N. In 1.6 miles, keep right and continue onto PA 696 S, following the route for 2.1 miles. In Newburg, turn left onto Main Street and follow PA 641 E for 9.1 miles. In Newville, turn right onto S High Street, and continue to follow PA 233 S for 11.7 miles, the road ends at a T-intersection with Pine Grove Road/ PA 233. The park office is across the road, to the right. When you reach the office, follow the gravel driveway downhill. Park in the large lot between the furnace stack pavilion and a restroom building.

From the east, follow I-76 W toward Harrisburg. Take exit 226 and follow US 11 N, merging onto I-81 in 1.7 miles. Follow I-81 S for 14.5 miles, then take exit 37. Turn left onto PA 233 S at the end of the ramp and follow it for 8 miles. The road ends at a T-intersection with Pine Grove Road/PA 233. The park office is across the road, to the right. When you reach the office, follow the gravel driveway downhill. Park in the large lot between the furnace stack pavilion and a restroom building.

GPS Shortcut: In Google Maps, set "Pine Grove Furnace State Park Office and Visitor Center" as your destination. When you reach the office, follow the gravel driveway downhill. Park in the large lot between the furnace stack pavilion and a restroom building.

THE HIKE

Head uphill away from the parking area, and begin following the white-blazed Appalachian Trail at the northern end of the lot. Pass through a small grass

SUNSET ROCKS TRAIL NEAR TOMS RUN SHELTER

field and intersect with Bendersville Road. To the right is an old grist mill where the Appalachian Trail Museum is housed. This unique attraction is well worth making the time for, presuming their hours of operation line up with your itinerary. Turn left by an information kiosk and follow Bendersville Road for 450 feet, passing by the Pine Grove Furnace Store, home of the Half Gallon Challenge. The road splits beyond this general store. Bendersville Road turns to the left and heads downhill, while Bendersville Lane continues straight, lazily curling toward Pine Grove Road/ PA 233. Follow Bendersville Lane, making your way past a retaining wall below the Ironmaster's Mansion, a historic brick building now used as a bunkhouse and hostel for park visitors.

ANTIQUATED HALFWAY POINT ON THE APPALACHIAN TRAIL

Bendersville Lane ends at PA 233 in 0.1 mile. Veer to the left and walk PA 233 for an additional 0.1 mile before turning to the right and leaving the road, advancing uphill on a wide gravel road.

The Appalachian Trail follows the gravel road, ascending moderately past several private residences. Please respect the landowner rights and stay on the trail. Cross a private gravel road in 0.2 mile, and continue straight, following the white blazes. After 0.75 mile of hiking, the trail bends to the left in the midst of the expansive pine forest that gives the state park its name, leveling off briefly before resuming a moderate climb. At 1.1 miles in, the trail tips downhill and begins to descend the knoll you just climbed. Up until this point the terrain is relatively easy to traverse and the tread is well-graded. All that changes on this moderate descent, however, as large lumpy rocks begin to appear in the trail, threatening to trip careless hikers. This rough section of trail begins to peter out as the elevation levels out, and at mile 1.6 the Appalachian Trail arrives at Toms Run, emerging through a dense stand of white pine. The Sunset Rocks Trail leads sharply uphill to the left here, and an unmarked footpath leads to a small parking area to the right.

Continue straight on the Appalachian Trail, crossing Toms Run on a short wooden footbridge. After crossing Toms Run, work your way uphill following narrow singletrack for 0.2 mile, meeting Bunker Hill Road near where it ends next to a metal gate to the right of a private cabin. Veer left and follow the road for roughly 200 feet and enter the woods to the right by a sign marking the Appalachian Trail. You will ascend a moderately steep slope on rocky terrain, winding through a tract of declining forest. Many of the trees in this area are dying, if not already dead, due in part to an invasive plant commonly known as mile-a-minute, which can spread up to 30 feet in a single year. This plant is easily recognizable by its triangular leaves and barbed vines that climb and cover anything it can stick to.

Cross paved Michaux Road at mile marker 2.6, where you pass by a small information kiosk and duck behind a metal gate. From here the Appalachian Trail follows a wide, easily traversable woods road grade for approximately 1 mile to reach a sizable monument and trail register that marks the halfway point of the Appalachian Trail in 2011. You can now say that you walked to the halfway point of the A.T.! In another 0.2 mile, after crossing a small stream, you will arrive at the Toms Run Shelter area, which boasts an Adirondack-style shelter, a few tent sites, a privy, and a picnic table protected from the weather by a pavilion. This is a great place to stop and take a break and relax before moving on.

From the shelter, continue to follow the Appalachian Trail, crossing the flow of a spring just past the pavilion, and cross Toms Run on a wooden footbridge. A short distance after crossing Toms Run, turn left onto the blue-blazed Sunset Rocks Trail, leaving the Appalachian Trail behind. Follow this narrow, rocky path back toward Michaux Road for 0.5 mile before it widens and joins the remains of an old road grade. The quality of this road fluctuates terrifically, alternating between a smooth wide tread and extremely rocky, narrow segments. The trail passes through a soggy, marshy area on well-placed boardwalks, and it meets with Michaux Road 0.2 mile later, 5.1 miles in.

Turn right and walk down Michaux Road for 0.2 mile. The Sunset Rocks Trail enters the woods on the left side

SCRAMBLING ALONG THE CREST OF LITTLE ROCKY RIDGE

of the road, heading down a driveway for about 20 feet before breaking off to the right and circling around behind a hunting cabin. Pay close attention to the blazes to avoid trespassing on private property. Thankfully, this area is very well marked and the trail should be very obvious. After passing a hunting cabin, the trail gently curves to the right and climbs steeply for a short distance to a treed-in rock outcropping that offers limited views of the surrounding forest. Turn back to the left at this point and continue to ascend sharply up the spine of Little Rocky Ridge. This piney ridge is appropriately named, as it crosses small areas of lichen-covered stones, eventually leading you to a couple of precipitous rock formations past the 5.5 mile marker. The trail generally splits at these points, with one spur leading to the left behind the rocks, while the other climbs up and over the formations themselves, before rejoining on the other side of the boulders. Pay close attention to the blazes, choose your route, and proceed carefully. The next 0.3 mile will twist and turn across the craggy, wooded ridgetop, passing over and through many chaotic, jumbled stone structures that at times require you to scramble with both your hands and feet.

Six miles after starting your hike, you will arrive at a trail junction on top of Little Rocky Ridge. The Sunset Rocks Trail descends to the left while a rough, rocky spur trail that leads to the Sunset Rocks viewpoint lies straight ahead. Continue straight for 0.1 mile to visit the vista, which looks to the south from two parallel stone slabs that jut out from the mountainside. The view from this protruding formation is one of the best in Michaux State Forest; hardly any sign of civilization can be seen from here due to the topography of the surrounding landscape. As the name implies, the sunset from the viewpoint is spectacular—just be sure you have a headlamp or flashlight should you decide to linger here until nightfall.

Return back down to where the trail splits and turn right to begin descending on the Sunset Rocks Trail. The first leg of the descent off the ridge follows wide, bumpy trail and is without a doubt the steepest part of the entire hike. Depending on your disposition you will either be very glad or very displeased to be descending on this sharply dropping terrain. As you continue making your way downhill, the grade of descent slowly eases as you pass through patches of young, spindly beech and birch trees. You will meet with the Appalachian Trail just before the first footbridge spanning Toms Run 0.3 mile after leaving the ridgetop. At this point you have completed the loop portion of the hike. Turn to the right here and follow the Appalachian Trail for 1.3 miles to reach PA 233. Turn left onto PA 233 and backtrack along Bendersville Lane, making your way back through Pine Grove Furnace State Park to return to your vehicle.

THE VISTA AT SUNSET ROCKS

Pole Steeple Loop

DISTANCE: 6 miles	
DIFFICULTY: Moderate	
HIKING TIME: 3 hours	
TYPE: Loop	
TOTAL ELEVATION GAIN: 629'	
MAXIMUM ELEVATION: 1,319'	

Pine Grove Furnace State Park gets its name from the Pine Grove Iron Works, a smelting facility that was built in the late 1700s. Many features of the park seen today were used long ago in the refining process, including some sections of trail, the flow of Mountain Creek, and Laurel Lake and Fuller Lake. The furnace stack used for smelting, which still stands at the heart of the park, is now a historic landmark echoing the area's industrial past. The surrounding pine forest was used to make charcoal that powered the furnace until 1874. This power source was ultimately replaced by coal in 1879. The facility continued to produce iron for 16 more years before shutting down in 1895. The land was sold to the state in 1913, and a portion of it became Pine Grove Furnace State Park.

Ascending to Pole Steeple, while not terribly strenuous, rewards hikers with a remarkably breathtaking view. The vista looks north over Laurel Lake, and the view is particularly dramatic in autumn when the surrounding foliage explodes with color. When the weather is agreeable, this popular viewpoint sees dozens of visitors over the course of a day, in part due to a parking area just south of Laurel Lake that allows hikers and rock climbers easy access to all that the overlook has to offer. By parking at Laurel Lake, hikers can climb a short, steep embankment to the rocky viewpoint and back to their car relatively quickly—but there is much more to enjoy about Pole Steeple than a quick view!

This hike starts a few hundred feet south of the Pine Grove Furnace State Park Office, from the same parking lot as the Sunset Rocks Loop entry. It features a relaxing walk on the historic Appalachian Trail along Mountain Creek and spectacular views of the surrounding forest from Pole Steeple. One steep trail

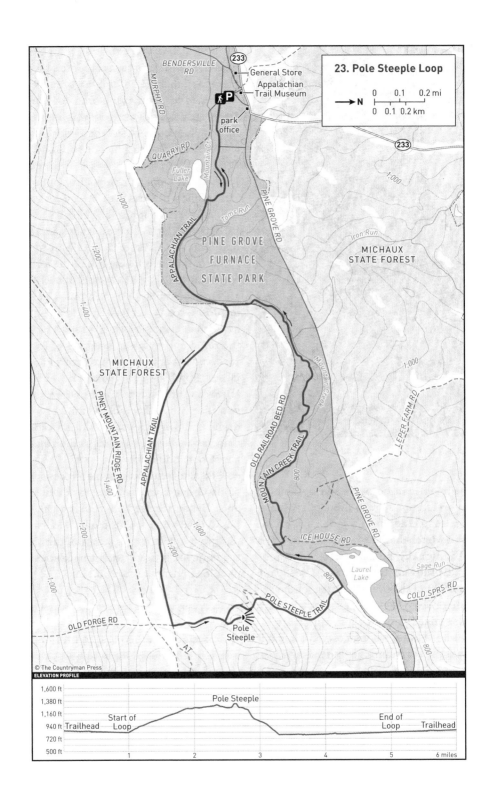

TRAIL SIGN POINTING THE WAY TO POLE STEEPLE

PA 696 S, following the route for 2.1 miles. In Newburg, turn left onto Main Street and follow PA 641 E for 9.1 miles. In Newville, turn right onto S High Street, and continue to follow PA 233 S for 11.7 miles, where the road ends at a T-intersection with Pine Grove Road/PA 233. The park office is across the road, to the right. When you reach the office, follow the gravel driveway downhill. Park in the large lot between the furnace stack pavilion and a restroom building.

From the east, follow I-76 W toward Harrisburg. Take exit 226 and follow US 11 N, merging onto I-81 in 1.7 miles. Follow I-81 S for 14.5 miles, then take exit 37. Turn left onto PA 233 S at the end of the ramp and follow it for 8 miles. The road ends at a T-intersection with Pine Grove Road/PA 233. The park office is across the road, to the right. When you reach the office, follow the gravel driveway downhill. Park in the large lot between the furnace stack pavilion and a restroom building.

GPS Shortcut: In Google Maps, set "Pine Grove Furnace State Park Office and Visitor Center" as your destination. When you reach the office, follow the gravel driveway downhill. Park in the large lot between the furnace stack pavilion and a restroom building.

THE HIKE

Head south from the parking area and turn left onto the white-blazed Appalachian Trail. Continue on the wide paved path for 0.3 mile as it follows the flow of Mountain Creek on the right, passing by another large parking area in a short distance. The trail turns to the left to go around the concession stand, changing from pavement to gravel tread. Pass through a large grassy field and in 0.2

segment can be bypassed by using a short alternate route, although most hikers should not have a problem with the steep pitch thanks to brilliant trail work. Additionally, an easy roadwalk can be substituted for the Mountain Creek Trail portion of this hike. Because of the relatively easy tread and route flexibility, this hike is an excellent candidate for winter hiking when snowy trails deter many hikers from enjoying the outdoors.

GETTING THERE

From the west, drive I-76 E toward Harrisburg and take exit 201 toward Shippensburg/Chambersburg. At the end of the ramp, turn left onto PA 997 N. In 1.6 miles, keep right and continue onto mile cross a footbridge over Mountain Creek as you approach Fuller Lake. This constructed lake, once an ore pit for the Pine Grove Iron Works, is now a popular destination for fishing and swimming.

Turn left and continue to follow the broad, flat gravel path that was once used as a railroad, immediately crossing the outlet of Fuller Lake, which flows into Mountain Creek. In 0.25 mile, you pass by the Swamp Trail to your right, which unsurprisingly forms a short loop through a swamp. Keep going down this relaxing path, following the flow of Mountain Creek for another 0.25 mile.

One mile after beginning your hike, pass behind a metal gate, and then turn to the right, heading uphill on the Appalachian Trail.

This leg of the hike follows the rutted remnants of a woods road to the east-northeast, climbing moderately on the bumpy tread through mixed forest. Due to the wide breadth of this old road grade, you should be able to pick out a course that avoids the worst of the ruts, roots, and rocks. The terrain continues to get tougher as you ascend, but the trail is well-graded (save for a few isolated incidents of narrow, water-eroded

THE FURNACE STACK AT PINE GROVE FURNACE STATE PARK

THE SWEEPING VIEW FROM ROCKY POLE STEEPLE

channels) and relatively easy to traverse, never becoming too cumbersome. After 1 mile of climbing, as mountain laurels begin to narrow the trail and fill out the surrounding woodland, the angle of ascent relaxes dramatically. The trail continues ambling through the forest, occasionally climbing gradually, for another 0.4 mile.

At mile marker 2.4, a sign marking the blue-blazed Pole Steeple Trail points to the left. Turn off the Appalachian Trail here and begin following the Pole Steeple Trail, paying close attention to the blazes. Another dilapidated road grade heads away from the Appalachian Trail from this point, heading in the same direction. Avoid this road grade and follow the Pole Steeple Trail, which descends slightly to the north, sharply bending first to the left, then back to the right, before gently meandering through the woods on a fairly similar, level course.

After walking the Pole Steeple Trail for 0.75 mile, you reach a fork in the trail by a wooden bench. Turn to the right here and ascend a rock-covered knoll on stone steps for about 0.1 mile to reach the viewpoint at Pole Steeple. From this sprawling exposed stone vista, you can gaze over the treetops at the surrounding wooded ridges almost 180 degrees to the northwest. Laurel Lake is notable in the valley below. It is another recreation destination that was also utilized by the Pine Grove Iron Works. Pole Steeple is popular with hikers and rock climbers of

all ages and fitness levels due to the relatively easy hike to reach the summit, as well as its proximity to nearby roads, so bear in mind that the area can become crowded on weekends and holidays when the weather is agreeable. It is rare to experience solitude at this particular viewpoint.

When you are finished enjoying the view, head back down the rocky path to the split in the trail and head moderately downhill toward Laurel Lake on the other leg of the fork, continuing to follow blue blazes. A short distance later, an easier alternate route turns off to the left and heads downhill, avoiding a very steep section of trail ahead. If you take this trail, you will rejoin the main trail roughly 0.2 mile later. Beyond the alternate route, you pass below the jutting

outcrop of Pole Steeple at a wide berth, with a few herd paths leading to climbing routes breaking off toward the cliff. The trail quickly bends to the left and heads very steeply downhill on large, sturdy stone steps. This steep section is intense but brief, and it meets with the end of the alternate route around the 3-mile mark. Continue to descend on rough, rugged terrain, passing more stone steps and rustic log benches, arriving at Old Railroad Bed Road at mile 3.5, where a small parking area borders the edge of Laurel Lake.

Turn left here and walk along the road, heading away from Laurel Lake. In 0.3 mile, just past a piped spring built into the side of the road, the yellow blazes of the Mountain Creek Trail turn off to the right down Ice House Road.

A CLOSER LOOK AT LAUREL LAKE FROM THE VISTA

This trail crosses the creek on a short bridge before turning to the left and continuing to follow the flow upstream. You have the option here of taking either the Mountain Creek Trail or continuing on the road. The Mountain Creek Trail can be wet and muddy during periods of high rainfall, as it winds through marshy areas and crosses the creek a handful of times. Should you decide to take the trail, turn right when you rejoin the paved road. If you decide not to follow the trail, continue up the road, passing several privately owned cabins. Both routes are 1.4 miles long.

About 0.1 mile past the point where the Mountain Creek Trail rejoins Old Railroad Bed Road, you come to the metal gate you passed earlier. The Appalachian Trail heads uphill to the left, signaling that you have completed the loop portion of this hike, at the 5-mile mark. Continue straight on the old gravel railroad bed for 1 mile and turn right to cross Mountain Creek near Fuller Lake. Continue to follow the path back past the concession stand to return to your vehicle at the furnace stack pavilion area of the park.

Flat Rock

DISTANCE: 4.6 miles	
DIFFICULTY: Difficult	
HIKING TIME: 2.5 hours	
TYPE: Out and Back	
TOTAL ELEVATION GAIN: 1,408'	
MAXIMUM ELEVATION: 1,986'	

Tucked within the Tuscarora State Forest, circling Doubling Gap Lake, sits Colonel Denning State Park. The park, which was opened in 1936, is named in honor of Revolutionary War veteran William Denning, who, despite the noble title given to him by the park, was never a colonel. He became an important figure in his day, making wrought iron cannons for the Continental Army during the Revolutionary War. After the war ended, he settled in nearby Newville. The Flat Rock Trail begins here, near the flow of Doubling Gap Run.

The hike to Flat Rock follows a demanding route in hardwood forest, passing at times through dense stands of mountain laurels. In springtime, their cup-shaped white and pink flowers bloom, dappling the trail with specks of color and immersing the woods with their subtle scent. Near the top of the ridge at a unique junction called the Wagon Wheel, the Flat Rock Trail joins and shares tread with the Tuscarora Trail, a 252-mile long backpacking trail that runs from Virginia to Pennsylvania, running roughly parallel to the Appalachian Trail (A.T.) to the west. The Tuscarora Trail connects to the Appalachian Trail at Mathews Arm Campground in Shenandoah National Park and on Blue Mountain west of the Susquehanna River. The trail was built in a wider woodland corridor as a potential alternative to the A.T. when fears of development in the 1960s threatened to close large chunks of the Appalachian Trail altogether. The viewpoint on the top of Blue Mountain rewards hikers with an excellent view of the Cumberland Valley.

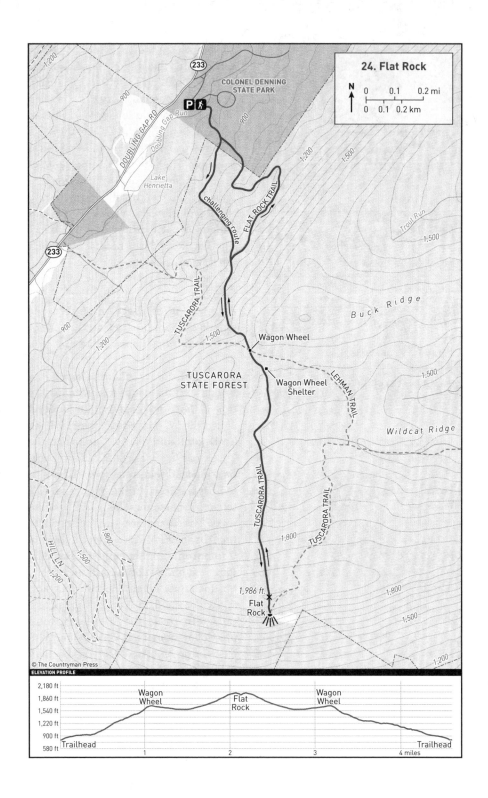

24. Flat Rock

N
0   0.1   0.2 mi
0   0.1   0.2 km

COLONEL DENNING
STATE PARK

233

DOUBLING GAP RD.

Doubling Gap Run

Lake
Henrietta

233

challenging route

FLAT ROCK TRAIL

Trout Run

1,500

1,200

900

B u c k   R i d g e

1,500

Wagon Wheel

TUSCARORA TRAIL

1,500

LEHMAN TRAIL

TUSCARORA
STATE FOREST

Wagon Wheel
Shelter

W i l d c a t   R i d g e

1,500

1,200

HILL LN

1,800

1,500

1,200

TUSCARORA TRAIL

1,800

TUSCARORA TRAIL

1,800

1,500

1,986 ft.
✕
Flat
Rock

1,200

© The Countryman Press

ELEVATION PROFILE

2,180 ft
1,860 ft   Wagon   Flat   Wagon
1,540 ft   Wheel   Rock   Wheel
1,220 ft
900 ft
580 ft Trailhead   Trailhead
            1   2   3   4 miles

GETTING THERE

From the west, follow I-76 E toward Harrisburg. Take exit 201 toward Shippensburg/Chambersburg and turn left onto PA 997 N. In 1.6 miles, continue on the road as it makes a slight turn to the left. Follow the PA 997 N for 10.7 miles to where it ends at the junction with PA 233. Turn left and follow PA 233 N. In 3.3 miles, turn right into Colonel Denning State Park. Follow the signs for the parking area and trailhead located downhill near Doubling Gap Run.

From the east, follow I-76 W toward Harrisburg. Take exit 226 and merge onto US 11 N. In 1.7 miles, take the ramp onto I-81 S. Follow I-81 S for 14.5 miles, then take exit 37 toward Newville. Turn right at the end of the ramp and follow PA 233 N for 12.7 miles. Turn right into Colonel Denning State Park. Follow the signs for the parking area and trailhead located downhill near Doubling Gap Run.

GPS Shortcut: Search Google Maps for "Flat Rock Trailhead" near the borough of Newville and your GPS will direct you to the parking area.

THE HIKE

The hike to Flat Rock starts at the southeastern end of the parking area, beyond the nature program pavilion and an amphitheater. A large wooden sign marks the start of the trail. The sign lists a quick breakdown of the trail and provides basic safety instructions. Walk past the sign and cross Doubling Gap Run on a wooden footbridge. Immediately after crossing the run, the yellow-blazed Flat Rock Trail begins climbing, first on a short flight of wooden steps, then on rugged trail interwoven with roots. Follow this bumpy

BOARDWALK OVER THE HEADWATERS OF WILDCAT RUN

trail for 0.2 mile as it bends to the right and ascends moderately to reach a fork in the trail. To the left lies the "preferred route," a newer stretch of trail that bypasses a section of steep climbing and gently curves uphill on smoother, very well-graded trail. To the right is the "challenging route," a more direct line of ascent that, as the name implies, is at times fairly difficult. The preferred route is slightly longer than the challenging route. Choose whichever path you like, but note that the hike described here

WAGON WHEEL SHELTER ON THE TUSCARORA TRAIL

ascends on the challenging route and returns on the preferred route.

Turn right and follow the faded red blazes of the challenging route. Despite its name, the trail follows straightforward, easy terrain, dipping briefly into a small ravine to cross a seasonal drainage before arriving at the tread of an old dirt road 0.2 mile from the trail split. Turn left and begin climbing a moderately steep uphill on this wide flat road grade. You will pass two small springhouses 0.1 mile later, where the dirt road ends. Skirt to the right of them and continue ascending very steeply on difficult, rocky terrain. At the 0.7-mile marker, the challenging route and the preferred route reconnect. Continuing from here you will once again follow yellow blazes.

Advance steeply up the trail on stone steps and jumbled rocks. This stretch of the trail climbs relentlessly, slowing your pace as you quickly gain elevation. Thankfully, there are plenty of good sitting rocks along the trailside, so be sure to take advantage of them and enjoy the scenery when you need a break. You will notice hemlocks begin to dot the mountainside, along with a large quantity of lush mountain laurels. At mile 0.9, the trail bends back sharply to the left and begins to curve uphill on switchbacks paved with yet more neat, lengthy stone steps. Continue to follow this rustic staircase, and about 0.3 mile later, arrive at the Wagon Wheel. The Flat Rock Trail, Tuscarora Trail, Warner Trail, Lehman Trail, and Woodburn Trail all mingle at this point. This junction is named as such due to the trails that all meet here, forming what would no doubt resemble the hub of a wagon wheel should you view it from above. The Flat Rock Trail merges with the Tuscarora Trail at this point. Continue straight through the Wagon Wheel and begin to follow yellow and blue blazes.

Past the Wagon Wheel, you will tread a very wide, flat, easy trail and pass a small Adirondack-style shelter that features a picnic table, a fire ring, and a privy. This is the aptly named Wagon Wheel Shelter, built in the year 2000 as an Eagle Scout project. Continue on past the shelter, trending downhill as the trail becomes rockier. At mile 1.5, turn to the left and walk on expertly placed stepping-stones and a wooden boardwalk to cross the headwaters of Wildcat Run. Seemingly as soon as you step off the boardwalk, the trail begins to climb once more. The angle of ascent is slightly less steep than the climb up to the Wagon Wheel, but the climb is just as relentless,

BIRDS OF PREY SOARING ABOVE THE CUMBERLAND VALLEY

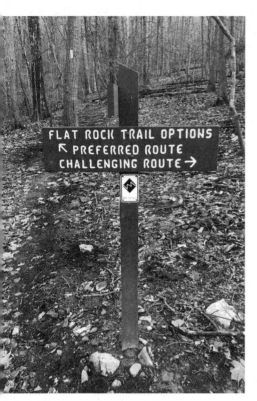

FLAT ROCK TRAIL OPTIONS
↖ PREFERRED ROUTE
CHALLENGING ROUTE →

TRAIL SPLIT ON THE WAY TO FLAT ROCK

due in no small part to the prevalence of lumpy rocks littering the wide trail. At the 2-mile mark, the grade begins to ease, depositing you near the top of the summit 0.1 mile later. Follow the trail down the crest of the ridge for another 0.1 mile to reach the southward-facing vista at the end of the Flat Rock Trail, 2.2 miles after beginning your hike. This large rock outcropping sits above a scree field, offering an outstanding view spanning almost 180 degrees, which looks out over the wide Cumberland Valley below. Vultures and other birds of prey can be seen here many times of year, circling upward on thermals.

When you are ready to continue, turn around and head back up and over the spine of the ridge, retracing your course back to the Wagon Wheel and down the Flat Rock Trail. When you come to where the challenging route and the preferred route split, stay to the right and follow the preferred route on easy, well-maintained sidehill trail. The preferred route eventually bends idly to the left, descending gradually to meet with the challenging route a short distance later. From here, turn to the right and follow the Flat Rock Trail back to where it begins, just over Doubling Gap Run.

White Rocks Trail and Center Point Knob

DISTANCE: 3 miles

DIFFICULTY: Difficult

HIKING TIME: 2 hours

TYPE: Out and Back

TOTAL ELEVATION GAIN: 565'

MAXIMUM ELEVATION: 1,095'

When construction of the Appalachian Trail was completed in 1937, it stretched more than 2,000 miles from Mount Oglethorpe in Georgia to Mount Katahdin in Maine. Since then, the southern terminus has changed to Springer Mountain in Georgia, and the trail has been lengthened and rerouted substantially. The original halfway point of the Appalachian Trail sits atop Center Point Knob in Cumberland County, Pennsylvania. And at the peak of Center Point Knob, sits a small boulder bearing a weathered bronze plaque celebrating the original halfway mark on this historic trail.

While Center Point Knob can be reached by following the Appalachian Trail from either the north or the south, the most exciting and challenging path to the summit is certainly on the White Rocks Trail. This route follows the crest of a slender ridge, eventually ending where it meets the Appalachian Trail. Along the way, you will visit several decent viewpoints and have plenty of opportunities to experience the rocks firsthand, as the trail passes up, over, down, and around the jagged formations.

GETTING THERE

From the west, take I-76 E to exit 226 and merge onto US 11 N. In 0.5 mile, turn right onto S Middlesex Road and follow it. In 3.4 miles, S Middlesex Road makes a left-hand turn onto Lisburn Road. In 0.1 mile, turn right to stay on S Middlesex Road. Continue on the road for 1 mile, then turn left onto PA 74 S. In 2.3 miles, turn right onto Ledigh Drive. In 1.1 miles, turn left onto Creek Road. Creek Road continues straight and becomes Kuhn Road in 0.2 mile. Follow Kuhn Road for 0.5 mile to reach the trailhead on the right side of the road.

From the east, follow I-76 W and take

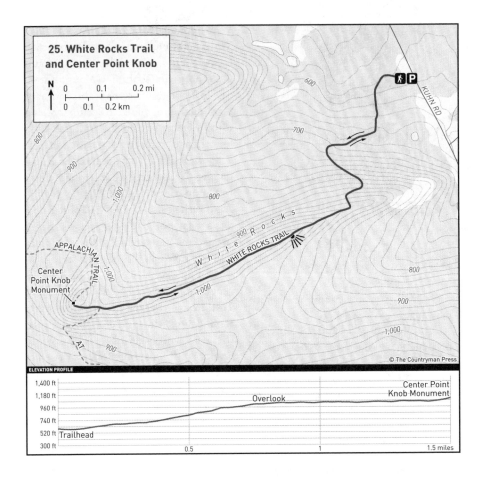

25. White Rocks Trail
and Center Point Knob

N
0   0.1   0.2 mi
0   0.1   0.2 km

APPALACHIAN TRAIL

Center
Point Knob
Monument

White Rocks

WHITE ROCKS TRAIL

AT

© The Countryman Press

ELEVATION PROFILE

1,400 ft
1,180 ft
960 ft
740 ft
520 ft   Trailhead
300 ft

Overlook

Center Point
Knob Monument

0.5   1   1.5 miles

exit 236 to merge onto US 15 S toward Gettysburg. After following US 15 S for 5.1 miles, turn right onto Spring Lane Road. In 1.2 miles, turn right onto PA 74 N and continue for 1.4 miles before turning left onto Creek Road. Follow Creek Road for 1.8 miles, then turn left onto Kuhn Road. The trailhead will be on the right side of the road in 0.5 mile.

GPS Shortcut: Enter "White Rocks Trail" into Google Maps. The trailhead is located near the town of Boiling Springs.

THE HIKE

Follow the blue blazes of the White Rocks Trail from the trailhead at the northwestern corner of the parking lot, next to a small information board. The trail is fairly wide, well marked, and very easy to follow as you leave the parking area. You will quickly cross over a small seasonal drainage culvert on a uniquely designed footbridge made of dozens of sticks thrown together in a seemingly haphazard manner. Climb moderately uphill on rocky terrain for 0.25 mile and turn to the right. The trail briefly follows the remains of an old woods road, rolling gently uphill. A short distance later, turn to the left as the road grade peters out and the trail narrows. Ascend steeply from here on rocky terrain. The tread in this section is at times a chaotic jumble

SCALING STONE OUTCROPPINGS ON THE WHITE ROCKS TRAIL

THE ORIGINAL HALFWAY POINT OF THE APPALACHIAN TRAIL

often meanders beside and through these craggy arrangements. About 0.75 mile in, the trail splits at the foot of a prodigious stone tower. From here you can scramble up the rocks, or you can bypass the structure altogether by veering slightly to the right to pass by it. You will have to use both hands and feet to climb up and down the towering precipice, but you will be rewarded with an excellent view looking southeast from a flat rock that sits in the shade underneath a pine tree.

The trail continues to send you over, around, and through interesting rock formations as you follow the ridgetop, gradually ascending and often giving you glimpses of the nearby mountains. The terrain at this point is extremely rough, composed largely of angular rocks that are tightly packed together and pointing up in all directions. This forces you to slow your pace and carefully consider your foot placement. At mile 1.3, as you progress through pine forest on the narrow ridge, the rocks begin to abate and give way to an easier dirt path. In another 0.1 mile, the White Rocks Trail ends where it meets with the Appalachian Trail. From here, go straight and hike a moderately steep uphill on a similar dirt tread. At the 1.5-mile marker, you reach the top of Center Point Knob, which is marked with an upright boulder bearing a bronze plaque that commemorates the original halfway point of the Appalachian Trail. Peering through the trees, you can catch limited, partially obstructed views of the surrounding countryside.

When you are finished at Center Point Knob, turn around and descend back to the White Rocks Trail. Follow the rocky ridge back the way you came to return to the parking lot.

of pointy boulders, so pay close attention to where you step as you climb.

After 0.6 mile of hiking, after several switchbacks and lots and lots of rocks, the White Rocks Trail reaches the crest of the narrow ridge and turns to the right. Continue on, gaining elevation as you follow the backbone of this ridge on yet more rocks. Moving forward, the terrain continues to grow more and more rugged, and the size of the rocks begins to increase as well. You will start to pass by massive formations made of cracked and crumbling stone that form large walls and chunky pillars as they jut up from the spine. Pay attention to the blazes, as the trail

Hawk Rock

DISTANCE: 1.7 miles

DIFFICULTY: Difficult

HIKING TIME: 1.5 hours

TYPE: Out and Back

TOTAL ELEVATION GAIN: 698'

MAXIMUM ELEVATION: 1,065'

Near the point where the Juniata River flows into the Susquehanna River, Hawk Rock protrudes from the northern tip of Cove Mountain's forked ridge. A mighty view unfolds from this lofty vantage point, looking to the north over the countryside. Below the rocky vista, one can see the serpentine flow of Sherman Creek making its way through the narrow valley toward the wide waters of the Susquehanna River. On the western shore of the river is Duncannon, a small town that received official Appalachian Trail Community status in 2012. The town hosts a free trail festival each year in celebration of this designation, with food, vendors, local trail clubs, and entertainment for all ages.

The hike to Hawk Rock is a short but challenging climb up long stretches of exquisite stone steps. This popular excursion follows the Appalachian Trail most of the way up the ridge. Expect to see lots of other day hikers (and the occasional thru-hiker) on warm summer days when the woods are lush and green. After your hike, consider grabbing a bite to eat at the historic Doyle Hotel in downtown Duncannon. Despite its shabby appearance, this quirky bar has been in business for over a century. It proudly welcomes hikers, and provides them with good food and drink at a reasonable price.

GETTING THERE

From the west, navigate toward State College, then follow US 322 E for 65.1 miles. Take the exit for US 15 S/US 22 S and follow the highway toward Camp Hill for 3 miles. Take the exit for PA 274 toward Duncannon and go straight at the end of the ramp. Follow Main Street for 0.4 mile and turn right onto Little Boston Road after crossing Sherman Creek.

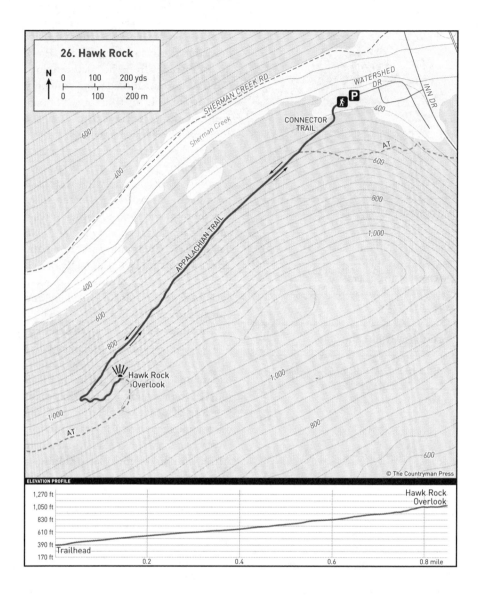

26. Hawk Rock

N

| 0 | 100 | 200 yds |
| 0 | 100 | 200 m |

SHERMAN CREEK RD

Sherman Creek

WATERSHED DR

INN DR

P

CONNECTOR TRAIL

AT

400

600

600

800

1,000

APPALACHIAN TRAIL

600

800

Hawk Rock Overlook

1,000

1,000

800

AT

600

© The Countryman Press

ELEVATION PROFILE

1,270 ft				Hawk Rock Overlook
1,050 ft				
830 ft				
610 ft				
390 ft				
170 ft	Trailhead			
	0.2	0.4	0.6	0.8 mile

A block later, turn right onto Watershed Drive and follow signs toward the recycling center. Park at the gravel lot about 0.1 mile down Watershed Drive. A large sign marks the trailhead.

From the east, follow I-76 W and take exit 247. Merge onto I-283 N toward Hershey/Harrisburg. In about 3 miles, merge onto I-83 N and follow it for 3.7 miles. Take exit 51A and merge onto I-81 S. Just under 2 miles later, take exit 67B and merge onto US 22 W/US 322 W toward Lewistown and State College. After 12.2 miles, shortly after crossing the Susquehanna River, turn left onto PA 849 W and follow signs for Duncannon. Continue straight onto Market Street and in 1.3 miles turn left onto Main Street. Turn right onto Little Boston Road after crossing Sherman Creek. A block later, turn right onto Watershed Drive and follow signs toward the

STONE STEPS LEADING UPWARD TO HAWK ROCK

recycling center. Park at the gravel lot about 0.1 mile down Watershed Drive. A large sign marks the trailhead.

   GPS Shortcut: The parking area is located just outside the borough of Duncannon. Enter "Hawk Rock Parking Area" into Google Maps and your GPS will direct you to the parking lot.

THE HIKE

Head into the woods from the southwest corner of the parking area. Look for a bulletin board and a sign pointing to the Hawk Rock Overlook. The blue-blazed trail twists and turns immediately, briefly climbing a small flight of

THE VIEW LOOKING NORTH FROM HAWK ROCK OVERLOOK

stone stairs before joining a wider grade and continuing to ascend moderately, heading away from a gravel access road that parallels Sherman Creek. About 0.1 mile after leaving the parking lot, the trail meets with the Appalachian Trail, which comes in sharply from the left, joins the blue trail, and proceeds to head straight, following your current trajectory. From here you will follow the white blazes of the A.T. all the way to the vista.

As you hike upward, the bumpy terrain will continue to get rougher and rockier. There are several stone benches along this portion of the trail that provide a relaxing reprieve from the arduous climb. When the leaves are off the trees, you will be able to see glimpses of the landscape surrounding Cove Mountain by peering out through the forest. After walking the Appalachian Trail for 0.4 mile, you will begin hiking up a series of impressive stone steps. To the right side of the trail, the mountainside drops off steeply. You may be able to make out the relatively level gravel access road below, which will give you a good idea of how quickly you are gaining elevation.

Beyond this point the trail almost exclusively follows stone stairs built and maintained by volunteer trail builders, passing at times through strips of pointy, angular scree that would otherwise be nearly impassable. In certain places you may see signs of hikers who have walked next to the stone steps. Doing this erodes the trail and can cause the stone steps to fail over time, so stay on the rock-paved path as much as possible. The Appalachian Trail turns left abruptly after 0.75 mile of hiking and continues to climb steeply. The trail then levels out briefly and, after one more short uphill push on rooty terrain, arrives at the Hawk Rock Overlook. The vista faces north, spanning almost 180 degrees, providing stunning views of the Susquehanna River Valley, the town of Duncannon, and the surrounding countryside.

When you are finished at the overlook, head back down the Appalachian Trail, passing over the rustic stone stairs once more. When you are about 0.1 mile away from the parking area, stay to the left and leave the tread of the Appalachian Trail, following the short blue-blazed trail back to your car.

Clarks Ferry Loop

DISTANCE: 4 miles	
DIFFICULTY: Difficult	
HIKING TIME: 2.5 hours	
TYPE: Loop	
TOTAL ELEVATION GAIN: 1,003'	
MAXIMUM ELEVATION: 1,291'	

For early American settlers seeking to travel west toward Pittsburgh, crossing the Susquehanna River posed a substantial challenge. The shoulders of the surrounding mountains dropped steeply to the wide waters of the Susquehanna and gave way to rocky rapids downriver from the confluence of the Juniata River. A ferry was established in 1788 by Daniel Clark, who eventually passed down the operation to his son, who in turn passed it down to his son, firmly cementing the Clark family name to the area. In 1828, a 2,088-foot covered bridge was built, thought to be the longest covered bridge in the world at the time. Since then, the bridge has been updated several times. The current bridge spanning the water was built in 1986, replacing a concrete toll bridge.

From the eastern shore of the Susquehanna River, this hike climbs the precipitous shoulder of Peters Mountain, following the Appalachian Trail on its northeastern trajectory through Pennsylvania. The top of the mountain features challenging terrain and an awe-inspiring view of the Susquehanna River Valley. While tough, this relatively short excursion into the woods is excellent as a standalone hike or as a supplement to the Hawk Rock hike, which follows the continuation of the Peters Mountain ridge, climbing to the top of Cove Mountain on the western shore.

GETTING THERE

From the west, navigate toward State College, then take US 322 E. Follow US 322 E toward Duncannon and Harrisburg for 67.3 miles. Cross the Susquehanna River on the Clarks Ferry Bridge and take the off-ramp for PA 147 N toward Halifax. At the end of the ramp,

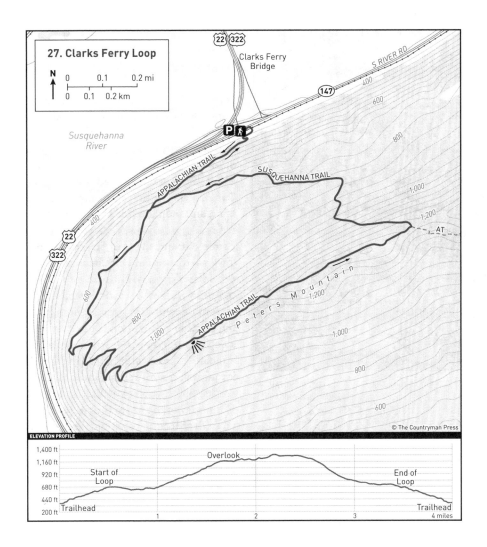

you will arrive at a park and ride lot on the right side of the road. The hike starts from here. There is additional overflow parking up the road to the left.

From the east, follow I-76 W and take exit 247. Merge onto I-283 N toward Hershey/Harrisburg. In about 3 miles, merge onto I-83 N and follow it for 3.7 miles. Take exit 51A and merge onto I-81 S. Just under 2 miles later, take exit 67B and merge onto US 22 W/US 322 W toward Lewistown and State College. Follow the highway for 11.5 miles and just before crossing over the Susquehanna River take the PA 147 N exit toward Halifax. At the end of the ramp, park in the park and ride lot, which is located on the left side of the road. Overflow parking is available farther up PA 147.

GPS Shortcut: Type "Clarks Ferry Park & Ride" into Google Maps. Your GPS will direct you to the parking area, located near the borough of Duncannon, on the eastern side of the Susquehanna River.

SWITCHBACKING UP THE HEAD OF PETERS MOUNTAIN

THE HIKE

Head east from the park and ride lot. Use caution to, first, cross the road, and then to cross an active railroad. An information board maintained by the York Hiking Club is located next to a retaining wall. After consulting it, head uphill on a few steps before picking up narrow singletrack trail as you enter the woods. Follow the white blazes of the Appalachian Trail, ascending aggressively on switchbacks, which give way to intermediate terrain that follows sidehill tread. After hiking for 0.3 mile, pass directly underneath a towering rock formation that angles slightly out over the trail. In another 0.1 mile, you will reach the point where the blue-blazed Susquehanna Trail meets with the Appalachian Trail, coming in from the left. You will return to this point later on to connect the loop

portion of the hike. For now, continue to follow the Appalachian Trail.

After this junction, the grade levels significantly but briefly as you walk across a broad, flat shelf partway up Peters Mountain. Follow the trail as it descends slightly then resumes climbing gradually, turning to the left just after passing the dilapidated remains of a building foundation made out of stone. Turn to the right a few hundred feet later, and then join the wide tread of an old road grade. This wide tread quickly peters out and the trail once again follows narrow sidehill singletrack. At the 1-mile mark, you will begin an intense 0.4-mile ascent on switchbacks. The terrain becomes very rocky here, adding another element of difficulty to the steep climb. When the switchbacks end almost 0.5 mile later, pass by several large rock outcroppings and continue. At this point, you have climbed almost all the way to the top of the ridge. While you will still gain elevation, the grade of ascent should be much more manageable and the terrain will become slightly less rocky.

When you gain the wooded spine of the mountain, the trail passes long, sloping slabs of stone, sometimes crossing over them as if they were a sidewalk, and other times passing beside them as if they were a crude crib wall. At 1.6 miles in, along a stretch of particularly slanty rock slab, there is an excellent viewpoint that looks to the southeast over the Susquehanna River Valley. Just after the viewpoint, the trail dips to the right, descending slightly to the south off the very top of the mountain to avoid a jagged rock outcropping. A few hundred feet later, briefly rejoin the spine before crossing over it, and then walk on the rocky tread just north of the ridgetop. The trail crisscrosses the

THE SUSQUEHANNA RIVER FROM THE CREST OF PETERS MOUNTAIN

jagged spine several times over the 0.5 mile, generally trending uphill.

After 2.4 miles, as the ridgetop broadens and the tread begins to descend, you meet the other end of the Susquehanna Trail. Turn to the left here and follow the blue blazes, heading back in the direction of the river, descending a moderately steep slope on the northern side of the elongated peak. The Susquehanna Trail drops steadily on jumbled rocky terrain and short spans of tall stone steps, switchbacking occasionally. Just before the 3-mile mark, the trail turns to the left. At this point the majority of the rocks impeding the trail disappear, and the grade of descent eases. Follow the trail, trending downhill, and cross an old woods road at the 3-mile mark. Beyond the woods road, the trail curves to the left and follows the rounded edge of the flat shelf part of the way up the mountain. You will reach the end of the Susquehanna Trail in 0.6 mile. Turn to the right here and descend along the narrow tread of the Appalachian Trail. You will reach the parking area and your vehicle in 0.4 mile.

THE EASTERN TERMINUS OF THE SUSQUEHANNA TRAIL

Stony Mountain Lookout Tower

DISTANCE: 7.3 miles	
DIFFICULTY: Difficult	
HIKING TIME: 3.5 hours	
TYPE: Loop	
TOTAL ELEVATION GAIN: 1,314'	
MAXIMUM ELEVATION: 1,661'	

Featuring a unique wraparound observation platform, this hike takes you to the lookout tower on Stony Mountain. The tower stretches 100 feet into the air, and it provides a lofty look at DeHart Reservoir and far-reaching views of the ridges and valleys of State Game Lands No. 211 that spread out below. The tower, which was built in 1922 by the Philadelphia & Reading Coal & Iron Company, was originally used by fire wardens to spot potential forest fires. It was relocated farther down the mountain in the 1970s and is now listed in the National Historic Lookout Register.

The hike described here follows a number of trails, including one named after the late Henry L. Knauber. Knauber, known informally as Hike Along Henry, was a local trail maintainer who regularly enjoyed walking along these rugged trails. On this circuitous route that explores the forest, you will encounter tough sections of climbing that contrast sharply with easy dirt road tread. Along the way, you will pass by a few relics likely left behind by the Philadelphia & Reading Coal & Iron Company, hinting at the land's industrial history. The lookout tower, known to locals as the Moon Tower, provides excellent views of the surrounding landscape during the day, and it is an excellent place to stargaze at night due to the clear view from the observation deck. The tower should only be climbed at your own risk.

GETTING THERE

From the west, navigate toward State College, then take US 322 E. Follow US 322 E toward Duncannon and Harrisburg for 67.3 miles. Cross the Susquehanna River and continue on US 322 E for 5 miles. Take the exit for PA 225 N toward Halifax. At the end of the ramp,

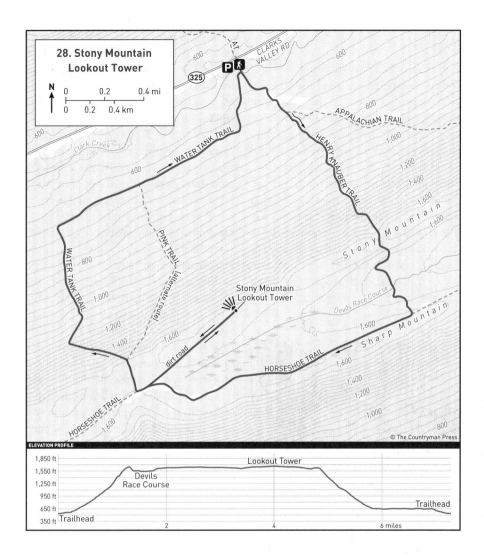

28. Stony Mountain Lookout Tower

ELEVATION PROFILE

turn right onto Allegheny Street, then turn left on PA 225 N. In 1.7 miles, turn right onto PA 325 E. In 10 miles, arrive at the parking area on the right side of the road, and down a short gravel drive.

From the east, follow I-76 W and take exit 247. Merge onto I-283 N toward Hershey/Harrisburg. In about 3 miles, merge onto I-83 N and follow it for 3.7 miles. Take exit 51A and merge onto I-81 S. Just under 2 miles later, take exit 67B and merge onto US 22 W/US 322 W toward Lewistown and State College.

Follow the highway for 6.1 miles and take the exit for PA 225 N toward Halifax. At the end of the ramp, drive PA 225 N for 1.7 miles, then turn right onto PA 325 E. In 10 miles, arrive at the parking area on the right side of the road and down a short gravel drive.

GPS Shortcut: Enter "Clarks Valley Road Appalachian Trail Access" into Google Maps, and your GPS will navigate to the trailhead. It is approximately 2 miles west of DeHart Reservoir.

THE HIKE

From the parking lot, enter the woods to the southeast, passing behind a metal gate. Immediately cross Clark Creek on a concrete culvert. Approach an information board and continue up a wide gravel road, then turn to the left and begin walking the Appalachian Trail, following its iconic white blazes through hemlocks and rhododendrons. The trail follows fairly easy terrain that gradually ascends, and it crosses a pipeline swath in 0.1 mile. In another 0.1 mile, the trail gently bends to the left as it passes a pleasant mountain spring. Beyond the spring, the angle of ascent intensifies,

steadily climbing on increasingly rocky terrain. After 0.4 mile of hiking, reach the junction with the red-blazed Henry Knauber Trail. A wooden sign marks the start of the trail, as it breaks off to the right, heading toward the ridgetop.

Follow the Henry Knauber Trail, promptly entering a stand of small white pines. This footpath climbs a moderately steep uphill slope on rocky terrain, passing through a mixed hardwood forest composed of oak, beech, birch, and plenty of mountain laurel. Despite the tough, bumpy terrain, the trail often feels like the only navigable route through the forest, due to the sea of scree boulders that periodically butt up against the trailside. You will reach the top of the ridge 0.9 mile after turning onto the Henry Knauber Trail, meandering occasionally to avoid the aforementioned scree fields. The last 0.3-mile chunk of this climb is especially physically demanding, and it will almost certainly feel much longer than it actually is. Upon gaining the ridgetop, the red-blazed trail intersects with an old road grade and turns to the left at a small cairn, following the roadbed briefly downhill before bending to the right.

The trail continues across the flat mountaintop, passing by a miniscule pond a short distance later. Beyond this clear reflecting pool, the trail enters dense evergreen forest and crosses a number of mucky, marshy areas and their trickling drainage outlets. These waters combine downhill and form the Devils Race Course, a stream that flows off the mountain to the east, eventually emptying into Rattling Run. The thick foliage on either side of the trail keeps you directly on the narrow walkway. During times of high rainfall, it may be impossible to follow this trail without

TOUGH TERRAIN ON THE HENRY KNAUBER TRAIL

FAR-FLUNG RIDGES SEEN FROM THE TOP OF THE TOWER

getting wet and muddy. Continue to hike across the top of the mountain, and reach another wide woods road at mile marker 1.9, after a short, abrupt ascent. The Henry Knauber Trail ends here. Turn to the right and begin following the old grassy road, which is part of the Horse-Shoe Trail, a 140-mile hiking and equestrian trail that begins in Valley Forge National Historical Park and ends on State Game Lands No. 211, a few miles east of the intersection with the Henry Knauber Trail.

Continue along the broad mountaintop, following this forest road. In 0.2 mile, you pass a large, rusty water tank on the left side of the trail. The road grade will come as a welcome reprieve from the rocky, damp terrain you encountered earlier, as it journeys through scenic forest, giving you a chance to take in your surroundings as you walk. The Horse-Shoe Trail reaches a wide, grassy meadow, and when you reach it you will have hiked 1 mile from the intersection with the Henry Knauber Trail. Pass through the meadow and continue on the other side as red pines and occasional birches begin to become more prominent. Follow the wide grassy tread, passing a few vernal ponds, to reach yet another woods

STONY MOUNTAIN LOOKOUT TOWER

you choose to go all the way to the observation platform at the very top of the tower, a grated walkway at the very top of the tower provides unobstructed 360-degree views.

When ready, head back down the gravel road and turn right to rejoin the Horse-Shoe Trail, continuing on your previous trajectory. In 0.1 mile, on the right side of the road grade, a small cairn marks the juncture of the blue-blazed Water Tank Trail, a narrow, somewhat faint footpath heading north. This cairn is easy to miss, so be sure to keep an eye out for it. Turn off the wide Horse-Shoe Trail here, and begin walking the Water Tank Trail. In another 0.2 mile, just before beginning to descend steeply off the mountaintop, the trail splits. The blue blazes of the Water Tank Trail head left and descend on rugged, rocky terrain. A pink-blazed trail breaks off to the right and descends at a slightly less intense angle. Take whichever trail you choose, as they both join with a logging road at the foot of the extended ridge in about 1 mile. Taking the pink-blazed trail will shorten the mileage listed in this book by about 0.5 mile.

Go down on whichever trail you choose, passing over rough, rugged terrain. When you reach the logging road at the foot of the mountain, turn right and follow its wide, smooth tread. The road is parallel to the ridgetop and bends to the left, heading downhill moderately at 6.9 miles. Walk over a wooden bridge that crosses the pipeline swath you passed earlier and arrive back at the parking area next to Clark Creek shortly thereafter.

road, which cuts back sharply to the right at mile marker 3.4. Turn here and follow the straight course of this trail as it passes a brushy, clear-cut area. The short gravel road grade ends in 0.5 mile at the foot of Stony Mountain Lookout Tower. Ascending the winding stairs of the tower will give you an amazing view of the DeHart Reservoir and the ridges and valleys that spread from here, running east and west. Should

Yellow Springs Loop

DISTANCE: 8.1 miles	
DIFFICULTY: Difficult	
HIKING TIME: 4 hours	
TYPE: Loop	
TOTAL ELEVATION GAIN: 1,362'	
MAXIMUM ELEVATION: 1,629'	

Nestled in the mountains of the ridge and valley region of Pennsylvania, the coal town of Yellow Springs supplied coal to the nearby Schuylkill and Susquehanna Railroad in the mid-1800s. One of five towns that inhabited Stony Valley (now State Game Lands No. 211), Yellow Springs and the surrounding communities began to diminish when the quality of the coal mined there was found to be subpar. The area was lumbered, but the railroad ceased operations once the trees were cut down, effectively cutting off the valley residents from any source of income. By the time the Great Depression struck, Yellow Springs was completely abandoned. The railway of the Schuylkill and Susquehanna Railroad has been transformed into the nearby Stony Valley Rail Trail, and the ghost town of Yellow Springs lies directly on the Appalachian Trail.

The hike described here rambles along several footpaths that wander State Game Lands No. 211, passing briefly through a rocky scree field to reach the ridgetop of Stony Mountain. From here, the circuit passes a large stone tower used in the coal mining process. It then descends to the ruins of Yellow Springs, where the shaft of an old well and several stone foundations can be found. A short side trail a few miles later leads to The General, an archaic excavator left behind to rust in the woods. Lastly, curious individuals can get a view of the valley looking toward Second Mountain from a small vista. Note that the trail immediately crosses the rapid flow of Clark Creek on a large log. This makeshift bridge can be slippery in wet conditions, and when the water level is high, the crossing may not be possible. Later in the hike, you will have to cross Rausch Creek. This stream flows more slowly but can be

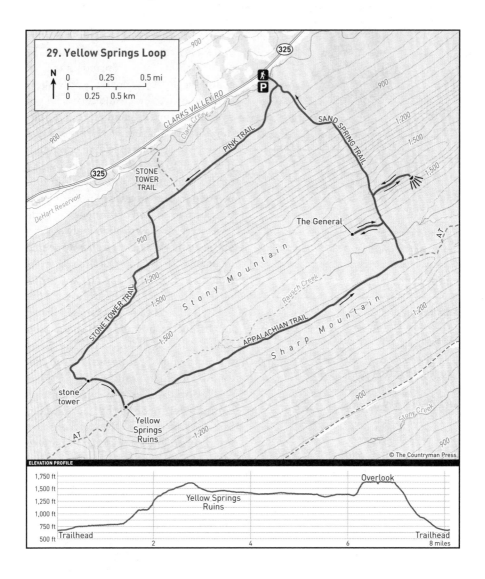

ELEVATION PROFILE

very difficult to cross without getting wet, so plan appropriately.

GETTING THERE

From the west, navigate toward State College, then take US 322 E. Follow US 322 E toward Duncannon and Harrisburg for 67.3 miles. Cross the Susquehanna River and continue on US 322 E for 5 miles. Take the exit for PA 225 N toward Halifax. At the end of the ramp, turn right onto Allegheny Street, then turn left on PA 225 N. In 1.7 miles, turn right onto PA 325 E. In 17.4 miles, the trailhead will be on the right side of the road. Park on the gravel shoulder of the road.

From the east, follow I-76 W and take exit 247. Merge onto I-283 N toward Hershey/Harrisburg. In about 3 miles, merge onto I-83 N and follow it for 3.7 miles. Take exit 51A and merge onto I-81 S. Just under 2 miles later, take exit

67B and merge onto US 22 W/US 322 W toward Lewistown and State College. Follow the highway for 6.1 miles and take the exit for PA 225 N toward Halifax. At the end of the ramp, drive PA 225 N for 1.7 miles, then turn right onto PA 325 E. In 17.4 miles, the trailhead will be on the right side of the road. Park on the gravel shoulder of the road.

GPS Shortcut: In Google Maps, search for "Trailhead Access for Sand Springs Trail/AT/Stone Tower/The General" and set it as your destination. Your GPS will navigate to the trailhead.

THE HIKE

Enter the woods on the south side of the road, and head down the blue-blazed Sand Spring Trail a short distance, less than a 0.1 mile. Approach Clark Creek, which flows rapidly, and cross it on a large log. This log can be very slippery when it is wet, and the creek may be altogether impassable during periods of heavy rainfall. After crossing Clark Creek, continue to follow the footpath into the woods a few hundred feet and meet with a pink-blazed trail that breaks off the Sand Spring Trail to the right, heading west. Follow this trail, passing through serene, dark hemlock groves and dense mountain laurels, roughly paralleling the line of the ridge to your left. As you progress, walking on fairly easy terrain, the forest opens up at several diminutive boulder fields, giving you a break from the close proximity and relative shade of the evergreens. After 1.1 miles of hiking, the pink-blazed trail ends. The hike continues from here on the red-blazed Stone Tower Trail. This trail comes in from the right and turns to follow the same trajectory as the pink-blazed trail, again paralleling the line of the ridge above.

CRUMBLING RUINS ON THE STONE TOWER TRAIL

Walk the Stone Tower Trail for 0.25 mile, and follow it as it turns to the left beside two small cairns. From here the trail climbs steeply on increasingly rocky terrain for 0.3 mile. At the end of this abrupt ascent, turn to the right and walk the remains of an old railroad grade. The terrain is still quite rocky here, but the level grade will give you a much-needed chance to catch your breath. About 0.2 mile later, the trail again turns to the left and resumes the aggressive climb, which continues through a sloping scree field. Carefully make your way through this difficult terrain, and take care not to stray from the trail. While extremely steep and treacherous, the scree field is relatively short. Emerge from the rocks in 0.2 mile and bend to the right, advancing lazily toward the ridge at an acute angle. The angle of ascent will mellow out significantly the farther you go on this portion of the Stone Tower Trail, in stark contrast to the brief ramble through the boulders.

In 0.7 mile after leaving the scree field, the trail turns to the left and arrives on the top of Stony Mountain a short distance later. A small cairn on the lengthy summit marks the blue-blazed Yellow Springs Trail, which follows the ridgeline to the right, and then descends to the left, sharing tread with the Stone Tower Trail. Turn left

ARRIVING AT THE GHOST TOWN OF YELLOW SPRINGS

and follow the red and blue blazes of the Stone Tower Trail, heading down the other side of the mountain. About 0.1 mile later, you will reach a massive handmade stone tower on the right side of the trail. This crumbling tower, the namesake of the Stone Tower Trail, was likely used in the coal mining operation that took place here, although its exact purpose is still debated. Continue downhill, descending moderately on tread that can be somewhat indistinct during the fall and winter months, when leaves and snow cover the trail. As you drop into the valley separating Stony Mountain from Second Mountain, the grade levels almost entirely and becomes very easy to walk.

The Yellow Springs Trail ends 0.5 mile later, intersecting at a right angle with the Appalachian Trail. A mailbox placed along the A.T. contains a trail register. On top of the mailbox, a wooden sign marks the ruins of the village of Yellow Springs, an area now used primarily as a campsite for backpackers. If you take some time to explore this area, you will find several signs of a bygone era, including the deteriorating foundations of buildings, pieces of brick, and an old dry well. When ready, turn to the northeast and begin following the Appalachian Trail, heading away from the Yellow Springs area, in between the seemingly endless ridges. The trail in this shallow channel, hemmed in on either side by mountain laurels, passes by several unreliable springs that drain into Rausch Creek, which flows in the woods to the left. When they are flowing, the springs rarely interrupt the trail, thanks to many large stepping-stones and expert trail maintenance. There is hardly any elevation gain or loss during this stretch, and the walking,

FOLLOWING THE APPALACHIAN TRAIL NORTH THROUGH THICK FOLIAGE

while occasionally rocky, is relaxing and easy.

After following the Appalachian Trail for 2.2 miles, you will notice a blue-blazed trail turning into the woods to the left. This is the Sand Spring Trail, which you started the hike on. Turn onto the trail and descend gradually into the thick underbrush of the forest. In about 0.2 mile, the trail arrives at the edge of Rausch Creek. This watercourse can be challenging to cross without getting wet, even during dry spells. Cross Rausch Creek and

General, an abandoned rusty excavator that got its name from an inscription engraved on the chassis. When you are finished surveying The General, head back down the spur trail and turn left onto the Sand Spring Trail.

Beyond the spur trail, the Sand Spring trail begins to ascend directly up to the top of Stony Mountain once more, reaching the ridgeline in 0.2 mile. Just before the crest of the ridge, a faint spur trail turns off to the right. A small viewpoint sits at the end of this spur trail, 0.3 mile from the tread of the Sand Spring Trail, looking southeast from a bumpy boulder. This trail is marked with fading yellow blazes and can be vague and overgrown with brush, so exercise good judgment if you are having trouble following it.

Continue to follow the Sand Spring Trail and begin to head down the northern side of the mountain. Immediately after beginning to descend, the terrain becomes extremely rocky and drops directly and steeply off the mountainside. As you approach the bottom of the valley, the trail reenters the cover of the hemlock trees. About 1 mile after leaving the top of the ridge, you will pass the pink-blazed trail that you walked earlier. It will be on your left. Continue straight ahead, cross back over Clark Creek, and arrive at your vehicle a short distance later.

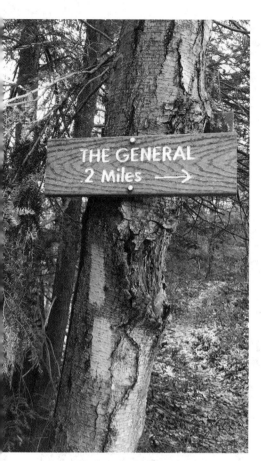

SIGN MARKING THE SPUR TRAIL LEADING TOWARD THE GENERAL

keep going. After another 0.1 mile, a spur trail marked by an enigmatic sign breaks off to the left. Following this trail for 0.2 mile will lead you to The

Worlds End State Park

DISTANCE: 6.1 miles

DIFFICULTY: Difficult

HIKING TIME: 3 hours

TYPE: Loop

TOTAL ELEVATION GAIN: 1,445'

MAXIMUM ELEVATION: 1,765'

When people hear the phrase "worlds end" it often elicits the vaguely science fiction–esque, apocalyptic scenes of scorched earth and dead cities, the air choked with black smoke. When the residents of Sullivan County hear the phrase, they imagine the calm, quiet forests, babbling streams, and breathtaking views of Worlds End State Park. The park's name is of uncertain origin, and the park has historically also been referred to as Whirls End and Whirls Glen as recently as the mid-20th century. Theories exist as to the etymology of each of these names, ranging from the sheer drop-off of the surrounding ridges to a whirlpool that existed nearby in Loyalsock Creek.

The hike described here rambles through the park on the Canyon Vista Trail, Loyalsock Trail, Link Trail, and the Double Run Nature Trail. The route features several attractions, including a pleasant walk beside Loyalsock Creek, a nice look at the falling waters of Cottonwood Falls, and a wide, panoramic view from Canyon Vista. Options exist for shortening or lengthening the hike. Moreover, across the creek, the northern side of the park offers a completely different set of trails and viewpoints. The 59-mile Loyalsock Trail winds through the park, visiting many of these vistas and taking advantage of everything the area provides.

GETTING THERE

From the west, follow I-80 E. Take exit 178 for US 220 N toward Lock Haven. Follow US 220 N for 31.5 miles and continue onto I-180 E. Take exit 21 and turn left onto PA 87 N, following it for 30.6 miles. In Forksville, turn right onto PA 154 E. In 3.6 miles arrive at the parking area, located on the left side of the road.

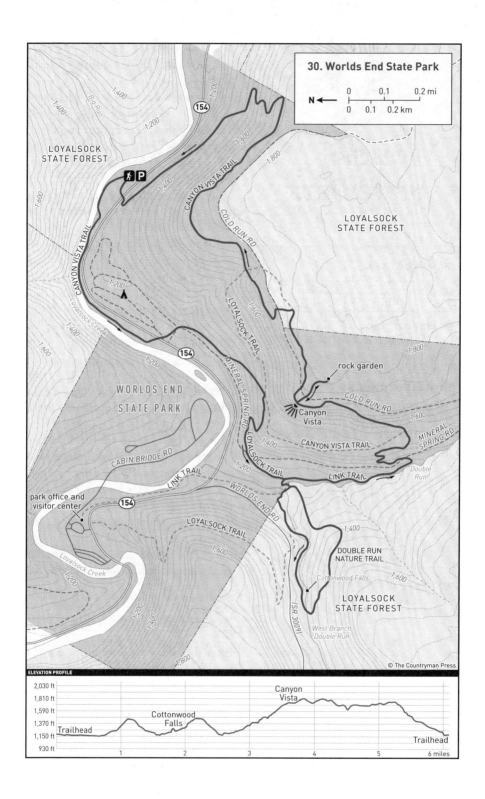

30. Worlds End State Park

N ←

| 0 | 0.1 | 0.2 mi |
| 0 | 0.1 | 0.2 km |

154

LOYALSOCK
STATE FOREST

1,400

1,200

1,600

1,400

1,200

Big Run

Loyalsock Creek

CANYON VISTA TRAIL

CANYON VISTA TRAIL

COLD RUN RD

LOYALSOCK TRAIL

1,600

1,800

LOYALSOCK
STATE FOREST

1,800

1,600

rock garden

Canyon
Vista

COLD RUN RD

CANYON VISTA TRAIL

MINERAL SPRING RD

WORLDS END
STATE PARK

154

CABIN BRIDGE RD

LINK TRAIL

MINERAL SPRING RD

LOYALSOCK TRAIL

1,400

1,200

LINK TRAIL

Double
Run

park office and
visitor center

154

WORLDS END RD

LOYALSOCK TRAIL

1,600

1,400

DOUBLE RUN
NATURE TRAIL

Cottonwood Falls

1,600

Loyalsock Creek

1,200

1,400

(SR 3009)

West Branch
Double Run

LOYALSOCK
STATE FOREST

1,800

© The Countryman Press

ELEVATION PROFILE

2,030 ft				Canyon		
1,810 ft				Vista		
1,590 ft		Cottonwood				
1,370 ft		Falls				
1,150 ft	Trailhead					
930 ft						Trailhead
	1	2	3	4	5	6 miles

The trail starts in the gravel lot on the shoulder and is marked by a sign.

From the east, follow I-80 W. Take exit 232 toward PA 42 N. Turn right onto PA 42 N, following signs for Millville. In 10.1 miles, turn right to stay on PA 42 N, continuing for another 7.9 miles. Turn left onto PA 118 W for 0.3 mile, then turn right to rejoin PA 42 N. In 7.4 miles, turn right and follow US 220 N. In 1.1 miles, turn left to once again rejoin PA 42 N. Drive 4.4 miles. Turn to the left at Worlds End Road and drive 5.7 miles, all the way to where it ends at PA 154. Make a sharp right onto PA 154 E. In 1.2 miles, arrive at the parking area, located on the left side of the road. The trail starts in the gravel lot on the shoulder and is marked by a sign.

GPS Shortcut: In Google Maps, set "Canyon Vista Trailhead" as your destination. Your GPS will direct you to the

FOOTBRIDGE OVER DOUBLE RUN

trailhead, which is located near the borough of Forksville.

THE HIKE

Enter the woods, passing under an awning that marks the blue-blazed Canyon Vista Trail. Two different segments of the Canyon Vista Trail meet here. One emerges to the left as soon as you enter the woods. This is the path you will take to arrive back at the parking area at the end of your hike, so ignore it for now and continue to head northeast, toward Loyalsock Creek. Less than 0.1 mile from the parking area, turn to the left and begin walking along the creek, mirroring the flow of the water on sandy, rooty tread. The Canyon Vista Trail passes through a narrow swath of forest between the

TRAIL SIGN ON THE CANYON VISTA TRAIL

EXPLORING THE ROCK GARDEN AT THE TOP OF THE CANYON

creek and the roadway of PA 154, gently meandering back and forth, occasionally approaching the edge of one before veering toward the other.

After 0.6 mile of easy hiking, turn to the left away from the creek and cross the road. From here the Canyon Vista Trail passes through a large family campground and leads to the right of Mineral Springs Road, paralleling it for a short distance before crossing the dirt road. After crossing Mineral Springs Road, the trail begins an ascent on smooth, narrow singletrack, growing steeper and rougher as you climb. Off to your right you will be able to see Mineral Springs Road in the canyon below, appearing to fall away as you gain elevation. Continue climbing, and at mile marker 1.1, arrive at a trail intersection where the Loyalsock Trail crosses the Canyon Vista Trail. Following the Loyalsock Trail from here will send you toward Double Run and Cottonwood Falls. If you wish to skip these features and shorten the hike by 2.2 miles, stay straight and follow the blue blazes. Otherwise, veer to the right onto Loyalsock Trail and follow the red and yellow blazes.

The terrain of the Loyalsock Trail is immediately much more challenging than the Canyon Vista Trail. Descend moderately on bouldery switchbacks for 0.3 mile, then cross Mineral Springs Road to stay on the trail. Continue beyond the dirt tread of the road for 0.1 mile. At this point, the Loyalsock Trail turns to the right and continues downhill on stone steps, dropping into the ravine where Double Run flows. Once in the ravine, the trail bends to the left and crosses the east branch of Double Run on a wooden footbridge. After this crossing you will notice that the trail is marked with three separate sets of blazes: the red and yellow blazes of the Loyalsock Trail, the red X (inside a yellow circle) blazes of the Link Trail, and the green blazes of the Double Run Nature Trail. Turn to the right and cross two more footbridges. A short distance beyond the third footbridge, the Link Trail veers to the right, while the Loyalsock Trail and Double Run Nature Trail bend to the left. Turn left, leaving the Link Trail behind for now.

The tread of the combined Loyalsock Trail and Double Run Nature Trail ascends moderately uphill, at times passing areas where the run bends and cascades over rocks. Continue along this shared tread for 0.2 mile. At this point, the Loyalsock Trail continues straight on, heading uphill as it approaches Worlds End Road. Turn to the left to follow the Double Run Nature Trail and descend toward the water. The green blazes follow a narrow walkway, gradually ascending up the west branch of Double Run, passing several mossy boulders. In 0.2 mile after leaving the Loyalsock Trail, you will reach Cottonwood Falls. This beautiful area gazes over a wide circular pool of water, where Double Run flows through a narrow stone chute and falls about 10 feet into the shallow basin below. Take your time here. When you are ready, continue up the trail.

Less than 0.1 mile past Cottonwood Falls, the Double Run Nature Trail splits. One leg continues straight on, following the run. The other crosses the run on a wooden footbridge. Turn left here and cross the run. On the other side, the trail begins a steady climb on a series of wooden stairs, which feels somewhat out

COTTONWOOD FALLS

of place here in the forest. Upon reaching the top of the stairs, the trail continues to ascend fairly directly for about 0.2 mile, after which the course almost entirely levels out and continues on a wide grade on the rounded shelf that separates the two branches of the run. Eventually, you will begin to descend toward the east branch of Double Run, dropping moderately over root-laden terrain. Follow this fun little descent as it twists and turns regularly, reaching the footbridge where you crossed over the east branch of the run. The Link Trail and Loyalsock Trail meet with the Double Run Nature Trail at this location, right at the 2.6 mile marker. Recross the bridge, leave the tread of the Double Run Nature Trail, retake the Loyalsock Trail, and retrace your footsteps uphill to the top of the stone steps you descended earlier.

At the top of the steps, turn to the right and begin following the Link Trail. Its blazes consist of a red X inside a yellow circle. The Link Trail ascends gradually up the east branch of Double Run, traversing rough terrain along

WALKING BESIDE DOUBLE RUN ON THE LINK TRAIL

the water's edge. At several points the scenic run spills over short ledges in tuneful cascades, creating a tranquil atmosphere that permeates the ravine. After 0.5 mile along Double Run, the Link Trail turns to the left away from the creek and ascends on long switchbacks, soon crossing Mineral Spring Road one more time. You will pass some interesting rock outcroppings that protrude from the hillside as you continue along these switchbacks. At the 3.5 mile mark, you will come to the junction with the Canyon Vista Trail, which comes in from the left. The Link Trail merges with the Canyon Vista Trail at this point, and, together, they bend to the left and continue uphill on a narrow sidehill tread following a very direct trajectory. Climb steeply, heading in the direction of the creek in the valley below. In 0.1 mile, a tiny spur trail on the left side of the trail leads about 15 feet to a view of a rock formation known as Ticklish Rock, named presumably for the way the formation curves away from the canyon wall as though it were being tickled.

As you continue to climb, you will notice that the Canyon Vista Trail alternates between stretches of smooth, well-graded terrain, and areas of roots and rocks. About 0.3 mile after the Ticklish Rock spur, the Canyon Vista Trail comes alongside the gravel surface of Cold Run Road. The road parallels the hiking trail and and both arrive at the Canyon Vista viewpoint a short distance later. This expansive viewpoint affords a sweeping view of Loyalsock Creek and the surrounding peaks and valleys that make up Loyalsock State Forest to the northwest. Just before the vista, the Loyalsock Trail merges with the Link Trail and the Canyon Vista Trail. Behind the vista is a small parking area and a restroom building. Take

your time here and enjoy the view, but before continuing down the trail, pass behind the restrooms and follow a wide unmarked footpath for 500 feet, ending at a rock garden. Narrow crevices snake between the massive boulders here, providing plenty of areas to explore.

Return to the vista and turn right on the combined treads of the Loyalsock Trail, Link Trail, and Canyon Vista Trail. The trail crosses Cold Run Road, and it continues to ramble along the top of the canyon, following rough, rocky terrain. In 4.1 miles, after passing by a natural stone wall on your right, you will arrive at a fork in the trail marked by a cairn. This is where the Loyalsock Trail, the Link Trail, and the Canyon Vista Trail split. Turn left onto the Canyon Vista Trail, following the blue blazes downhill, crossing back over Cold Run Road in 0.1 mile. After crossing the road, the trail bends to the right and the grade levels, leading you along the rounded edge of the canyon rim on rolling terrain for 0.9 mile. One mile after leaving the Loyalsock Trail and the Link Trail, the blue blazes begin winding through an area similar to the rock garden by the vista. Twist and turn through the towering, mossy boulders for 0.1 mile to reach the Cold Spring Trail, an extension of the Canyon Vista Trail that passes several waterfalls over its course. Should you decide to take this extension, it will add 1.5 miles to your hike.

Turn left and follow the Canyon Vista Trail away from the rocky area as you descend into the canyon, heading back and forth on well-graded switchbacks. You will reach the other end of the Cold Spring Trail after 0.2 mile. At the 6-mile mark, the trail drops down a particularly steep switchback onto the shoulder of PA 154. Cross the road and turn to the right. You will arrive back at the parking area 0.1 mile later.

Rock Run

DISTANCE: 3 miles	
DIFFICULTY: Moderate	
HIKING TIME: 1.5 hours	
TYPE: Out and Back	
TOTAL ELEVATION GAIN: 613'	
MAXIMUM ELEVATION: 1,952'	

One of Pennsylvania's gems, the Rock Run area is gorgeous any time of year, although it is most popular in the summertime. Located in the Loyalsock State Forest, the stream has a reputation as Pennsylvania's prettiest, due to the twisting channels of smooth, water-carved stone; exposed bedrock platforms that overlook the flow; a wide, cool swimming hole; and the confluence of Yellow Dog Run, which tumbles down a series of ledges into Rock Run. A number of campsites are located near the water's edge on both runs. Because of the scenic nature of this area, it is often busy on weekends and holidays.

The walk to Rock Run detailed here is a relatively easy jaunt through classic Pennsylvania forest on wide, sloping tread. The hike is suitable for children, although a short section near the parking area can be wet and muddy after periods of rain. The hike follows the Old Loggers Path exclusively, an orange-blazed footpath that forms a 27-mile loop through Loyalsock State Forest. The Old Loggers Path is an excellent introduction to backpacking, and it visits a number of scenic viewpoints and the ghost town of Masten, as well as Rock Run.

GETTING THERE

From the west, drive I-80 E. Take exit 178 toward Lock Haven. At the end of the ramp, turn left onto US 220 N. Follow US 220 N for 31 miles. Take exit 29, merging onto US 15 N. Follow US 15 N for 12.8 miles, then take the exit onto PA 14 for Trout Run. At the end of the ramp, merge onto PA 14 N and drive for 11.1 miles. In the town of Ralston, turn right onto Thompson Street. In 0.7 mile, continue straight on Rock Run Road. In 3.5 miles, turn to the right onto Yellow Dog Road,

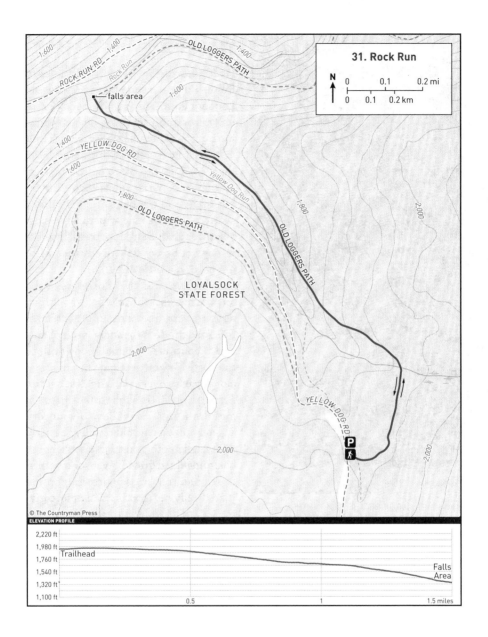

31. Rock Run

LOYALSOCK
STATE FOREST

ELEVATION PROFILE

2,220 ft	
1,980 ft	Trailhead
1,760 ft	
1,540 ft	Falls Area
1,320 ft	
1,100 ft	

© The Countryman Press

immediately crossing the run itself. Follow Yellow Dog Road for 1.8 miles to reach the gravel parking area, located on the left side of the road. If you reach Ellenton Ridge Road, you have gone 0.4 mile too far.

From the east, drive I-80 W. Take exit 210B, merging onto US 15 N at the end of the ramp. Follow US 15 N 16.5 miles, then turn left to merge onto I-180 W at Williamsport. In 1.7 miles, keep right and continue to follow US 15 N. In 12.6 miles, take the exit onto PA 14 for Trout Run. At the end of the ramp, merge onto PA 14 N and drive for 11.1 miles. In the town of Ralston, turn right onto Thompson Street. In 0.7 mile continue straight on Rock Run Road. In 3.5 miles, turn to

THE HIKE

Head into the woods toward the east, following the orange blazes of the Old Loggers Path. The trail descends gradually, crossing a small stream and entering a grove of hemlock trees on the other side. Follow a narrow drainage ditch, then turn left onto the remains of a wide, swampy, stagnant woods road. A number of stepping-stones and tree limbs scattered on the mucky path will assist you through this stretch of trail. Even so, it may not be possible to advance without getting a little dirty.

After 0.1 mile, the trail veers to the left and merges with another woods road as you escape from the mud. The tread of this road grade is in much better shape, and it continues gradually downhill to the north. As you descend you will occasionally pass over small trickles that run across the trail through rutted channels and drain into the valley to your left. The terrain on this old roadbed is fairly rocky, advancing through areas of cobbles and mixed gravel. At several points, brush and tall grasses growing on the road briefly narrow the trail before giving way to its wide course farther downhill. The trail drops steadily, although never more than moderately.

As you descend, you will be able to hear the burgeoning flow of Yellow Dog Run in the ravine to your left. At 0.9 mile, looking down into the ravine through the trees, a decently sized waterfall becomes visible, though it is fairly far away. In 0.2 mile, the incline of the trail intensifies slightly, continuing downhill. You will notice the sounds of the run getting closer as you advance, and at mile marker 1.5, you will arrive at the confluence of Yellow Dog Run to your left and Rock Run, which lies

WINTER MORNING ON THE OLD LOGGERS PATH

the right onto Yellow Dog Road immediately crossing the run itself. Follow Yellow Dog Road for 1.8 miles to reach the gravel parking area, located on the left side of the road. If you reach Ellenton Ridge Road, you have gone 0.4 mile too far.

GPS Shortcut: Search Google Maps for the intersection of "Ellenton Ridge Road and Yellow Dog Road near McIntyre Township." The parking area is a small gravel lot on Yellow Dog Road, about 0.4 mile away from this intersection.

CONFLUENCE OF ROCK RUN AND YELLOW DOG RUN

directly ahead, flowing perpendicular to your current course.

There is plenty to enjoy in this gorgeous area. There are a number of flat ledges on Rock Run that make excellent viewing platforms for a look down into the channel that the run flows through. From these ledges you can see the smooth, water-carved stone walls of the channel, and a small cascade farther upstream. Yellow Dog Run flows over jumbles of rounded boulders upstream, giving way to wide, smooth slabs of stone, which form an abrupt and uneven staircase that the water splashes down just before joining Rock Run. At the bottom of this little waterfall sits a wide, placid pool that makes a great swimming hole in the hot summer months. The easiest way to reach this area is

THE GENTLE FLOW OF ROCK RUN WEST OF THE FALLS AREA

by carefully crossing Yellow Dog Run through an eroding campsite, turning to the right on the other side, and descending to the edge of the water.

When you are finished here, head back uphill, roughly mirroring the flow of Yellow Dog Run, and retrace your footsteps back to the parking area on Yellow Dog Road.

32

Haunted Vista

DISTANCE: 3.9 miles	
DIFFICULTY: Difficult	
HIKING TIME: 2 hours	
TYPE: Out and Back	
TOTAL ELEVATION GAIN: 842'	
MAXIMUM ELEVATION: 1,691'	

The Anna S mine, located atop Rattler Mountain in Tioga State Forest, originally operated in the early 20th century, when it extracted coal from the mountainside. The mine closed in 1937 due to financial problems stemming from the Great Depression, but the land still bears scars left behind by the operation in the form of road tread, acid pollution, rusting machinery debris, and a steeply sloping clear-cut hillside littered with shale that has come to be known as the Haunted Vista. This site allegedly claimed the lives of several workers back when the Anna S mine was running. Since then, sightings of ghostly, forlorn figures dressed in filthy mining garb—supposedly the spirits of these unfortunate individuals—have been periodically reported to wander the area.

The hike to the Haunted Vista follows the Mid State Trail, Pennsylvania's longest and arguably most rugged long-distance footpath. The trail crosses three oddly colored streams. Two still display the neon orange signs of acid pollution. The third is a milky white color. This is a byproduct of acid pollution treatment, the white color resulting from precipitated aluminum hydroxide. Also of interest is a stretch of trail that follows a long stone ledge made up of flat-topped boulders separated by channels up to a foot wide. You will have to step over these crevices to continue on the Mid State Trail, taking care not to fall into these deep gaps. For those interested in geology, this area might be the highlight of the entire hike. A bypass trail mirrors this portion of the hike from the foot of these rocks, and it is useful in slippery conditions. The parking area is located on Rattler Road, and because this road is not maintained in the wintertime, this hike is best done when the ground is clear of snow and ice.

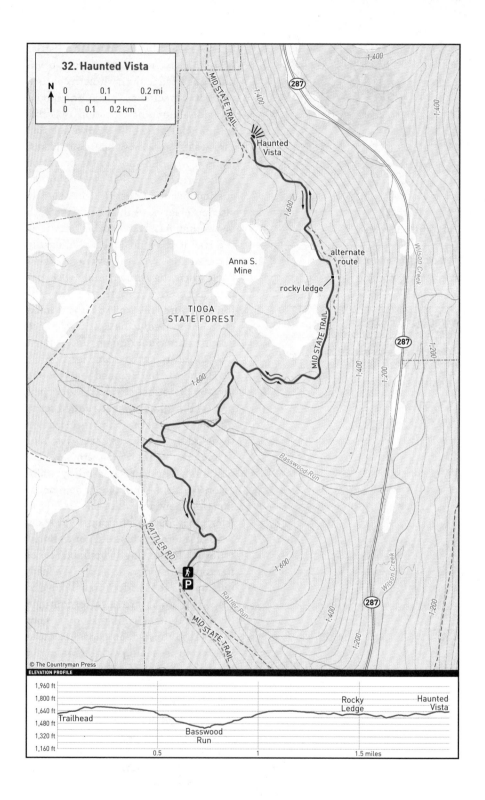

32. Haunted Vista

N

| 0 | 0.1 | 0.2 mi |
| 0 | 0.1 | 0.2 km |

Haunted
Vista

MID STATE TRAIL

alternate
route

rocky ledge

Anna S.
Mine

TIOGA
STATE FOREST

MID STATE TRAIL

Wilson Creek

287

Basswood Run

RATTLER RD

Rattler Run

MID STATE TRAIL

287

Wilson Creek

© The Countryman Press

ELEVATION PROFILE

1,960 ft			
1,800 ft		Rocky	Haunted
1,640 ft		Ledge	Vista
	Trailhead		
1,480 ft			
1,320 ft		Basswood	
1,160 ft		Run	
	0.5	1	1.5 miles

The Mid State Trail is the only trail system in Pennsylvania whose governing body uses the metric system to measure distance and elevation. For the sake of continuity within this guide, the US standard system is used in this entry.

GETTING THERE

From the west, follow I-80 E. Take exit 178 for US 220 N toward Lock Haven. At the end of the ramp, turn left onto US 220 N and follow it for 21 miles. Turn left onto PA 287 N, and follow for 28.3 miles to the town of Morris. Turn left to stay on PA 287 N, and in 0.4 mile turn left onto Rattler Road. The parking area is located about 1 mile up Rattler Road on the right side. It is marked by a wooden Mid State Trail sign.

From the east, follow I-80 W. Take exit 210B, merging onto US 15 N toward Williamsport. Drive 16.5 miles. Immediately after crossing the Susquehanna River, turn left and merge onto I-180 W, keeping right. In 1.7 miles take exit 29 and continue on US 15 N. Drive for 27.2 miles. Take the exit for PA 414 toward Morris/Liberty. At the end of the ramp, turn left onto PA 414 W. Continue for 9.8 miles, pass through the town of Morris, and then continue straight onto PA 287 N. In 0.4 mile, turn left onto Rattler Road and continue uphill for about 1 mile. The parking area will be on the right side of the road, marked by a wooden Mid State Trail sign.

GPS Shortcut: The nearest searchable location in Google Maps is "Slide Hollow Lane, Morris Township." The trailhead is located on Rattler Road just outside of Morris. When you arrive at Slide Hollow Lane, simply continue on Rattler Road and take it uphill for 0.9 mile to reach the small parking area on the right side of the road.

JUST BEFORE THE LEDGES ON THE MID STATE TRAIL

THE HIKE

Follow the orange blazes of the Mid State Trail into the woods, heading north. The trail winds uphill along rocky tread, passing through cool, shady hemlock groves and ledges of stacked rock slab for 0.1 mile. At this point, the trail grade levels out, leading along the top of the plateau for 0.3 mile before beginning a steep descent as the trail turns to the right. The trail drops very directly, briefly following tough, rocky terrain that leads toward a much easier woods road grade. Follow the woods road as it passes alongside Basswood Run in the ravine below for 0.3 mile, then make an abrupt left turn, leaving the road grade to continue on the Mid State Trail.

VIEW FROM THE HAUNTED VISTA LOOKING NORTH

The trail descends into the ravine and crosses the main flow of Basswood Run on awkward, uneven stepping-stones. You will cross a second branch of Basswood Run immediately afterward, just before it joins with the main branch. This smaller branch of the run is separated from the main flow by a triangular crest. After the water crossing, the trail rejoins a wide grassy road grade that heads moderately uphill, following the northern branch of Basswood Run upstream. The pools and rocks of this branch are tinted an unnatural neon orange, a sign of acid pollution from the mining days. Continue upward on a moderately steep ascent on this road grade for 0.2 mile, passing through more hemlock and a good number of birch trees.

Turn right and head away from the north branch of Basswood Run on a narrow singletrack tread, passing through more birches and patches of very young beech trees on rocky terrain. The trail turns to the right in a short distance, skirting the bottom of a short cliff ledge before ascending through a cleft in the stone and emerging onto the top of the plateau that features a brushy forest populated with many mountain laurels. From here, the trail heads east, approaching the edge of the rim and turns to the left along the wooded plateau. The terrain grows rockier and rockier as you advance, and in 1.3 miles you will come to a trail split marked by a sign. Continuing straight from here, the Mid State Trail follows the top of a long, rocky ledge composed of wide, flat-topped boulders that are separated by deep gaps up to two feet across. A highlight of this hike, this 0.3-mile-long stretch of trail is lots of fun to explore, so be sure to take your time.

If you decide that you do not want to walk along the top of the rocks, the yellow-blazed Rock Bypass turns to the right at this trail split and follows the foot of the ledge, paralleling the tread of the Mid State Trail. The Rock Bypass is on a wide road grade through very young forest and can be wet and muddy occasionally. Near the end of the Rock Bypass, the trail descends steeply a short distance, then turns to the left and ascends just as sharply to rejoin the Mid State Trail. The Rock Bypass is approximately as long as the ledge portion of the Mid State Trail.

At mile marker 1.6, the Mid State Trail reaches the other end of the Rock Bypass at the edge of a milky-white stream. This discoloration is caused by the presence of aluminum hydroxide, a byproduct of treating the acid runoff from the nearby mine site. Cross the stream on slippery stepping-stones, and bend to the left, climbing the top of another ledge. From this point, the trail follows a wide path cut into the mountainside, passing some odd slag boulders and some rusty machine parts left behind when the mine closed. The trail follows a relatively flat course for about 0.3 mile before bending to the left once more and ascending a short embankment, arriving at the Haunted Vista 1.9 miles after leaving the parking area. The view from this wide expanse on the edge of the plateau looks to the northeast, over PA 287 toward the town of Antrim on the other side of the canyon. The vista, as indicated by its name, is supposed to be haunted by the ghosts of miners. While the roaming spirits of these deceased individuals may or may not make themselves known to you, the area certainly has an eerie feeling to it, due to the black coal waste covering the ground and the scarcity of plants along this clearing.

When you are finished at the viewpoint, turn around and follow the Mid State Trail back the way you came to return to your vehicle.

SURVEYING THE LANDSCAPE FROM THE HAUNTED VISTA

33

West Rim Trail Day Hike

DISTANCE: 14.6 miles	
DIFFICULTY: Very Difficult	
HIKING TIME: 7 hours	
TYPE: Loop	
TOTAL ELEVATION GAIN: 2,061'	
MAXIMUM ELEVATION: 1,868'	

The West Rim Trail is a 30-mile point-to-point hiking trail that runs along the top of the Pine Creek Gorge. The trail runs north to south, starting near the town of Ansonia in the north and ending at Rattlesnake Rock near the village of Blackwell in the south. The West Rim Trail features many scenic views of the Pine Creek Gorge, which is designated as a National Natural Landmark by the National Park Service, and this trail makes an excellent weekend excursion for avid backpackers who usually complete the whole trail in two or three days. Near the northern terminus, Pine Creek Outfitters offers shuttle services for hikers, transporting either hikers or vehicles to the southern terminus. Using this service, the trail can be hiked in either direction.

The hike detailed here follows about a quarter of the West Rim Trail. This hike goes north before beginning a short loop, and then it returns back down the West Rim Trail in the opposite direction. As you hike you will pass a number of excellent viewpoints, babbling brooks, and some quaint campsites that allow for overnight camping options. The hike is considered very difficult, due largely to its length, although two connector trails can be used to shorten the hike by either 2 or 3 miles.

To shorten the hike by 2 miles, when you first arrive at Bradley Wales Road, continue driving up West Rim Road for 0.9 miles, then make a very sharp turn to the right onto Painter Leetonia Road. Park on the gravel shoulder about 0.7 mile north up Painter Leetonia Road to access the trailhead for the Ice Break Trail. To shorten the hike by 3 miles, continue driving roughly 1.6 miles past the hairpin on Painter Leetonia Road and park on the gravel shoulder at the trailhead for the Slate Run Trail.

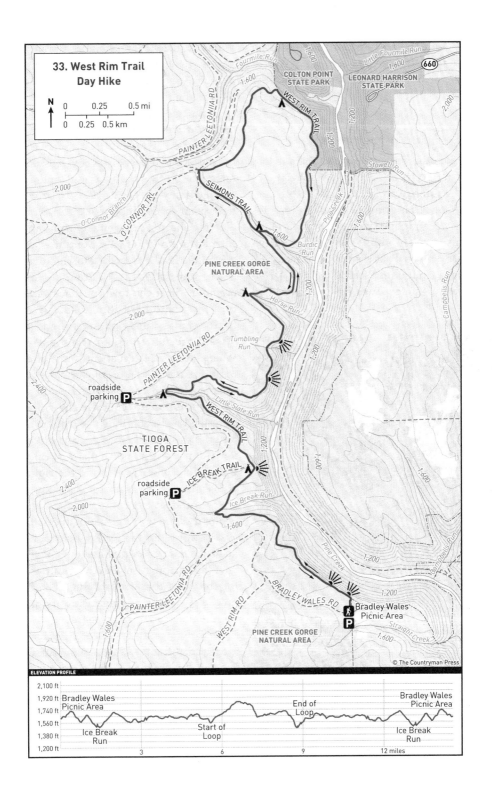

33. West Rim Trail
Day Hike

N

| 0 | 0.25 | 0.5 mi |
| 0 | 0.25 | 0.5 km |

COLTON POINT
STATE PARK

LEONARD HARRISON
STATE PARK

660

WEST RIM TRAIL

PAINTER LEETONIIA RD

SEIMONS TRAIL

PINE CREEK GORGE
NATURAL AREA

O'CONNOR TRL

Tumbling
Run

roadside
parking P

TIOGA
STATE FOREST

WEST RIM TRAIL

Little Slate Run

roadside
parking P

ICE BREAK TRAIL

Ice Break Run

PAINTER LEETONIIA RD

WEST RIM RD

BRADLEY WALES RD

Bradley Wales
Picnic Area

PINE CREEK GORGE
NATURAL AREA

© The Countryman Press

Fourmile Run

Little Fourmile Run

Stowell Run

Pine Creek

Burdic Run

Horse Run

Campbells Run

Pine Creek

Straight Creek

ELEVATION PROFILE

2,100 ft			
1,920 ft	Bradley Wales	End of	Bradley Wales
1,740 ft	Picnic Area	Loop	Picnic Area
1,560 ft			
1,380 ft	Ice Break	Start of	Ice Break
1,200 ft	Run	Loop	Run
	3	6	9	12 miles

Be advised that the roads leading to the parking area at Bradley Wales Picnic Area are not maintained in the wintertime.

GETTING THERE

From the west, follow I-80 E. Take exit 178 toward Lock Haven. At the end of the ramp, turn left onto US 220 N and follow it for 21 miles. Turn left onto PA 287 N and continue for 27.7 miles. Make a sharp left onto PA 414 W, and drive for 6 miles. Past the town of Blackwell, turn right onto West Rim Road. Drive for 10.9 miles. Turn right onto Bradley

HIKING ALONG THE SIDEHILL TREAD ON THE WEST RIM TRAIL

Wales Road, following signs for Bradley Wales Picnic Area. In about 1 mile, the parking area will be on the left side of the road, in front of a pit toilet building.

From the east, follow I-80 W. Take exit 210B, merging onto US 15 N toward Williamsport. Immediately after crossing the Susquehanna River, turn left and merge onto I-180 W. Keep right, and in 1.7 miles take exit 29 onto US 15 N. Drive for 27.2 miles, then take exit 162 toward Morris/Liberty. At the end of the ramp, turn left onto PA 414 W. Continue for 9.8 miles. In the town of Morris, turn left to stay on PA 141 W. Continue for 6.7 miles. Past the town of Blackwell, turn right onto West Rim Road. Drive for 10.9 miles. Turn right onto Bradley Wales Road, following signs for Bradley Wales Picnic Area. In about 1 mile, the parking area will be on the left side of the road, in front of a pit toilet building.

If you wish to shorten the hike described here, continue past the turn for Bradley Wales Picnic Area and drive for 0.9 mile farther north up West Rim Road. Make a hairpin turn to the right onto Painter Leetonia Road. Continue up the road and look for signs marking connector trails on the right side of the road. The trailhead for the Ice Break Trail is about 0.7 mile up Painter Leetonia Road past the hairpin turn, and the trailhead for the Slate Run Trail is roughly 1.6 miles beyond the hairpin turn. Park on the shoulder to access these trails.

GPS Shortcut: In Google Maps, search for "Bradley Wales Picnic Area, Bradley Wales Road." The parking lot is near the end of the road next to a pit toilet and a grassy field with some scattered picnic tables. Be advised that there is another area nearby mistakenly labeled "Bradley Wales Picnic Area" on Google Maps. The correct trailhead is the one located on Bradley Wales Road.

LOOKING DOWN INTO THE PINE CREEK GORGE

THE HIKE

From the parking area, head east up the dirt road following the orange blazes of the West Rim Trail. After 0.1 mile, approach the edge of the canyon rim and turn to the left, leaving the road grade behind. Immediately after leaving the dirt road, the trail enters a dark wooded area shaded by a large quantity of evergreen trees. Begin walking along the edge of the canyon, passing two impressive vistas over 0.2 miles. These fenced-in viewpoints look north up the wide expanse of the gorge. Pine Creek and a rail trail are visible in the deep ravine.

After passing the second vista, the trail begins a long, gradual descent that hugs the side of the canyon wall. Turn to the left 0.75 mile after leaving

the parking area and continue descending into a hollow, eventually crossing a small seasonal stream and ascending out of the hollow on the other side. About 1 mile in, the trail briefly levels before again descending, passing through a small clear-cut field on the way downhill. After descending for 0.4 mile, curve around an occasionally soggy bend in the trail, home to a seasonal spring. A short distance beyond this spring is the larger, more consistent flow of Ice Break Run. As before, cross the flow and begin ascending out of the hollow on the other side. The West Rim Trail often follows this routine, dropping down sloping folds in the canyon wall, crossing a stream, and then ascending out of the diminutive water-carved ravine.

Follow the footpath away from Ice Break Run, climbing moderately. While the West Rim Trail gains and loses elevation often, the ascents and descents are never terribly steep. Furthermore, the tread of the trail up until this point, while fairly narrow and occasionally laced with protruding roots, is mostly void of sharp pointy rocks, and it is relatively easy to traverse. After climbing for 0.5 mile, you will reach another fenced-in vista that provides another glimpse into the Pine Creek Gorge. There is a dry campsite here, as well as a trail register for hikers to sign, should they wish to. A short distance beyond the viewpoint, the Ice Break Trail breaks off to the left, leading to Painter Leetonia Road. Continue straight past this junction and keep hiking as the trail widens and gradually descends for 1 mile to Little Slate Run. There are several decent campsites on either side of the run. The Slate Run Trail heads uphill to the left toward Painter Leetonia Road. Continue over Little Slate Run on a wooden footbridge and head up the other side of the ravine.

Over the next 0.3 mile, cross two small seasonal streams as the terrain becomes briefly rougher, lazily approaching the edge of the drop-off into the canyon. There are limited views of the surrounding countryside on this stretch of trail as the orange blazes lead you along the edge of the rim through this pleasant Pennsylvania forest. After 4.2 miles of hiking, cross the petite flow of Tumbling Run that, as its name implies, tumbles cheerfully downhill, eventually joining Pine Creek at the bottom of the gorge, nearly 2,000 feet below. In 0.1 mile after crossing Tumbling Run, pass a large open campsite on the right side of the trail. There is a decent, slightly obstructed, view from this campsite, and here is a great place to take a break

from hiking. Continue following the trail north and bend to the left, descending gracefully for 0.6 mile into another hollow to cross Horse Run. Cross Horse Run and continue uphill, away from the flow, passing a mediocre viewpoint and some small campsites nestled among moody hemlock trees in another 0.3 mile. Farther north, the trail once more bends to the left and gradually descends, reaching Burdic Run at mile marker 5.8, 1 mile after crossing Horse Run.

From this point, leave the West Rim Trail and stay straight to follow the Seimons Trail, beginning the loop portion of the hike. The Seimons Trail heads moderately uphill, roughly following Burdic Run on a wide, lumpy trail, before crossing the dwindling flow at mile 6.1. The Seimons Trail is soggy at random intervals and is only marked sporadically, but it is still very easy to follow. As you progress, bend to the right and parallel the dirt tread of Painter Leetonia Road for 0.1 mile before reaching the road grade, where the Seimons Trail ends. The West Rim Trail reappears here, crossing Painter Leetonia Road on its northbound ramble. Instead of crossing the road, turn to the right here and head uphill, following the West Rim Trail southward to begin looping back to where you picked up the Seimons Trail.

After a short, steep climb, the West Rim Trail passes behind a metal gate and continues along on a fairly level course through tall, stately deciduous trees and brushy forest. Follow the orange blazes through rolling terrain for 0.7 mile, then make a short, quick descent to join a wide woods road grade under dark hemlocks. Emerging onto the shady road grade, the yellow-blazed Refuge Trail heads to the left toward

Painter Leetonia Road. Turn to the right and continue on the orange-blazed West Rim Trail, heading south for about 1.3 miles, passing through alternating patches of hemlock and beech trees, all the while skirting the edge of the canyon. As you advance, the trail bends to the right and begins descending moderately, crossing Burdic Run and reaching the junction with the Seimons Trail at the 9-mile mark, completing the loop portion of the hike.

At this point, turn to the left and retrace your footsteps, heading south on the West Rim Trail to return to your vehicle at the Bradley Wales Picnic Area in 5.6 miles. You will reach the turnoff for the Slate Run Trail in 2.6 miles and the turnoff for the Ice Break Trail in 4.1 miles.

34

Black Forest Trail Day Hike

DISTANCE: 15.6 miles

DIFFICULTY: Very Difficult

HIKING TIME: 8 hours

TYPE: Loop

TOTAL ELEVATION GAIN: 2,913'

MAXIMUM ELEVATION: 2,061'

The Black Forest Trail, a grueling 42-mile backpacking trail just west of the Pine Creek Gorge, gets its name from the evergreen trees that grow in abundance in the area, and which shade the footpath. The trail forms a loop that twists and turns through the Tiadaghton State Forest, ascending and descending numerous steep slopes. Along the way, the trail provides expansive, panoramic views of the wide, creek-carved gorges. For this reason, the trail is widely considered to be the most challenging—and most rewarding—backpacking that Pennsylvania has to offer. Several side trails and woods roads make it possible to piece together smaller day hikes along the Black Forest Trail.

Described here is a hard, circuitous day hike that may also be completed as a short backpacking trip. The route climbs in and out of the Slate Run valley several times, following a variety of terrains and visiting a myriad of viewpoints on both sides of Slate Run, as well as an old slate quarry toward the end of the hike. The Old Supply Trail runs between and connects two segments of the Black Forest Trail, following a stretch of Manor Fork, which eventually empties into Slate Run. Be advised that the Old Supply Trail crosses Manor Fork several times, and during periods of high rainfall these crossings can be difficult and dangerous.

GETTING THERE

From the west, follow I-80 E. Take exit 178 for US 220 N toward Lock Haven. At the end of the ramp, turn left onto US 220 N. Follow it for 16.5 miles. Take exit 120 for PA 44 N toward Pine Creek. Turn left at the end of the ramp, and on PA 44 N drive for 12.3 miles. Continue straight onto PA 414 E for 14.1 miles,

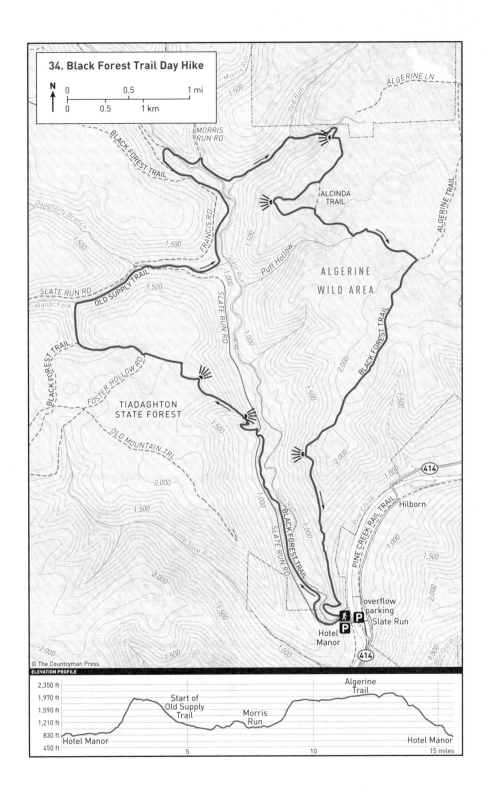

34. Black Forest Trail Day Hike

N

0   0.5   1 mi

0   0.5   1 km

MORRIS RUN RD

BLACK FOREST TRAIL

ALGERINE LN

Morris Run

Red Run

1,500

ALGERINE TRAIL

ALCINDA TRAIL

Daugherty Branch

FRANCIS RD

1,500

1,500

Putt Hollow

ALGERINE WILD AREA

1,500

Slate Run

BLACK FOREST TRAIL

1,000

SLATE RUN RD

OLD SUPPLY TRAIL

SLATE RUN RD

1,500

Manor Fork

BLACK FOREST TRAIL

1,000

2,000

2,000

1,500

1,500

FOSTER HOLLOW RD

TIADAGHTON STATE FOREST

1,500

OLD MOUNTAIN TRL

2,000

414

Hilborn

1,000

1,000

1,500

1,000

Little Slate Run

1,500

Slate Run

2,000

BLACK FOREST TRAIL

SLATE RUN RD

Pine Creek

PINE CREEK RAIL TRAIL

1,000

2,000

overflow parking
Slate Run

1,500

Bonnell Run

2,000

1,500

1,000

Hotel Manor

414

© The Countryman Press

ELEVATION PROFILE

2,350 ft		Algerine Trail	
1,970 ft	Start of Old Supply Trail		
1,590 ft		Morris Run	
1,210 ft			
830 ft	Hotel Manor		Hotel Manor
450 ft		5 10 15 miles	

UNDER THE EVERGREEN TREES ON THE BLACK FOREST TRAIL

then turn left onto Slate Run Road. Cross Pine Creek and turn to the right at the T-intersection. Drive a short distance to the Hotel Manor, and behind it park in the designated day use parking spaces. Overflow or overnight parking is available on the opposite side of Pine Creek in the gravel Slate Run boat access lot.

From the east, follow I-80 W. Take exit 210B, merging onto US 15 N toward Williamsport. Immediately after crossing the Susquehanna River, turn left and merge onto I-180 W. Keeping left, in 1.7 miles continue on US 220 S. Drive for 14.6 miles and take exit 120 for PA 44 N toward Pine Creek. Turn right at the end of the ramp, and on PA 44 N drive for 12.3 miles. Continue straight onto PA 414 E for 14.1 miles, then turn left onto Slate Run Road. Cross Pine Creek and then turn to the right at the

T-intersection. Drive a short distance to the Hotel Manor, and park behind it in the designated day use parking spaces. Overflow or overnight parking is available on the opposite side of Pine Creek in the gravel Slate Run boat access lot.

GPS Shortcut: Search for "Hotel Manor + Bar" in Slate Run and follow your GPS to the day use parking area behind the inn. Overnight parking is available on the opposite side of Pine Creek in a large gravel lot.

THE HIKE

From the parking area, turn to the left next to an information kiosk and pick up the orange blazes of the Black Forest Trail, ascending up the shoulder and onto the paved tread of Slate Run Road. Turn to the right and begin following the road, which continues moderately uphill for 0.25 mile, passing several private residences and cabins. Veer to the right at a sign marking a rerouted segment of the Black Forest Trail and enter the woods, passing through tall evergreen trees

ENTERING ALGERINE WILD AREA

on narrow singletrack tread. Descend moderately toward Slate Run, then turn to the left and head gradually uphill on old railroad grade, paralleling Slate Run against its flow. Continue on the flat, well-graded path through towering white pines and diminutive hemlocks.

After 0.6 mile, an orange-blazed spur trail breaks off the Black Forest Trail to the left next to a trail register, leading to another parking area. Continue straight to stay on the Black Forest Trail, which dips shortly after this junction, joining another railroad grade. This section of the trail gently weaves back and forth several times, leaving one rail grade and traversing rolling terrain to join another. Continue for 1.4 miles, then make an abrupt left turn as you approach a stream that feeds into Slate Run and ascend a short distance to reach Slate Run Road

yet again. Turn to the right and cross the road, reentering the woods on the opposite side. Continue to follow the orange blazes, climbing a fairly steep incline up long stretches of narrow sidehill and short uneven switchbacks before following the crest of this protruding feature, which leads more directly uphill. After 0.4 mile, about halfway to the top of the plateau, the trail briefly passes through an open area of exposed rock that boasts one of the best views in the entire Black Forest Trail system, looking eastward over Slate Run toward the Algerine Wild Area. From here, continue up the steep, rocky spine for another 0.5 mile, taking care to stay on the trail as the ground drops away steeply to the either side.

Near the top of the plateau, the Black Forest Trail bends to the right among dense, shrubby stands of mountain

GAZING NORTHEAST OVER SLATE RUN GORGE

ONE OF MANY PANORAMIC VIEWS ON THE BLACK FOREST TRAIL

laurel, arriving at another excellent viewpoint 0.1 mile later. Turn to the left here and follow the narrow trail across the broad, relatively flat plateau, passing the junction with the Old Black Forest Trail on the left side of the trail at the 3.2-mile marker. Turn right here and continue for 0.4 mile through more mountain laurel and dense ferns. At this point, the Black Forest Trail approaches the privately owned Foster Hollow hunting camp. The trail passes in front of the flagpole, skirting the property to the southwest, then follows a small stream that feeds into a pond behind the cabin. Reenter the shade of the evergreen trees at the far end of the pond and continue on the Black Forest Trail, steadily descending into a densely wooded ravine next to the outlet of the pond on rocky tread that crisscrosses the flow several times.

Near the bottom of the ravine, at mile 4.2, you will reach the junction with the Old Supply Trail. The Black Forest turns to the left and begins leading uphill at this point. Turn right onto the Old Supply Trail and continue heading downhill next to the stream, immediately passing a campsite as you begin to follow

the yellow blazes. The trail descends for another 0.4 mile along the edge of the cascading water, passing some interesting rock formations on the way. At this point the stream empties into the larger flow of Manor Fork. Turn right and follow the yellow blazes for 0.7 mile as it meanders alongside Manor Fork on rolling, occasionally treacherous side-hill trail, arriving at the gravel tread of Slate Run Road once again at mile 5.3.

The following section of the Old Supply Trail crosses Manor Fork a few times. During periods of high rainfall or snowmelt, crossing the stream can be difficult and potentially dangerous. To bypass this section, turn left and walk down Slate Run Road about 0.1 mile and turn right onto Francis Road. Walk the dirt tread of Francis Road for 1.4 miles to meet the Black Forest Trail where the Old Supply Trail ends. If you choose to skip the second part of the Old Supply Trail, then skip the following paragraph.

To continue on the Old Supply Trail, cross the road, passing behind a guardrail, and drop down to the edge of Manor Fork, continuing to follow the yellow blazes as they lead along

point, the Black Forest Trail bends to the right and begins descending aggressively, arriving at the bumpy, eroded tread of Morris Run Road in 0.2 mile. Turn right and follow Morris Run Road, first crossing Slate Run on a bridge, then passing two campsites for motorized vehicles as the road ascends moderately. At the 7.8-mile mark, the Black Forest Trail turns to the right and leaves Morris Run Road, descending the short, steep bank to reach a tributary that feeds Slate Run. This is Morris Run, which features a small waterfall, a picturesque reflecting pool, and some smooth, carved rock formations. Cross the stream on a wooden footbridge, follow the trail into a dense stand of mountain laurel, and enter Algerine Wild Area.

The trail circles the base of a rounded shoulder protruding from the plateau following well-graded trail tread, and then it begins a long, steady ascent on rocky terrain. This ascent follows Red Run, another stream that eventually empties into Slate Run. Pass some large, mossy boulders and several pleasant gurgling cascades as you ascend. Cross Red Run 0.9 mile after entering Algerine Wild Area and continue to climb, ascending steadily for another 0.1 mile. At this point, the Black Forest Trail turns to the right and begins climbing very directly and very steeply uphill on a mess of jumbled boulders, following another stream that feeds into the main flow of Red Run. Follow the trail uphill for 0.6 mile to reach the rim of the plateau on the eastern side of Slate Run. Toward the top, the trail begins to bend to the right, away from the stream, and enters another patch of dense mountain laurel. You will be rewarded for the arduous climb with two excellent views looking to the west from rocky precipices at the 9.4-mile mark.

the flowing water. The Old Supply Trail crosses the stream several times over the next 0.8 mile. At some points it is impossible to cross without getting wet, so be prepared to ford Manor Fork, which can occasionally be knee-deep even during the dry summer months. At mile 6.1, the trail approaches two cabins in a grassy clearing and turns to the left, skirting the private property before bending back into the woods a short distance later. Climb steadily uphill, away from these cabins, alternating between wide tread and very narrow singletrack above Slate Run in the gorge below. Make your way downhill, passing closer to the run, then make a left turn and follow the trail up a series of short switchbacks to a wide road grade. The Old Supply Trail continues, moderately ascending. This trail ends where it joins the tread of Francis Road as well as the Black Forest Trail at the 7-mile mark.

Turn right and once again follow the orange blazes of the Black Forest Trail down Francis Road. In 0.2 mile the trail turns to the right, leaving Francis Road and continuing on a dirt path that parallels the road for another 0.1 mile. At this

TAKING IN THE VIEW FROM ALGERINE WILD AREA

Continue along the plateau on the Black Forest Trail. In 0.5 mile, come to the junction of the yellow-blazed Alcinda Trail. This 0.25-mile trail bypasses a stretch of the Black Forest Trail and, if you wish, can be used to shorten the hike by about 0.7 mile. Turn to the right and continue on the Black Forest Trail along the edge of the plateau, dropping a short distance over rocky terrain to a vista in another 0.4 mile. Half a mile later, you will reach the other end of the Alcinda Trail. Turn to the right and follow the Black Forest Trail along the relatively flat plateau, through mixed forest and the ever-present mountain laurels. The Algerine Trail meets with the Black Forest Trail, coming in from the left at the 11.9-mile mark. Bend right to stay on the Black Forest Trail. Continue on suspiciously flat terrain that gives way to rolling ups and downs before descending moderately on a narrow sidehill trail, arriving at a magnificent, open, west-facing viewpoint 2 miles later at the site of a disused slate quarry. Enjoy the view, but keep an eye out for rattlesnakes, which have been known to enjoy the exposed rocky slope in the summer months.

The Black Forest Trail passes through this short area, then it continues steadily downhill on wide grassy road grade. In another 0.6 mile, you will reach another quarry site amid tall, sheer stone walls, with a similar viewpoint on the right side of the trail. At a cleft in the wall on the left side of the trail, there are some oddly shaped stone sculptures, apparently made by some creative, industrious individuals. For the next 0.7 mile, the Black Forest Trail follows the rocky spine gradually downhill of the ridge, passing through teetering stacks of slate and beautiful white pine forest.

At mile 15.2, the trail begins to descend more aggressively as the town of Slate Run comes into view directly ahead. In another 0.2 mile, turn left onto the obvious remains of an old railroad grade. Follow this wide tread down one more easy descent, and in another 0.2 mile cross the footbridge that spans Slate Run to arrive back at your vehicle.

35

Golden Eagle Trail

DISTANCE: 9.6 miles

DIFFICULTY: Very Difficult

HIKING TIME: 5 hours

TYPE: Loop

TOTAL ELEVATION GAIN: 2,390'

MAXIMUM ELEVATION: 2,172'

The popular Golden Eagle Trail has earned an impressive reputation over the years as the best day hike in Pennsylvania. While the validity of this claim is often hotly debated in hiking circles, it cannot be denied that it is a splendid hike, traversing a variety of terrains in the Wolf Run Wild Area. The Golden Eagle Trail was built and maintained in part by local legend Bob Webber, who had a major role in the creation of many of the hiking trails in the Pennsylvania Wilds region. More information about Bob Webber can be found in the entry for the Bob Webber Trail, which starts only a few miles from the Golden Eagle Trail and is equally breathtaking in more ways than one.

The Golden Eagle Trail starts at the bottom of Pine Creek Gorge at the Utceter Station canoe access parking lot and follows beside Bonnell Run, ascending to the top of the plateau, eventually arriving at two excellent vistas before beginning a moderate descent following Wolf Run. Near the end of the hike the trail visits the Raven's Horn, a flat rock outcropping on the spine of the ridge. From this vantage point, one can take in spectacular views of Wolf Run Bald and Pine Creek far below. During periods of high runoff, both Wolf Run and Bonnell Run may be difficult to cross without getting wet feet, so plan accordingly and keep an extra pair of socks in your pack or vehicle.

GETTING THERE

From the west, follow I-80 E. Take exit 178 for US 220 N toward Lock Haven. At the end of the ramp, turn left onto US 220 N. Follow it for 16.5 miles. Take exit 120 for PA 44 N toward Pine Creek. Turn left at the end of the ramp, and on PA 44 N drive for 12.3 miles. Continue straight

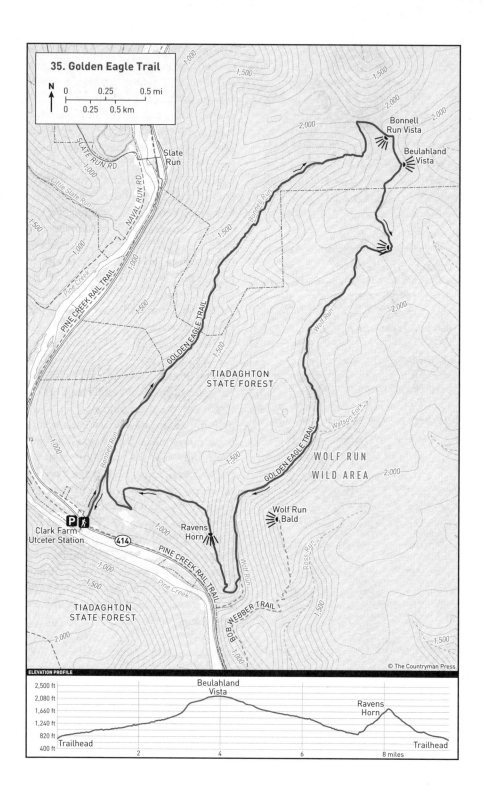

35. Golden Eagle Trail

N
0   0.25   0.5 mi
0   0.25   0.5 km

Bonnell Run Vista

Beulahland Vista

Slate Run

SLATE RUN RD

NAVAL RUN RD

Little Slate Run

Pine Creek

PINE CREEK RAIL TRAIL

Bonnell Run

GOLDEN EAGLE TRAIL

TIADAGHTON STATE FOREST

Bonnell Run

Wolf Run

Watson Fork

GOLDEN EAGLE TRAIL

WOLF RUN WILD AREA

Wolf Run Bald

Ross Run

Clark Farm Utceter Station

P

414

Ravens Horn

PINE CREEK RAIL TRAIL

Pine Creek

Wolf Run

BOB WEBBER TRAIL

TIADAGHTON STATE FOREST

© The Countryman Press

ELEVATION PROFILE

2,500 ft
2,080 ft
1,660 ft
1,240 ft
820 ft
400 ft

Trailhead

Beulahland Vista

Ravens Horn

Trailhead

2   4   6   8 miles

onto PA 414 E and drive for 11.5 miles to reach the parking area on the left side of the road. The gravel lot is marked by a sign for Clark Farm Utceter Station canoe access.

From the east, follow I-80 W. Take exit 210B, merging onto US 15 N toward Williamsport. Drive 16.5 miles. Immediately after crossing the Susquehanna River, turn left and merge onto I-180 W, keeping left, and in 1.7 miles continue on US 220 S. Drive for 14.6 miles, and take exit 120 for PA 44 N toward Pine Creek. Turn right at the end of the ramp, and on PA 44 N drive for 12.3 miles. Continue straight onto PA 414 E for 11.5 miles to reach the parking area on the left side of the road, marked by a sign for Clark Farm Utceter Station canoe access.

GPS Shortcut: The parking lot is located near Cammal. Search Google Maps for "Golden Eagle Trail" or "Utceter Station Canoe Access" and your GPS will navigate you to the trailhead at the Clark Farm Utceter Station recreational parking lot.

THE GOLDEN EAGLE TRAIL APPROACHING WOLF RUN

THE HIKE

Head east from the parking lot and cross the rail trail and PA 414. Cross to the other side of the road and enter the woods next to a wooden sign that marks the start of the Golden Eagle Trail. Begin following the orange-blazed Golden Eagle Trail, climbing consistently uphill on steep root-laced sidehill above Bonnell Run in the ravine to the left. In 0.4 mile, arrive at a trail split, marking the start of the loop portion of the Golden Eagle Trail. Continue straight ahead, roughly paralleling Bonnell Run on the ascending trail. As you walk, the course of Bonnell Run rises, leveling with the tread of the trail. In another 0.4 mile,

the trail veers to the right and climbs up the side of the steep ravine, heading away from the run before descending back to the edge of the water a short distance later. The Golden Eagle Trail crosses Bonnell Run several times as you advance through the scenic ravine, following well-trodden trail on moderate terrain. The trail ascends fairly gradually, occasionally going over short lumpy hills that bulge from the sloping sides of the ravine.

Continue alongside the stream for 2 miles, passing through classic Pennsylvania forest composed of oaks, hemlocks, and beech trees, as well as plenty

PINE CREEK GORGE FROM THE RAVEN'S HORN

of rhododendrons and mountain laurel. As you make your way up the trail, the ravine will start to narrow, and the flow of Bonnell Run will start to dwindle. At this point, the trail bends gently to the right and climbs moderately, the grade of ascent quickly intensifying the higher you climb. The trail climbs very steeply for about 0.3 mile, going over loose rocky terrain that only makes the ascent more difficult. After this very steep stretch, the Golden Eagle Trail bends to the left and the slope of the trail relaxes slightly.

At the 3.5-mile mark, you will reach the grassy tread of a wide woods road. Turn to the right here and follow the orange blazes as they lead along the road. The broad, grassy trail ascends at a much more gradual rate, which should be a welcome reprieve from the grueling climb up to the road. In 0.2 mile, arrive at the Bonnell Run Vista, a wide, shrubby area that looks out from the woods road to the west and over the Bonnell Run ravine toward Pine Creek. Continue up the trail, turning to the right to stay on the woods road, and reach a second viewpoint in another 0.2 mile. This is the Beulahland Vista, which surveys the forest that spreads out to the east. Enjoy the view and resume, following the Golden Eagle Trail for another 0.2 mile to reach the end of the woods road in a big circular clearing.

Turn to the left and reenter the cover of the thick forest on winding singletrack trail, descending moderately through tall oak and fragrant white pine trees on fairly easy terrain. An unnamed vista, located down a very short spur trail, appears on the right side of the trail at the 4.5-mile mark. It offers limited views to the west. Continue descending on the Golden Eagle Trail for another 0.6 mile and enter a shady stand of mature hemlocks as you begin to follow the meager flow of Wolf Run. Emerge from the hemlocks into a primarily deciduous forest as you continue the lengthy descent, while the flow of Wolf Run strengthens in the ravine and spills over rocky shelves, forming diminutive waterfalls. As you continue along the trail, you will cross the run a few times and follow rolling terrain on the sides of the deepening ravine.

In 7.3 miles, the Golden Eagle Trail turns to the right and begins climbing once more, heading away from Wolf Run. While the entire Golden Eagle Trail is very well-marked, this turn can be somewhat easy to miss thanks to a connector trail that continues following Wolf Run downstream, so be sure to keep an eye on the orange blazes. The trail wraps around the southern tip of the ancient plateau, getting steeper as you ascend and switchbacking a few times to reach the narrow spine of this raised landmark. Continue up the spine, treading over flat stone platforms and passing by several uniquely textured rock formations. After climbing for 0.6 mile, you will arrive at the Raven's Horn, an impressive sloping stone shelf protruding from the hillside. Excellent views of Pine Creek can be seen from here by looking toward the south. Across the wide Wolf Run valley to the east is Wolf Run Bald, which can be accessed on foot by the Bob Webber Trail. The Bob Webber Trail is described later in this book.

When you are finished at the Raven's Horn, continue up the ridge, arriving at the top in another 0.2 mile. Follow the Golden Eagle Trail as it bends to the left and heads downhill on a moderately steep slope, descending consistently toward Pine Creek. In another 0.5 mile, the trail bends to the left and continues losing elevation as the trail widens. Follow the trail as it meanders downhill and finish the loop portion of the hike at mile marker 9.2.

From here, turn left and retrace your footsteps back toward the parking area to reach your vehicle.

A short trail leads from the parking area to the rocky the edge of Pine Creek. This little shore is a great place to enjoy a posthike foot soak during the hot summer months, and the large quantity of smooth flat rocks make for excellent stone skipping.

36

Bob Webber Trail

DISTANCE: 3.7 miles

DIFFICULTY: Very Difficult

HIKING TIME: 3 hours

TYPE: Out and Back

TOTAL ELEVATION GAIN: 1,426'

MAXIMUM ELEVATION: 1,962'

Spend some time on the trails in and around the Pine Creek Gorge and the name Bob Webber has a tendency to come up, always with an air of reverence. The former Pennsylvania Bureau of Forestry employee was extremely passionate about the place he called home, and he took great pleasure in introducing the public to the woods he had helped manage. Living with his wife Dottie in an off-the-grid cabin near Slate Run, Webber lived for more than 50 years without modern conveniences. He helped establish and maintain several trail systems in the Tiadaghton State Forest, and he hiked well into his 70s. Bob passed away at his cabin in the woods in 2015. The seasoned outdoorsman was 80 years old when he passed, but his legacy outlives him on the trails he built: the Black Forest Trail, the Golden Eagle Trail, and the Bob Webber Trail, which he had dug out almost entirely by hand.

The Bob Webber Trail may seem short, but don't let that fool you. While the start of the hike and the portion just before reaching the summit are relatively easy, the midsection of the trail climbs aggressively to the top of Wolf Run Bald, relentlessly ascending the slope of the canyon wall. The summit surveys the surrounding folds and creases of the Pennsylvania Grand Canyon, Pine Creek far below, and the beautiful Wolf Run Wild Area. From such a beautiful viewpoint it becomes easy to understand why Bob Webber loved this area so much.

GETTING THERE

From the west, follow I-80 E. Take exit 178 for US 220 N toward Lock Haven. At the end of the ramp, turn left onto US 220 N. Follow it for 16.5 miles. Take exit 120 for PA 44 N toward Pine Creek. Turn

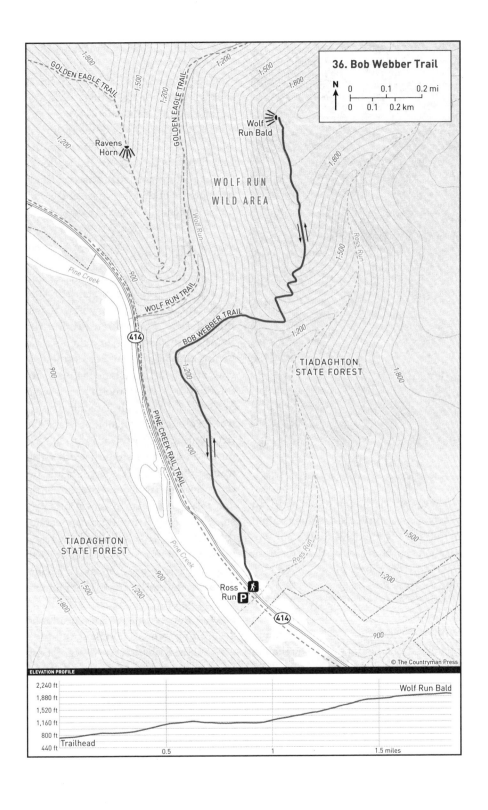

36. Bob Webber Trail

N

0   0.1   0.2 mi
0   0.1   0.2 km

GOLDEN EAGLE TRAIL

Ravens Horn

Wolf Run Bald

GOLDEN EAGLE TRAIL

WOLF RUN WILD AREA

Wolf Run

Pine Creek

WOLF RUN TRAIL

414

BOB WEBBER TRAIL

Ross Run

TIADAGHTON STATE FOREST

PINE CREEK RAIL TRAIL

Pine Creek

TIADAGHTON STATE FOREST

Ross Run

Ross Run

Ross Run

414

900

© The Countryman Press

ELEVATION PROFILE

| | | Wolf Run Bald |
2,240 ft
1,880 ft
1,520 ft
1,160 ft
800 ft
440 ft   Trailhead

0.5   1   1.5 miles

AT THE START OF THE BOB WEBBER TRAIL

left at the end of the ramp, and on PA 44 N drive for 12.3 miles. Continue straight onto PA 414 E and drive for 9.6 miles to reach the parking area on the left side of the road. The gravel lot is marked by a sign for Ross Run.

From the east, follow I-80 W. Take exit 210B, merging onto US 15 N toward Williamsport. Drive 16.5 miles. Immediately after crossing the Susquehanna River, turn left and merge onto I-180 W, keeping left, and in 1.7 miles continue on US 220 S. Drive for 14.6 miles, and take exit 120 for PA 44 N toward Pine Creek. Turn right at the end of the ramp, and on PA 44 N drive for 12.3 miles. Continue straight onto PA 414 E for 9.6 miles to reach the parking area on the left side

of the road. The gravel lot is marked by a sign for Ross Run.

GPS Shortcut: The parking lot is located near Cammal. Enter "Ross Run Campground" into Google Maps and your GPS will lead you to the trailhead. While the destination name implies that there is camping available, this is unfortunately not true. There is, however, plenty of parking space and canoe and boat access to Pine Creek.

THE HIKE

Head northeast to cross the rail trail and PA 414. Enter the woods next to a sign marking the start of the yellow-blazed Bob Webber Trail. Upon leaving the roadside, the trail veers to the left and begins climbing uphill. Pass a trail register after a short distance and ascend a moderately steep incline on a well-graded trail through a patch of pine trees. Follow the trail as it bends to the left, continuing northward through the pines on a flatter sidehill trail. After walking this relatively level grade for 0.1 mile, the trail bends to the right and resumes the steep ascent on fairly smooth terrain. After climbing for about 0.6 mile, the trail briefly levels and then begins a rolling descent on a rocky tread lined with neon-green moss. In a short distance, the trail turns to the right and begins heading deeper into the heart of Wolf Run Wild Area on a gradually descending trail. After making this turn, views of the Raven's Horn viewpoint can be seen high above through the trees depending on the density of the foliage.

As you walk on this brief respite from the intense climbing, you will appear to be approaching a towering hill straight on. At the 1-mile mark, the trail turns to the right and begins climbing up to a small col, or saddle, in between two lofty

THE RAVEN'S HORN AND PINE CREEK GORGE FROM WOLF RUN BALD

hills, following a very steep tread for 0.1 mile. The Bob Webber Trail levels just long enough for you to catch your breath, then it turns to the left and resumes the arduous climb. Continue up the canyon wall, on increasingly steep switchbacks that seem to never end, occasionally passing some chunky stone ledges that protrude from the sloping hillside. Shortly after the 1.4-mile mark, the trail switchbacks to the left one last time, and then it begins ascending more directly. This fairly straight trajectory appears in stark contrast to the previously twisting tread, and it will likely come as a welcome change of pace as you may have begun to feel as though the switchbacks were not really easing the ascent that much anyway.

After another 0.1 mile, the rate of ascent relaxes significantly. While the Bob Webber Trail still leads uphill, it is at a much easier grade, giving you a good chance to catch your breath and enjoy the forest on top of this rounded, ridgy shoulder. Continue for another 0.3 mile on this much easier grade and, shortly after mile 1.8, arrive at the vista on the wooded summit of Wolf Run Bald. A log bench and trail register under a pine tree provide a wonderful place to take a break. The Wolf Run Bald viewpoint

PEERING UP THROUGH THE TREES AT THE RAVEN'S HORN

faces west, showcasing the expansive spread of the Wolf Run ravine, which joins the Pine Creek Gorge to the south. Looking directly across the vast space, hikers with a keen eye can see the stone platform of the Raven's Horn vista, which is accessed via the Golden Eagle Trail, near the top of the closest ridge.

Enjoy the view from here and, when you are ready, turn around and head back down the Bob Webber Trail the way you came to return to your vehicle.

III.

EASTERN PENNSYLVANIA

37

Ricketts Glen Falls Trail

DISTANCE: 6.9 miles

DIFFICULTY: Difficult

HIKING TIME: 4 hours

TYPE: Loop

TOTAL ELEVATION GAIN: 1,010'

MAXIMUM ELEVATION: 2,215'

Located west of Scranton, Ricketts Glen State Park is home to more than 20 waterfalls that cascade down Kitchen Creek, ranging in height from the 11-foot Cayuga Falls to the towering 94-foot Ganoga Falls. The park is named after Robert Bruce Ricketts, a Civil War officer who owned the land the state park now occupies, as well as a good portion of the surrounding State Game Lands. After Ricketts's death in 1918, a large portion of the land east of the falls area was sold to the Pennsylvania Game Commission, and in 1935 plans were made to make Ricketts Glen into a national park. A year later, in the wake of the Great Depression, these plans were placed on indefinite hiatus and the funding was used for other projects. The area was eventually signed into legislation as Ricketts Glen State Park in 1941, officially opening two years later.

The hike described here loops through the park, visiting all the named waterfalls on a very popular route. This is a great hike for hot, early summer days, when cool mist from the falls feels particularly refreshing. Expect to see many people on the Falls Trail, especially on holidays and weekends. Unlike most of the hikes in this book, the Falls Trail is closed to hikers in the winter months due to ice buildup. After the trail is closed for the season, the park only allows very experienced hikers and climbers into the falls area, so long as they obtain a permit and are equipped with crampons, ice axes, and climbing ropes.

GETTING THERE

From the west, follow I-80 E. Take exit 212B. Merge onto I-180 W and follow it for 12.4 miles. Take exit 13 for PA 405 N toward Hughesville. Turn right at the end of the ramp. Follow PA 405 N for 3.4 miles,

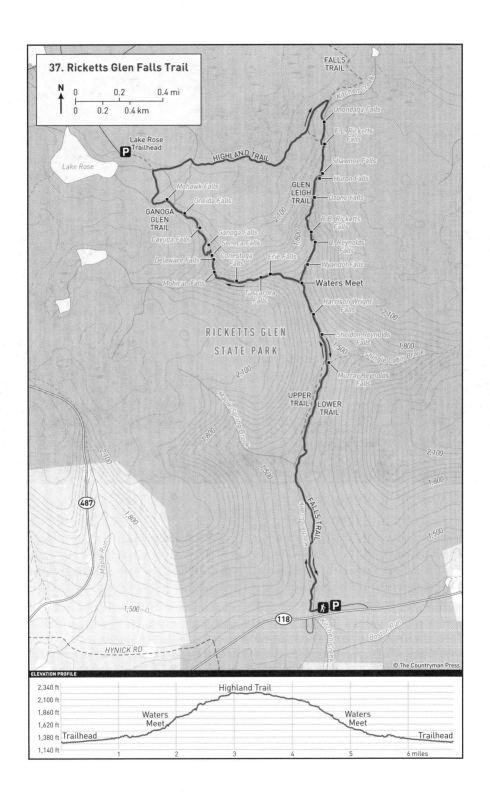

37. Ricketts Glen Falls Trail

ERIE FALLS ALONG THE GANOGA GLEN TRAIL

then turn right onto Water Street. Water Street becomes PA 118 E. Follow PA 118 E for 26 miles to reach the parking lot, located on the left side of the road.

From the east, follow I-476 N. Take exit 105 for PA 115 N toward Wilkes-Barre. At the end of the ramp, turn left and follow PA 115 N for 4 miles, then merge onto PA 309 N. Follow the road for 7 miles and turn left onto Hillside Road. Drive Hillside Road for 3.2 miles. Cross Huntsville Road and drive Old Route 115 for 3.4 miles. Turn left onto PA 118 W and follow the road for 12.6 miles to reach the large parking lot located on the right side of the road.

GPS Shortcut: Search Google Maps for "Rt. 118 Trailhead Parking" and your GPS will navigate to the proper trailhead.

THE HIKE

From the parking area, head west and pick up the Falls Trail. The beginning of the Falls Trail is signed but not marked by any blazes. Its tread is, however, very easy to discern due to its popularity. Turn right and begin following the Falls Trail, walking upstream beside Kitchen Creek. At 0.2 mile in, keep right at the junction with a park service road and cross a footbridge. Over the course of the hike, the trail crosses the creek on a number of footbridges as it progresses through the creek ravine, following relatively flat and easy terrain on an old disused dirt road grade.

Approximately 1 mile in, shortly after crossing two bridges in close succession, arrive at a split in the trail. To the right, the Lower Trail continues gradually upstream, closely adhering to the rocky bank of Kitchen Creek. The trail to the right, the Upper Trail, follows a similar trajectory on easier terrain at a slightly higher elevation. When the water level is high, the Lower Trail can be very difficult or impossible to follow safely, so keep this in mind as you choose your route. The Lower and Upper Trails reconvene in 0.3 mile just before reaching the first named waterfall, Murray Reynolds Falls. Over the next 0.5 mile, the Falls Trail passes two more named falls, Sheldon Reynolds Falls and Harrison Wright Falls. While Kitchen Creek features an abundance of smaller, tumbling cascades, each of the named falls is announced by a wooden sign bearing its name.

At the 1.8-mile mark, arrive at a confluence known as Waters Meet. At this point, the east and west branches of Kitchen Creek join, and the Falls Trail splits into two sections, each following a different branch. The forked trail is connected farther north by the Highland Trail, allowing both sections to be enjoyed as a loop. As such, the Falls Trail can be hiked in either direction. The hike described here follows the loop in the clockwise direction, so turn left and begin heading up the Ganoga Glen Trail. The Ganoga Glen Trail begins heading uphill at a more aggressive angle than before, arriving at Erie Falls in a short distance, and then at Tuscarora Falls very quickly thereafter. Both

falls are 47 feet tall, the tallest waterfalls yet to be seen on this hike. Conestoga Falls is the next waterfall the trail passes, and it is much smaller than the previous two.

Past Conestoga Falls, continue to make your way through the ravine, occasionally ascending on flights of stone steps. Due to their proximity to the falls, these steps can be slippery at any time of year, so use caution and place your feet carefully. The trail crosses a bridge over a stream that feeds into Kitchen Creek and then passes three waterfalls very close to each other: Mohican Falls, Delaware Falls, and Seneca Falls. At the diminutive Seneca Falls, the trail bends to the left and ascends steeply for a stretch, arriving at a junction with another trail on the left at the 2.5-mile mark. This trail connects to the Old Beaver Dam Road Trail, a multiuse loop that circles the plateau above, west of Kitchen Creek. Keep right to stay on the Falls Trail, continuing to ascend.

Shortly after passing the connector trail, the Falls Trail arrives at Ganoga Falls, the tallest waterfall in Ricketts Glen State Park at a whopping 94 feet. The Falls Trail continues up the ravine to the left of the falls to reach the top of this lofty waterfall. Just before heading uphill, however, an unmarked herd path breaks off to the right. This herd path provides access to the bottom of Ganoga Falls, where a unique perspective showcases just how massive this waterfall is. When you are finished at the base of Ganoga Falls, head up the trail to the top of the falls. The top of the falls is an open area, with a broad rocky outcropping near the waterfall's edge. It may be tempting to get as close to the edge as possible, but this is not advised. The rocks here are almost always slick, and a fall from the top would result in serious

SHAWNEE FALLS ON THE GLEN LEIGH TRAIL

injury or even death. Stay on the trail and be safe!

After leaving Ganoga Falls, the trail continues climbing at a much more relaxed angle. The next waterfalls you will pass are Cayuga Falls, the shortest named waterfall along the Falls Trail, followed by Oneida Falls, which is only marginally taller. Approximately 0.2 mile after Oneida Falls, the trail turns to the left, arriving at Mohawk Falls. A short distance past Mohawk Falls, the Ganoga Glen leg of the Falls Trail ends at an extension of the Old Beaver Dam Road Trail at mile 3.2. Turn right onto this trail and follow it toward the Lake Rose Trailhead, which is an alternate parking area for the Falls Trail system.

In 0.1 mile, make a right onto the Highland Trail, before reaching the Lake Rose Trailhead. As previously mentioned, the Highland Trail connects the two branches of the Falls Trail. Follow the Highland Trail along the relatively flat top of the plateau for 0.8 mile, passing through Midway Crevasse on the way. Near the end of the Highland Trail, a distinct spur trail breaks off to the right. This little trail can be used to access the other leg of the Falls Trail in Glen Leigh by descending down a steep rocky slope. Using this short connector will shorten the hike by 0.1 mile and skip one of the named waterfalls. Continue straight past this spur trail and make a sharp right in a short distance, just after the 4-mile mark.

Make your way downhill after the turn, following the eastern branch of Kitchen Creek. The Glen Leigh portion of the Falls Trail passes eight more named waterfalls over the next mile. In order, as you descend, they are Onondaga, F. L. Ricketts, Shawnee, Huron, Ozone, R. B. Ricketts, B. Reynolds, and lastly Wyandot Falls. Similarly to the Ganoga Glen leg of the hike, the trail often descends down flights of primitive stone steps. Again, use caution as the steps are often wet and slippery due to the nearby waterfalls.

At the 5.1-mile mark, a short distance past Wyandot Falls, arrive back at the Waters Meet junction. You have now completed the loop portion of this hike. From here, turn left and retrace your steps, following the flow of Kitchen Creek downstream to arrive back at the parking lot in 1.8 miles.

38

The Haystacks and Dutchman Falls

DISTANCE: 4.5 miles

DIFFICULTY: Moderate

HIKING TIME: 2.5 hours

TYPE: Loop

TOTAL ELEVATION GAIN: 497'

MAXIMUM ELEVATION: 1,741'

In the middle of Loyalsock Creek, a rock formation known as the Haystacks stands out as an oddity. The tall, rounded rocks that emerge from the depths of the waters are composed of much harder stone than the rest of the creek bed. The result is a wild rapids area, the raging waters bending around the more durable stone "haystacks" and continuing downstream. The sight is impressive, especially after a heavy rain when the creek swells with drainage from the nearby hills. Perhaps even more impressive is that geologists do not know how the Haystacks formed; the stone is unlike any other in the Appalachian Mountain region. The formation posed a serious problem for the lumber companies of the mid-1800s that used the Loyalsock Creek to transport their logs downstream. The timber would jam on the rocks, unable to move. The loggers tried eradicating the Haystacks with dynamite, but the stubborn rocks refused to move.

The hike to the Haystacks sends hikers along the easy tread of an old railroad and then puts them on a portion of the Loyalsock Trail along the creek to the rapids area. The full Loyalsock Trail, which was originally conceived in 1951, is a 59-mile backpacking trail that winds through Lycoming and Sullivan counties. After visiting the Haystacks, the trail heads back along Loyalsock Creek. Just before returning to the parking area, hikers can visit Dutchman Falls by following a short spur trail. Dutchman Falls is a two-tiered waterfall, cascading a combined 25 feet between both drop areas. The quick hike to Dutchman Falls is included in the total mileage. Choosing not to visit Dutchman Falls will shorten the hike by approximately 0.4 mile.

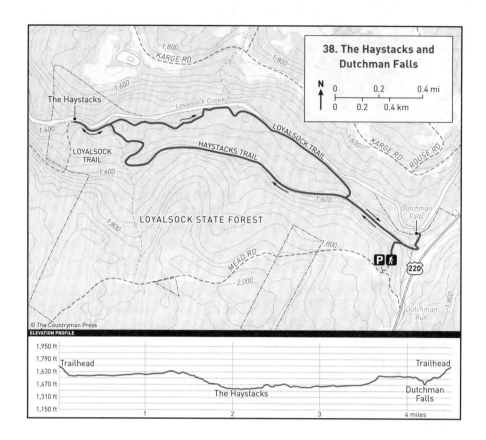

The Haystacks
1,800
KARGE RD
1,800
1,600
Loyalsock Creek
The Haystacks
1,400
LOYALSOCK
TRAIL
1,600
HAYSTACKS TRAIL
LOYALSOCK TRAIL
1,600
KARGE RD
ROUSE RD
1,600
Dutchman
Falls
1,800
LOYALSOCK STATE FOREST
MEAD RD
1,800
2,000
P
220
Dutchman
Run
1,800
© The Countryman Press

38. The Haystacks and Dutchman Falls

N
0   0.2   0.4 mi
0   0.2   0.4 km

ELEVATION PROFILE

1,950 ft
1,790 ft   Trailhead   Trailhead
1,630 ft
1,470 ft
1,310 ft   The Haystacks   Dutchman
1,150 ft   Falls
        1   2   3   4 miles

GETTING THERE

From the west, follow I-80 E. Take exit 212B. Merge onto I-180 W and follow it for 12.4 miles. Take exit 13 or PA 405 N toward Hughesville. Turn right at the end of the ramp. Follow PA 405 N for 3.8 miles and continue straight onto US 220 N. Follow US 220 N for 24.8 miles, then make a left onto Mead Road. The parking area is on this dirt road in 0.2 mile.

From the east, follow I-476 N. Take exit 105 for PA 115 N toward Wilkes-Barre. At the end of the ramp, turn left and follow PA 115 N for 4 miles, then merge onto PA 309 N. Follow the road for 7 miles and turn left onto Hillside Road. Drive Hillside Road for 3.2 miles. Cross Huntsville Road and drive Old Route 115 for 3.4

miles. Turn left onto PA 118 W and follow the road for 14.5 miles, then turn right on PA 487 N. Follow the road for 13.8 miles and turn right to stay on the route an additional 3.1 miles. Take a sharp left onto PA 564/Old Bernice Road and follow it to where it ends at US 220. Turn left onto US 220 S and continue for 2.8 miles. Make a sharp right onto Mead Road and drive 0.2 mile to reach the parking area.

GPS Shortcut: Type "Loyalsock Trailhead Dutchman Falls" into Google Maps and your GPS will send you to the trailhead.

THE HIKE

The trailhead is a large gravel parking lot with a restroom building and a few signs that highlight the history of the area. Head to the northeastern corner of the parking lot and enter the woods on the Loyalsock Trail, following its unique blazes. The trail is marked by either a yellow rectangular blaze with a horizontal red line passing through it or by a yellow circle encompassing a red LT. Begin descending on the Loyalsock Trail. While short, this steep descent follows very challenging terrain, passing over slanting rocks and tangled roots. Use caution as you make your way downhill, and after 0.1 mile you will reach the gravel tread of an old railroad grade. Turn left onto this wide walkway, continuing to follow the Loyalsock Trail while passing through shadowy hemlock groves. In 0.4 mile, the Loyalsock Trail turns to the right and descends the bank of this rail grade on narrow singletrack. For now, go straight and continue to follow the wide gravel path.

A short distance past this trail junction, the Haystacks Trail meets the rail grade, coming in from the left. This yellow-blazed trail leads back to the parking lot, following an easy tread. Again, go straight on the rail grade. This stretch of the hike follows a trail alternatingly marked with yellow rectangular blazes and circular yellow blazes with a red X in the middle. In 1.5 miles after leaving the parking area, you reach a gravel service road. Turn right and follow the yellow rectangular blazes downhill on the service road, leaving the abandoned railroad grade and its yellow and red X blazes. This access road winds downhill on a gently descending slope, immediately passing close to a stream whose waters cascade through the forest, eventually feeding into Loyalsock Creek.

Follow the service road for 0.4 mile to rejoin the Loyalsock Trail, approaching the bank of Loyalsock Creek. A sign here marks the end of the Haystacks Trail. Turn left and follow the flow of the creek on the Loyalsock Trail, crossing the aforementioned feeder stream very shortly. Walk the Loyalsock Trail for another 0.2 mile, passing underneath a towering rock formation at a bend in the creek just before reaching the Haystacks area. When the creek level is high, the turbulent waters flow around the exposed rocks and tumble downstream, forming surging rapids. There are a number of good places along the shore to take a break and enjoy the view of the powerful waters. There is a nice flat spot on the shore near the Haystacks that fits several tents. Camping is

A SCENIC VIEW BESIDE LOYALSOCK CREEK

DUTCHMAN FALLS

THE HAYSTACKS

allowed here, but fires are prohibited. Be aware that camping for more than one night requires a permit.

When you are finished taking in the rapids, turn around and head back to the terminus of the Haystacks Trail, but continue straight to stay on the Loyalsock Trail. Follow the trail as it climbs up a short, steep embankment on moderately challenging terrain. At the top of this little knoll, the trail leads beside a steep drop-off overlooking the creek below, and then it descends down the other side, approaching the water's edge once more. Cross a few seasonal runs that empty into the creek on your way downhill, and then bend to the right to stay on the trail after you reach Loyalsock Creek. The trail follows the creek upstream to the tune of gently rushing water, through pleasant, shady hemlock forest.

At mile 3.6, the trail leaves the creekside, turning to the right and climbing a moderately steep incline to reach the abandoned railroad grade 0.1 mile later. When you reach the railroad grade, turn left and head back toward the turnoff for the parking area. When you reach this point, continue straight past the turn and follow blue blazes to reach Dutchman Falls. The blue blazes lead about 300 feet down the rail grade before turning to the left and descending a relatively steep grade on narrow tread. Follow this short spur for 0.1 mile to reach the bottom of Dutchman Falls, very close to the edge of Loyalsock Creek in a somewhat cramped viewing area.

Enjoy the cascading waters of Dutchman Falls, then retrace your footsteps back to the railroad grade and the junction with the Loyalsock Trail. Turn left at the junction and climb steeply uphill for 0.1 mile to return to the parking area.

39

Big Pine Hill Loop

DISTANCE: 5.8 miles	
DIFFICULTY: Moderate	
HIKING TIME: 3 hours	
TYPE: Loop	
TOTAL ELEVATION GAIN: 489'	
MAXIMUM ELEVATION: 2,260'	

Pinchot State Forest, originally known as Lackawanna State Forest, is a collection of separate tracts of land located south of the city of Scranton. The name was changed in 2015 in honor of the late Gifford Pinchot, whose philosophy of forest conservation, management, use, and renewal were highly influential in the early 20th century. During the presidency of William McKinley, Pinchot served as head of the Department of Agriculture's Division of Forestry. When Theodore Roosevelt was elected president in 1901, Pinchot was appointed the first head of the U.S. Forest Service, an agency suggested to the president by Gifford Pinchot himself. After leaving office in 1910, Pinchot kept busy with political activism and conservation. He served as the governor of Pennsylvania for two terms, and continues to this day to be remembered for his political career and forest management philosophy.

The observation tower on Big Pine Hill is located in the Thornhurst Tract of the Pinchot State Forest. This tract of public land supports a robust trail system of dirt and gravel roads and narrow singletrack, including the 26-mile-long Pinchot Trail. The hike described here makes use of the Pinchot Trail and a handful of other shorter trails to make a loop that visits the tower, which offers a 360-degree view of the Pocono Plateau. This hike is pleasant year-round, but it is especially stunning in the wintertime when the elevated plateau gathers snow and transforms into a frozen utopia.

GETTING THERE

From the west, follow I-80 E. Take exit 260B to merge onto I-81 N. Drive I-81 N for 19.1 miles. Take exit 170A and merge onto PA 115 S. Follow PA 115 S for 9

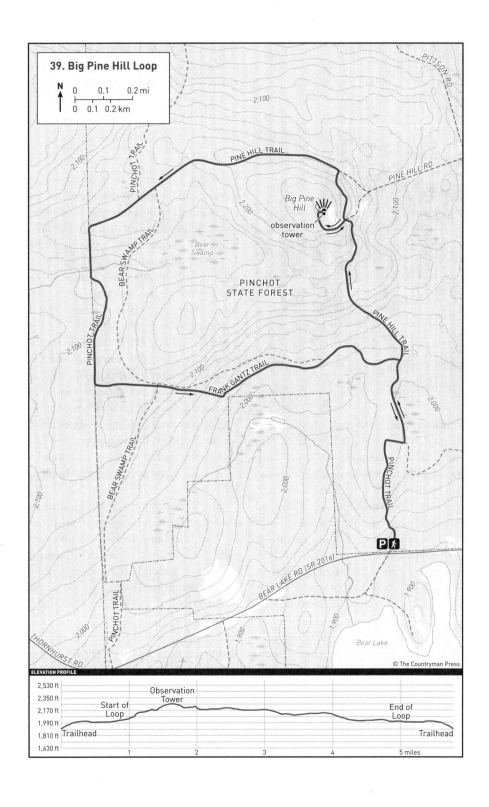

39. Big Pine Hill Loop

N

| 0 | 0.1 | 0.2 mi |
| 0 | 0.1 | 0.2 km |

PITTSON RD

2,100

PINCHOT TRAIL

PINE HILL TRAIL

PINE HILL RD

2,200

Big Pine Hill

observation tower

2,100

BEAR SWAMP TRAIL

Bear Swamp

PINCHOT STATE FOREST

2,100

PINCHOT TRAIL

PINE HILL TRAIL

2,100

FRANK GANTZ TRAIL

2,000

2,000

2,100

BEAR SWAMP TRAIL

2,000

PINCHOT TRAIL

P

BEAR LAKE RD (SR 2016)

1,900

1,900

PINCHOT TRAIL

THORNHURST RD

2,000

1,900

Bear Lake

© The Countryman Press

ELEVATION PROFILE

2,530 ft		Observation				
2,350 ft		Tower				
2,170 ft	Start of				End of	
1,990 ft	Loop				Loop	
1,810 ft	Trailhead				Trailhead	
1,630 ft						

1   2   3   4   5 miles

THE OBSERVATION TOWER ON BIG PINE HILL

miles, then turn left onto Meadow Run Road. Continue for 3.8 miles, then turn right and follow Thornhurst Road, which becomes Bear Lake Road. The trailhead will be on the left side of the road in 2.5 miles. It is a gravel lot about 100 feet off the road in a shady picnic area.

The trailhead is located northwest of Philadelphia, to the east of Wilkes-Barre. From the Philadelphia area, follow I-476 N. Take exit 105 to merge onto PA 115 S. Follow the route for 4.8 miles, then turn left onto Meadow Run Road. Continue for 3.8 miles, then turn right and follow Thornhurst Road, which becomes Bear Lake Road. The trailhead will be on the left side of the road in 2.5 miles, beneath a stand of large trees. There are a few picnic tables underneath the trees.

GPS Shortcut: In Google Maps, search for "Pinchot Trail Trailhead" and set it as your destination. According to Google Maps there is another parking area for the Pinchot Trail 0.4 mile to the east, on Pittson Road. For the purposes of this hike do not park at the eastern trailhead.

THE HIKE

Head into the woods at the north end of the parking lot. Follow the orange blazes of the Pinchot Trail and begin ascending immediately after entering the woods, climbing gradually but steadily. The Pinchot Trail passes a trail register very shortly after leaving the parking area and continues on somewhat rough terrain, continuing to gain elevation. After 0.2 mile, the trail grade levels out almost entirely. The Pinchot Trail gently meanders through mixed forest on this flat course and is closely hemmed in on either side by dense stands of mountain laurels for another 0.2 mile before turning abruptly to the right, at which point the forest opens up, allowing you to see farther off the trail into the shrubby woods.

Arrive at the junction with the Pine Hill Trail shortly after turning to the right. The Pinchot Trail continues straight ahead, joining tread with the Powder Magazine Trail. Turn onto the Pine Hill Trail and begin following its course, which is marked by yellow blazes, skirting the edge of a large stand of tall pine trees on the right. After turning onto the Pine Hill Trail, the terrain becomes much rougher, with many rocks and roots that pose tripping hazards. While certainly more challenging than the Pinchot Trail, this stretch of Pine Hill Trail is still fairly easy, as the tread is well-graded and level. In approximately 0.3 mile, the Pine Hill Trail passes the eastern end of the Frank Gantz Trail on the left side of the trail. Pass this junction and 0.1 mile later cross a very wide, grassy multiuse trail that runs east to west.

Continue to follow the Pine Hill Trail on the other side of the multiuse trail. The tread tips uphill, climbing gradually to moderately on rocky singletrack terrain through brushy forest. The trail passes a handful of short ledgy areas before arriving at a gravel road grade in 0.6 mile, just east of the summit of Big Pine Hill. Turn left and follow the gravel road, ascending roughly 50 feet over 0.1 mile to reach the observation tower on top of Big Pine Hill. This wooden platform is elevated just enough to reach above the windswept trees to provide a very good view of the Pocono Plateau in all directions. Enjoy the view, and when you are ready to keep hiking, head back down the gravel road and turn left to resume, following the yellow-blazed Pine Hill Trail.

Past the summit, the Pine Hill Trail gently weaves through dense, brushy forest, and passes through more mountain laurels and rhododendrons on the continued narrow, rocky trail. In 0.3 mile, the narrow trail joins another wide, grassy road grade. Turn left and follow the Pine Hill Trail along this forest road, trending very gradually downhill on its easy, well-graded terrain. The equally broad Bear Swamp Trail breaks off this woods road on the left in 0.7 mile. Go straight, and less than 0.1 mile later meet with the orange blazes of the Pinchot Trail. The Pine Hill trail joins with the Pinchot Trail here, so go straight to continue heading west along the wide woods road. Pass a junction with the County Line Trail on the right in 0.2 mile, then in another 0.1 mile, turn left to stay on the Pinchot Trail, leaving the road grade behind.

Upon turning, the Pinchot Trail shares tread with the White Line Trail, following a straight, southbound course along the county line for Luzerne and Lackawanna Counties. In contrast to the wide road grade, this part of the Pinchot Trail is narrow and rocky, with lots of thick, thorny brush to grab at your clothing as you advance. Follow the orange blazes, crossing a plank footbridge over the outlet of nearby Bear Swamp, and make your way very gradually downhill. In 0.7 mile, arrive at the junction with the Frank Gantz Trail on the left. Turn here and begin following the yellow blazes, heading east for just over 0.2 mile. At this point the Frank Gantz Trail intersects with the wide, north-to-south tread

SNOWY SCENERY ON THE PINE HILL TRAIL

LOOKING OUT OVER THE FROZEN POCONO PLATEAU

of the Bear Swamp Trail, reentering the woods on the other side just south of another woods road that breaks off the Bear Swamp Trail to the east. Cross the Bear Swamp Trail and continue heading east on the Frank Gantz Trail. The remainder of the Frank Gantz Trail is similarly narrow and extremely brushy. It may be overgrown and difficult to follow, especially during the summer. If you are having trouble following the trail, or simply do not want to deal with the thick brush, the woods road that breaks off the Bear Swamp Trail can be followed, as it mirrors the course of the Frank Gantz Trail and is almost exactly the same length.

Follow the Frank Gantz Trail (or the wide woods road) for 0.9 mile, then turn left onto the Pine Hill Trail. Follow the yellow-blazed Pine Hill Trail south for 0.4 mile, then turn right onto the Pinchot Trail and retrace your footsteps back to the shady parking lot.

Pocono Environmental Education Center

DISTANCE: 6.7 miles

DIFFICULTY: Difficult

HIKING TIME: 3 hours

TYPE: Loop

TOTAL ELEVATION GAIN: 1,147'

MAXIMUM ELEVATION: 879'

Founded in 1972, the Pocono Environmental Education Center, often abbreviated as PEEC, is a private nonprofit organization that operates in close proximity to the Delaware Water Gap National Recreation Area. The nonprofit is the education partner with this national recreation area, and according to their mission statement, they seek to promote "environmental education, sustainable living, and appreciation for nature through hands-on experience." The land managed by PEEC features a number of geologic and historic oddities, all of which can be reached on hiking-only footpaths maintained by the center.

The hike described here loops through PEEC land on a moderate course that traverses the ripples and folds of the Pocono Plateau. The trails visit hemlock groves, idyllic streams, a waterfall, two historic ruins, and a few craggy cliffs, including an area along the edge of the plateau that surveys the expanse to the south. Most of the hike follows relatively easy terrain on rolling ups and downs. There are, however, a few steep trail segments that either climb or drop sharply. One such area on the Ridgeline Trail portion descends a rocky cliff face with the aid of a climbing rope tethered to trees. This section of trail can be bypassed by following the Scenic Gorge Trail instead of the Ridgeline Trail, and doing so will shorten the hike by about 2 miles.

GETTING THERE

From the west, follow I-80 E. Take exit 309 for US 209 N toward Marshalls Creek. After exiting, follow US 209 N for 11.1 miles, then turn left onto Bushkill Falls Road. Drive for 1.5 miles, then turn right onto Milford Road. Continue for 6.7

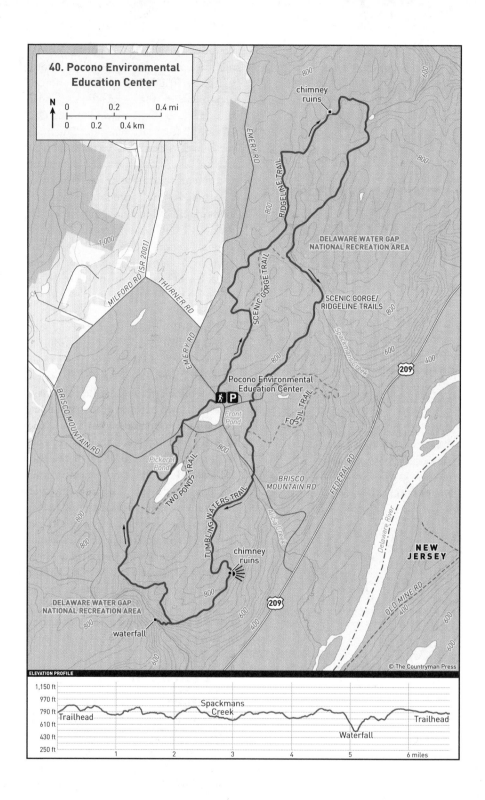

40. Pocono Environmental Education Center

N
0   0.2   0.4 mi
0   0.2   0.4 km

chimney
ruins

RIDGELINE TRAIL

EMERY RD

800

800

800

600

DELAWARE WATER GAP
NATIONAL RECREATION AREA

SCENIC GORGE/
RIDGELINE TRAILS

800

MILFORD RD (SR 2001)

1,000

THURNER RD

SCENIC GORGE TRAIL

EMERY RD

Spackmans Creek

600

400

209

800

Pocono Environmental
Education Center

P

Front
Pond

FOSSIL TRAIL

BRISCO MOUNTAIN RD

Pickerel
Pond

800

TWO PONDS TRAIL

BRISCO
MOUNTAIN RD

FEDERAL RD

Alicia Creek

TUMBLING WATERS TRAIL

800

800

chimney
ruins

Delaware River

NEW
JERSEY

209

OLD MINE RD

400

600

DELAWARE WATER GAP
NATIONAL RECREATION AREA

800

waterfall

600

400

© The Countryman Press

ELEVATION PROFILE

1,150 ft
970 ft
790 ft
610 ft
430 ft
250 ft

Trailhead

Spackmans
Creek

Waterfall

Trailhead

1   2   3   4   5   6 miles

miles. Turn right onto Thurner Road, and 0.3 mile later turn right onto Emery Road. Pocono Environmental Education Center will be on the left side of the road in 0.3 mile.

The Pocono Environmental Education Center is located north of Philadelphia. From the Philadelphia area, follow I-476 N and take exit 56 toward Lehigh Valley. Merge onto US 22 E and drive for 16.4 miles. Take the exit for PA 33 N toward Stroudsburg. Follow PA 33 N for 21.8 miles, then keep right and follow US 209 N. Drive for 4.2 miles, then merge onto I-80 E. Take exit 309 to US 209 N toward Marshalls Creek. Continue onto US 209 N. After 11.1 miles turn left onto Bushkill Falls Road. Drive for 1.5 miles, then turn right onto Milford Road. Continue for 6.7 miles. Turn right onto Thurner Road, and 0.3 mile later turn right onto Emery Road. Pocono Environmental Education Center will be on the left side of the road in 0.3 miles.

GPS Shortcut: Enter "Pocono Environmental Education Center" into Google Maps and your GPS will navigate you to the parking area.

THE HIKE

From the parking area, head north and begin following the yellow and red blazes of the Ridgeline and Scenic Gorge Trails, two overlapping footpaths that share tread along a few segments. The two trails climb gradually up well-graded singletrack that is mostly void of roots and rocks. After 0.2 mile, emerge onto an access road and walk to the right of a large radio tower, reentering the woods behind the tower site. Continue to follow the trails on lively rolling terrain and arrive at a signed junction in 0.2 mile. The Ridgeline Trail turns to the left here, while the Scenic Gorge

CHIMNEY RUINS ALONG THE TRAIL

Trail veers to the right, reconnecting with the Ridgeline Trail farther ahead. Turn left and follow the Ridgeline Trail, ascending and descending frequent rolling hills.

The Ridgeline Trail converges with the Scenic Gorge Trail in 0.5 mile, sharing tread again for a short distance on level grade. Approximately 200 feet after rejoining the Scenic Gorge Trail, the trails split once more. The Scenic Gorge Trail turns right and heads east, entering a stand of large hemlock trees. Stay on the Ridgeline Trail and continue to follow the yellow blazes, crossing a footbridge spanning a small stream immediately after the intersection. In 0.1 mile, the Ridgeline Trail enters a grove of short hemlock trees, then passes in between a vernal pond on the right and a rocky cliff face on the left. Skirt the

WATER CROSSING ON THE RIDGELINE TRAIL

demanding, requiring the use of both your hands and your feet. A knotted climbing rope is tethered between a tree near the top and a tree at the bottom to aid in the descent. After making this descent, the trail begins to bend to the east, lazily arcing back toward the environmental center on rolling terrain similar to what you have been following up until now. In 0.5 mile, the trail passes a stone chimney, the only standing remnant of an old cabin that used to exist here. Continue following the trail, gradually descending down to another sizable wetland area. Cross the inlet stream that feeds into the marsh and begin to climb at a moderate rate through a mature hemlock stand. After this sustained 0.2 mile climb, the trail largely resumes its trend of short, lumpy ups and downs, occasionally skirting small boggy areas in the depressions between the hills.

At mile 2.6, the trail meets with the genial flow of Spackmans Creek, following the edge of the water for a short distance before crossing it on a log bridge. In another 0.1 mile, the Ridgeline Trail crosses a small stream that feeds into Spackmans Creek, leading over a small waterfall on a wooden footbridge. After crossing the bridge, the Ridgeline Trail is joined by the Scenic Gorge Trail once more. Continue to follow Spackmans Creek downstream for approximately 0.3 mile, then bend to the right and begin ascending moderately in between two hills, heading away from the water. This segment of the trail ascends up the side of the westernmost hill, occasionally clambering over patches of exposed rock, to intersect with a paved road at mile 3.4. The red and yellow blazes end at the edge of the pavement. Veer right here and follow the road uphill a short distance, passing some cabins as you

base of this cliff for a short distance, then climb a moderately steep ascent up a sharp slope. This brief ascent follows a narrow trail as it approaches several craggy, oddly textured rock formations to reach the top of this lengthy ridge. Note that the trail on this ascent can be somewhat challenging due to its uneven tread, which slants toward the bottom of the gorge as it ascends.

On top of the ridge, the trail advances through a young pine forest and meanders along more short ups and downs. At the 1.4-mile mark, the yellow-blazed trail bends to the right and descends steeply into a crack in the ledge. While this descent is not very long, it is fairly

WATERFALL AT THE SOUTHERN END OF THE LOOP

head in the direction of the environmental center.

After 0.2 mile, turn left and leave the road shortly before reaching the parking area, entering the woods on the orange-blazed Tumbling Waters Trail and the blue-blazed Fossil Trail. A wooden sign marks the start of these two trails, which share tread for about 0.1 mile. After meandering through white pine forest past some oddly shaped boulders, these two trails split. Keep right and follow the orange blazes of the Tumbling Waters Trail. In 0.2 mile, cross Brisco Mountain Road and resume following the Tumbling Waters Trail on the other side of the road, passing over a small stream on stepping-stones. Immediately after crossing the stream, the trail joins with a wide, flat woods road grade. Continue along the old dirt road for 0.3 mile to meet with an emergency access road that bypasses a large portion of the Tumbling Waters Trail. Bend to the left and continue to follow the orange blazes.

Arrive at another chimney ruins at mile 4.6, as well as a scenic view from a

miniscule ledge nearby, looking southeast. Beyond the chimney and vista, the trail trends downhill on rocky terrain, following the edge of a steep drop-off for

TRAIL SIGN ON THE TUMBLING WATERS TRAIL

CROSSING SPACKMANS CREEK

they are shaded from the sunlight by thick evergreen trees.

Upon rejoining the Tumbling Waters Trail from the spur trail, turn left and begin heading steeply uphill on a short, rocky spine. In 0.2 mile, pass the other end of the emergency access trail. Stay left and continue following the orange blazes. The grade descends briefly, then climbs at a more relaxed angle for 0.4 mile on a narrow path through dense evergreen forest. Afterward, the trail widens and levels out significantly, entering a mixed forest and meeting with the Two Ponds Trail, which breaks off to the right. Stay straight and continue to follow the orange and white blazes. The trail leads along the western edge of Pickerel Pond for a short distance before bending back into the woods.

At 6.4 miles, cross back over Brisco Mountain Road and enter the woods on the opposite side under a small power line, and then approach Front Pond. The trail makes an abrupt right turn in 0.2 mile, descending a short distance to a wooden walkway. At the end of this boardwalk, and just before arriving back at the parking area, there is a bird blind. Enjoying the wildlife from this point is a great way to relax before ending your hike.

When you are finished at the bird blind, cross Emery Road to arrive back at the environmental center and your vehicle.

0.4 mile. There are several more excellent views to the southeast along this lip, as the trail constantly leads into the cover of the forest, then back out to the more exposed edge. At the 5-mile mark, just after descending on some deep, slanting, handmade steps, the Tumbling Waters Trail arrives at a junction with a spur trail. To the left, a series of wooden staircases winds steeply downhill, arriving at a frothy, two-tiered waterfall in 0.1 mile, the namesake of the Tumbling Waters Trail. Enjoy the falls, and then head back up to the orange-blazed trail when you are ready. Take your time going down and up the wooden stairs. They are often wet and slippery, because

Mount Minsi

DISTANCE: 4 miles

DIFFICULTY: Difficult

HIKING TIME: 2 hours

TYPE: Out and Back

TOTAL ELEVATION GAIN: 988'

MAXIMUM ELEVATION: 1,461'

On the western side of the Delaware River stands Mount Minsi. The 1,461-foot-tall mountain forms the western end of Delaware Water Gap National Recreation Area, and it is opposite Mount Tammany, which represents the continuation of the ridge on the New Jersey side of the river. The peak of Mount Minsi is a popular hiking destination, and it can be reached via the historic white-blazed Appalachian Trail. It is the last peak thru-hikers encounter in the state of Pennsylvania. From there, hikers delve into the town of Delaware Water Gap, Pennsylvania, before crossing the Delaware River and entering New Jersey.

The hike to the summit of Mount Minsi follows rocky tread that climbs consistently, and it occasionally ascends steep sections of trail. The wooded ridge is covered with rhododendrons, and it feels particularly lush and jungle-esque on hot, humid summer days. The hike features a handful of scenic viewpoints from rock outcroppings that look out over the Delaware River into New Jersey. Also of interest is the cheerful flow of Eureka Creek and the small constructed body of water known as Lenape Lake. Lenape Lake, which is fed by Caledonia Creek, is only a short walk from the parking lot. This still pool of water is furnished with a few wooden tables, and it is a superb place for a picnic or some posthike rock skipping.

GETTING THERE

From the west, follow I-80 E. Take exit 310 for PA 166 toward Delaware Water Gap. At the end of the ramp, enter the traffic circle and take the second exit, and continue on Broad Street for 0.5 mile. At the end of Broad Street, turn left onto Main Street and drive for 0.3 mile. Turn

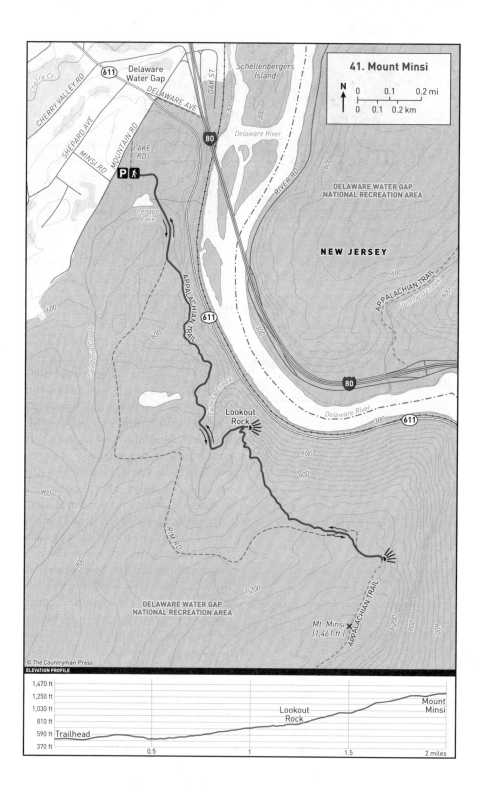

right onto Mountain Road and continue for 0.1 mile. Veer left onto Lake Road. Drive 0.1 mile, following signs toward Lake Lenape to reach a gravel parking area on the right side of the road. The hike starts in front of a metal gate across the Appalachian Trail, next to an information board.

Delaware Water Gap National Recreation Area is located due north of Philadelphia, on the Pennsylvania–New Jersey border. From the Philadelphia area, follow I-476 N and take exit 56 toward Lehigh Valley. At the end of the ramp, keep right and merge onto US 22 E. Drive US 22 E for 16.4 miles. Take the exit for PA 33 N toward Stroudsburg and drive for 21.8 miles. Keep right where PA 33 and US 209 split. Stay on US 209, following signs toward Stroudsburg. In 4.2 miles, merge onto I-80 E. Stay on the I-80 E for 4.2 miles, then take exit 310 toward Delaware Water Gap. At the end of the ramp, take the second exit on the traffic circle and follow Broad Street. Drive for 0.5 mile. At the end of Broad Street, turn left onto Main Street and drive for 0.3 mile. Turn right onto Mountain Road and continue for 0.1 mile. Veer left onto Lake Road. Drive 0.1 mile, following signs toward Lake Lenape to reach a gravel parking area on the right side of the road. The hike starts in front of a metal gate across the Appalachian Trail, next to an information board.

GPS Shortcut: Enter "Lenape Lake, Delaware Water Gap" into Google Maps and your GPS will direct you to the trailhead.

THE HIKE

Enter the woods next to a small sign at the southern end of the parking area and begin following the white blazes of the Appalachian Trail on an old woods road.

ON THE APPALACHIAN TRAIL

The historic footpath arrives at Lenape Lake after 0.1 mile of easy, flat walking. Continue on the woods road past the lake and ascend gradually on the same wide path for another 0.2 mile. At this point, the Appalachian Trail turns to the left and leaves the road grade, narrowing slightly and transitioning to very rocky and rooty terrain. The trail descends toward a lip that follows the side of the mountain, ascending and descending short hills, and occasionally offering partial views into the river valley below. Aside from being quite rocky, the trail is easy to follow, trending downhill through rhododendrons, often making use of large, blocky stone steps on the descents. After hiking for 0.5 mile, arrive at Council Rock on the left side of the trail. This flat rock outcropping used to present an impressive view across the Delaware River, but it has become overgrown recently.

After the gradual descent to Council Rock, the Appalachian Trail begins a long, drawn-out ascent, climbing steadily and sometimes steeply up the northern flank of Mount Minsi. The trail levels out briefly, only to cross Eureka Creek, resuming the climb on the other side through majestic, shady rhododendrons and navigating over stretches of exposed rock. After 0.7 mile of mostly moderate climbing, the Appalachian Trail bends to the right, very near a small clifftop on the mountainside, and ascends a steep flight of rustic stone steps, advancing through a small ledge area shortly thereafter. Before heading up the steps, continue straight on for

about 50 feet to reach the cliff, which features another view of the Delaware River looking due east. This point is known as Lookout Rock for obvious reasons. The turn leading up the steps can be easy to miss, as Lookout Rock generally garners more attention than the subtle bend in the Appalachian Trail, so keep an eye out for it. The short spur to Lookout Rock dead ends at the sheer drop-off, so if you miss the turn, you will know very quickly if you need to turn around.

Continue uphill, ascending a moderately steep incline past Lookout Rock, on short, quick switchbacks, then over an exposed rock face. The trail levels out for a short distance at mile 1.5, providing you with an opportunity to catch your breath, before once more ascending on stone steps through thick, lush rhododendrons. Hike for 0.3 mile, the grade becoming incrementally more

THE VIEW FROM LOOKOUT ROCK ACROSS THE DELAWARE RIVER

MOUNT TAMMANY AS SEEN FROM MOUNT MINSI

relaxed and the organized stone steps devolving into a messy jumble of rocks, until you eventually intersect with the same woods road that the hike started on. Turn left onto the road grade, then approximately 25 feet later, turn right to stay on the Appalachian Trail, leaving the wide grassy road. This short stretch is still extremely rocky, but much flatter, giving you another opportunity to catch your breath.

Less than 0.1 mile later, the Appalachian Trail rejoins the woods road and once more begins ascending. This last push to the summit of Mount Minsi climbs moderately under another grove of rhododendrons, following a strange segment of trail that mixes the wide, well-graded tread of the woods road with the intense, rocky terrain the Appalachian Trail is known for. Arrive at the top of Mount Minsi roughly 0.2 mile after rejoining the woods road. From this rocky clearing in the woods, an excellent view of Mount Tammany can be seen to the east. The folded, exposed crust of the ridge can be seen from here on the southern face of Mount Tammany, and it will surely intrigue amateur geologists.

From this point, turn around and head back down the Appalachian Trail, retracing your previous course to arrive back at the parking area in 2 miles.

42

Lehigh Gap Appalachian Trail Winter Loop

DISTANCE: 2.7 miles

DIFFICULTY: Very Difficult

HIKING TIME: 2 hours

TYPE: Loop

TOTAL ELEVATION GAIN: 956'

MAXIMUM ELEVATION: 1,421'

Frequently cited as one of the state high-lights for thru-hikers, the climb out of Lehigh Gap is a challenging one that features some of the only exposed climb-ing along the Appalachian Trail in Penn-sylvania. The route ascends sharply up from the Lehigh River and requires nontechnical scrambling up the rocky abutment near the top of the ridge. For their efforts, hikers are rewarded with a sweeping view of the countryside below, a sight regarded as one of the best along the Appalachian Trail in the state of Pennsylvania. For the most part, Pennsylvania epitomizes the concept of the "green tunnel," a phrase often used to describe the densely wooded scen-ery along the Appalachian Trail, but this brief break from underneath the thick canopy is a breath of fresh air for thru-hikers and day hikers alike.

This hike follows the Appalachian Trail, climbing out of Lehigh Gap on the eastern side of the river before break-ing off onto a blue-blazed connector trail and descending toward the river on the Winter Trail. The last leg of the hike follows an old railroad grade that sits above PA 248, skirting the foot of the mountain. While fairly short, the hike is physically demanding, and toward the top of the ridge requires hikers to use both hands and feet to scale a few stone faces. This vista is well-known and very popular, and it routinely becomes very crowded when the weather condi-tions are pleasant. If you are looking for a quieter but equally enjoyable hike, consider the nearby North Trail Loop on the western side of the Lehigh River. It is described in the next entry of this book. Enterprising hikers may wish to tackle both hikes in one day, gaining a view of Lehigh Gap from both sides of the river.

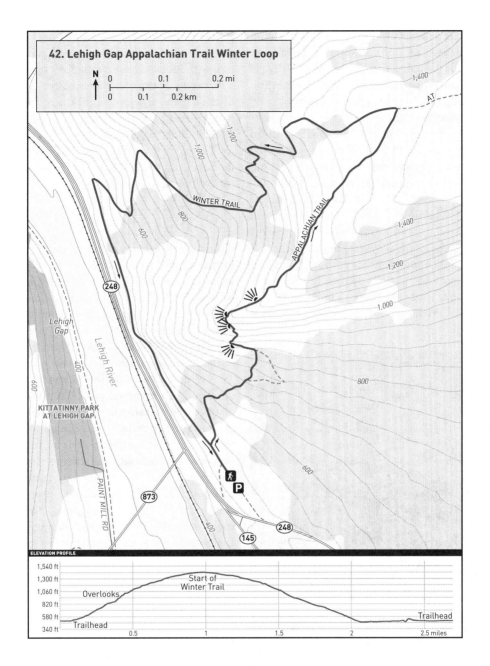

42. Lehigh Gap Appalachian Trail Winter Loop

ELEVATION PROFILE

1,540 ft
1,300 ft — Start of Winter Trail
1,060 ft — Overlooks
820 ft
580 ft — Trailhead ... Trailhead
340 ft

0.5   1   1.5   2   2.5 miles

GETTING THERE

From the west, follow I-76 E. Take exit 226 and merge onto US 11 N toward Harrisburg. Keep right and in 2.2 miles merge onto I-81 N. Follow I-81 N for 36.8 miles, then take exit 89 and merge onto I-78 E. Drive for 34.6 miles on I-78 E. Take exit 35 for PA 143 toward Lenhartsville. At the end of the ramp, turn left onto PA 143 N. Drive for 12.1 miles, then turn left onto Mosserville Road. In

1.8 miles, cross PA 309 and join Mountain Road. Continue on Mountain Road for 9.9 miles, then merge onto PA 873 N and cross the Lehigh River. After crossing the river, turn right onto PA 248 and drive for 0.2 mile. Just after a traffic light at the junction of PA 145, make a sharp left onto a dirt road. Follow the dirt road for 0.1 mile to reach the gravel parking area along the Appalachian Trail.

Lehigh Gap is located northwest of Philadelphia. From the Philadelphia area, follow I-476 N. Take exit 74 toward Mahoning Valley, keeping left at the end of the ramp to merge onto PA 209 S. Follow PA 209 S for 1.6 miles, then turn left onto PA 248 E. Drive 7.1 miles on PA 248 E, which parallels the Lehigh River and passes two bridges spanning the water. Just after the traffic signal at the junction with PA 145, make a sharp left onto a dirt road. Follow the dirt road for 0.1 mile to reach the gravel parking area along the Appalachian Trail.

GPS Shortcut: Search Google Maps for "Appalachian Trail Parking, Walnutport" and your GPS will navigate to the trailhead.

THE HIKE

Head to the north end of the flat parking lot past some large boulders and begin following the white blazes of the Appalachian Trail. A few hundred feet after leaving the parking area, the trail splits where the Appalachian Trail meets with the blue-blazed Winter Trail. This fork in the trail marks the start of the loop. The Winter Trail continues straight on from here, eventually reaching the vista on the ridgetop by following easier, less intense terrain. You can follow this loop in either direction but for the purposes of this hike, veer right to stay on the Appalachian Trail. It may seem counterintuitive to ascend the more difficult route here, but going up the rocky scramble in most cases is much easier and safer than descending steep, exposed obstacles.

The trail ascends from the junction, climbing a moderately steep incline on rocky terrain that features a few sporadic instances of wooden steps. The angle of ascent continues to intensify the farther you progress, always following the jumbled rocks that have garnered such an infamous reputation for the Appalachian Trail through Pennsylvania. In 0.2 mile, on the right side of the trail, a window through the treetops provides a slight view of the Lehigh Valley spreading out to the south.

SUNNY EXPOSURE ALONG THE CREST OF THE RIDGE

GAZING NORTH OVER THE LEHIGH RIVER

In 0.1 mile, the trail turns to the left, heading west a short distance before beginning a more aggressive climb directly toward the top of the ridge. This portion of the hike is largely exposed, traversing a very rocky spine that peeks above the tree line, and it continues to get steeper and steeper for 0.2 mile. Because of the exposure, incredible continuous views can be seen looking to the south and the west. There are a few points during this intense climb that require the use of both hands and feet to scale sheer walls of rock, meaning that you must make use of gaps and cracks in the imposing ledges to advance.

At the 0.5-mile mark, the trail gains the crest of the ridge amidst a field of weathered stone. From this point, excellent panoramic views can be enjoyed, with 180 degrees of exposure to the west. Looking north over the elongated hills toward the Pocono Plateau, the serpentine course of the Lehigh River can be seen as it flows through gaps in the ridges, making its way through the vast valley to the south and eventually emptying into the Delaware River along the New Jersey border. There is a notable rock formation protruding from the side of the ridge on the opposite side of the Lehigh River and is known as Devil's Pulpit. The bluff earned its name due to the extremely steep and difficult drop down to the outcropping and its precarious perch over the shallow river below. The optional route to Devil's Pulpit is described in the next entry of this book.

When you are ready to continue, resume following the Appalachian Trail on the north side of the spine. After arriving at the crest, the trail bends to the right and advances on the same rocky course, still ascending but at a much

CONTINUING NORTH ON THE APPALACHIAN TRAIL

more relaxed rate. Pay close attention to the blazes through this bouldery segment, as it can be easy to wander off trail here. In 0.1 mile, the trail bends gently to the left, slowly reentering the patchy tree cover amid white pines, hemlocks, and birches. The terrain at this point alternates between sharp, clunky rocks and smoother dirt grade, leveling off gradually for the next 0.4 mile. Partial spotty views can be seen on the left side of the trail, and a large fenced-in area will begin to appear on the right. This fenced-in plot is a restoration project to help recover the area from industrial damage done by a nearby zinc processing plant. The trail passes some signage along the fence that explains the effort in more detail.

At the 1-mile mark, the Appalachian Trail meets with the other end of the blue-blazed Winter Trail. Turn to the left and begin following the Winter Trail, leaving the Appalachian Trail behind. From the intersection, the Winter Trail descends moderately on a fairly straight trajectory, advancing over much more agreeable terrain through sparse, stunted forest. To keep the descent comparatively easy, the trail turns to the left in 0.2 mile and starts dropping on a series of switchbacks, reentering the cover of the trees in the process. These switchbacks grow rockier the farther the trail descends, becoming slightly steeper as they wind around the western flank of the ridge.

In 1.1 miles after leaving the Appalachian Trail on top of the ridge, the Winter Trail arrives at a flat, grassy railroad grade that runs to the left and the right. Turn to the left to stay on the blue-blazed trail and follow the wide path above the busy road below. The Winter Trail skirts the base of a tall cliff and crosses a few seasonal trickles that drain from the ridge toward the river, and in roughly 0.5 mile the trail arrives back at the start of the loop.

From this point, continue straight ahead a very short distance on the Appalachian Trail to return to the parking area.

43

North Trail Loop

DISTANCE: 6.8 miles

DIFFICULTY: Difficult

HIKING TIME: 3.5 hours

TYPE: Loop

TOTAL ELEVATION GAIN: 1,451'

MAXIMUM ELEVATION: 1,534'

Atop the long and gently curving ridge of Blue Mountain, and just west of the Lehigh River, is the North Trail, which forms a loop with the Appalachian Trail. The North Trail lies on land that was once devastated by industrial pollution from Palmerton nearby, but thanks to extensive cleanup projects the area is now rebounding. This area is jointly maintained by the Allentown Hiking Club and the Lehigh Gap Nature Center. The North Trail is notable for its exposed course through windswept grassland terrain, boasting almost continuous views to the north. Seeming somewhat out of place for the state of Pennsylvania and more akin to mountain trails bordering the plains of the Midwest, the North Trail is truly a hidden gem for the Keystone State.

The hike described here traverses the northern edge of Blue Mountain, following the ridge and providing sweeping panoramic views of the surrounding countryside to the north. The sight comes at a cost, though, as the route to the top of the ridge follows a gravel road grade, climbing relentlessly through the forest. Additionally, the terrain poses a challenge, as it is characteristically rocky and rough. For those willing to endure, however, an excellent sustained view and an impressive experience in a unique landscape await. An optional portion of the hike leads to the viewpoint on Devil's Pulpit. This precipice, while impressive, is extremely difficult to get to, as hikers must follow a faint, faded trail that is more akin to a bushwhack than a stroll down a maintained footpath. If you decide to head to Devil's Pulpit, use your best judgment and be prepared to turn around if necessary.

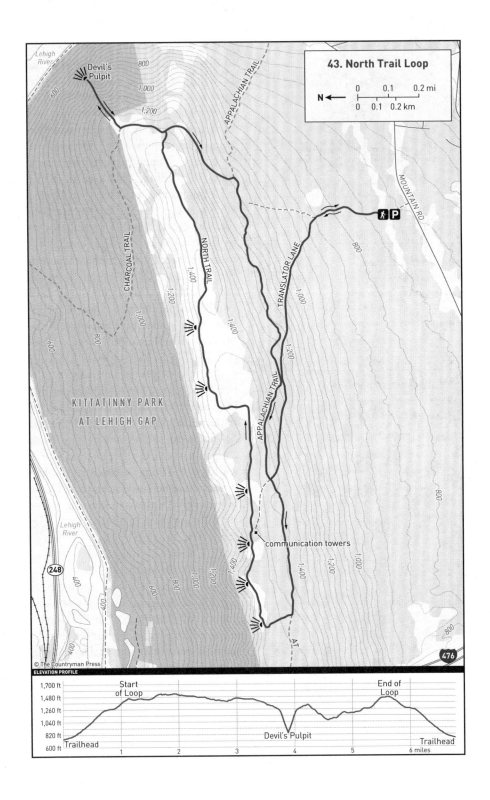

43. North Trail Loop

Lehigh River

Devil's Pulpit

APPALACHIAN TRAIL

MOUNTAIN RD.

CHARCOAL TRAIL

NORTH TRAIL

TRANSLATOR LANE

APPALACHIAN TRAIL

KITTATINNY PARK
AT LEHIGH GAP

Lehigh River

248

communication towers

AT

476

© The Countryman Press

N ←

0   0.1   0.2 mi
0   0.1   0.2 km

ELEVATION PROFILE

Start of Loop

End of Loop

Devil's Pulpit

Trailhead

Trailhead

1,700 ft
1,480 ft
1,260 ft
1,040 ft
820 ft
600 ft

1   2   3   4   5   6 miles

GETTING THERE

From the west, follow I-76 E. Take exit 226 and merge onto US 11 N toward Harrisburg. Keep right and in 2.2 miles merge onto I-81 N. Follow I-81 N for 36.8 miles, then take exit 89 and merge onto I-78 E. Drive for 34.6 miles on I-78 E. Take exit 35 for PA 143 toward Lenhartsville. At the end of the ramp, turn left onto PA 143 N. Drive for 12.1 miles, then turn left onto Mosserville Road. In 1.8 miles, cross PA 309 and join Mountain Road. Continue on Mountain Road for 9.1 miles. Turn left onto Translator Lane. Drive for 0.1 mile. Park in the gravel lot located in the power line swath. The hike starts from here.

The hike starts west of Lehigh Gap, which is northwest of Philadelphia. From the Philadelphia area, follow I-476 N. Take exit 56 toward Lehigh Valley. At the end of the ramp, keep right and follow US 22 E for 0.8 mile, then take the exit and merge onto PA 309 N. Drive for 6 miles. In Schnecksville, keep straight and merge onto PA 873 N. Follow PA 873 N for 3 miles. Keep right to stay on the route and continue for another 3.6 miles. In Slatington, turn left on PA 873 N just before crossing the Lehigh River. Continue on PA 873 N. In 2 miles, make a sharp left onto Mountain Road. Drive for 0.8 mile. Turn right onto Translator Lane. Drive for 0.1 mile. Park in the gravel parking lot located in the power line swath. The hike starts from here.

GPS Shortcut: There is no searchable destination for the parking area. The easiest way to navigate to trailhead is to enter "Translator Lane Slatington" into Google Maps and set it as your destination. Park in the large gravel lot located in the power line swath. Translator Lane continues up the mountain,

THE NORTH TRAIL ATOP BLUE MOUNTAIN

but a metal gate restricts vehicle access past this point.

THE HIKE

From the parking area beneath the power lines, head north up the gravel tread of Translator Lane, passing behind a metal gate as you enter the woods. While not marked, Translator Lane is extremely easy to follow albeit not terribly exciting; it advances up the ridge moderately while bending gently to the west. The terrain on the gravel access road is well-graded but tiresome the farther up you go due to the gradually steepening angle of ascent. After 1.1 miles, the road crosses the Appalachian Trail, very close to the top of the ridge. Translator

Lane continues straight ahead, eventually arriving at a privately owned radio tower. Turn left at this intersection and begin following the white blazes of the Appalachian Trail.

The tread of the Appalachian Trail traverses the ridgetop, passing through pleasant, shady pine forest. The terrain is much rockier and the trail is significantly narrower than that of the gravel road, although the course of the Appalachian Trail is relatively flat. In 0.5 mile, arrive at the western terminus of the North Trail, which breaks off the Appalachian Trail to the right. Turn here and begin following the North Trail. In a few hundred feet the trail crosses a dirt road next to a communications tower, bending to the left shortly thereafter. After 0.1 mile, make an abrupt right turn and begin following the blue blazes along the northern flank of the ridge. Heading

eastward, you will immediately emerge from underneath the tree cover and come to a rocky clearing just off the trail that offers excellent views of the countryside to the north.

As you continue, the North Trail follows the rounded lip of the sloping spine, providing exquisite, extended views of the ridges in the distance, the valley below, and the winding course of the Lehigh River. This part of the Blue Mountain Ridge is occupied by patches of grassy field that is sparsely treed. The lack of tree cover and the tall swaying grasses on the ridgetop feel out of place in the Keystone State, which is normally known for its heavily forested environment. For the next 0.3 mile, the terrain is rocky, advancing on narrow tread that trends very gradually uphill toward two more communications towers. After passing the towers, the trail

THE VIEW EAST FROM ABOVE DEVIL'S PULPIT

CONTINUOUS VIEWS ON THE GRASSY RIDGETOP

enters spotty, immature forest as it continues on a fairly straight trajectory for another 0.5 mile.

At the 2.5 mile mark, the North Trail turns to the left and descends approximately 50 feet off the top of the ridge before heading back to the crest in 0.4 mile. This slight drop in elevation continues along the lip of the ridge, giving hikers plenty more opportunities to enjoy the far-reaching view. After regaining the top of the mountain, the trail follows the gradually descending ridgeline, passing through more grassy field areas and a growing concentration of thicker forest.

The North Trail meets with the Charcoal Trail at mile marker 3.6. The Charcoal Trail is marked with orange blazes, turning off the North Trail to the left nearby to where the ridge descends into the Lehigh River Gap. If you want to visit Devil's Pulpit, turn left onto the Charcoal Trail and follow it for 0.2 mile. This optional out-and-back spur requires bushwhacking on very steep, very difficult terrain, and it should only be attempted by experienced hikers in good physical shape. Skipping this portion will subtract 0.8 mile from the hike. Just before entering land managed by the Lehigh Gap Nature Center, arrive at a wooden post that marks the boundary. A faintly discernible herd path is on the right side of the trail. This treacherous herd path, if followed carefully, leads to Devils Pulpit, a rock outcropping that surveys the eastern side of Lehigh Gap. The vista is 0.2 mile off the Charcoal Trail, but it drops on an extremely steep angle through thick brush and jumbled rocks and feels a lot longer than it

THE LEHIGH RIVER AND PALMERTON SEEN FROM THE NORTH TRAIL

actually is. It can be very easy to lose the trail. Turn around if you feel unsafe. Remember that the farther you drop, the farther you will have to climb back up to the Charcoal Trail. Even if you only make it part of the way down the steep incline, you will be rewarded with an excellent view to the east. When you are finished, return to the Charcoal Trail, turn left, and head back to the junction with the North Trail.

After rejoining the North Trail, descend moderately down the southern flank of the ridge. In a rocky 0.3 mile, reach the eastern terminus of the North Trail, ending at the Appalachian Trail just west of the George W. Outerbridge Shelter. Turn right onto the Appalachian Trail and follow its bumpy, ascending tread. The trail climbs at a moderate angle, occasionally going up short, steeper segments for 1 mile.

When the Appalachian Trail reaches Translator Lane, turn left and head downhill on the gravel road. You will arrive at the parking lot in 1.1 miles.

Bear Rocks and Knife's Edge

DISTANCE: 4.3 miles	
DIFFICULTY: Moderate	
HIKING TIME: 2.5 hours	
TYPE: Out and Back	
TOTAL ELEVATION GAIN: 350'	
MAXIMUM ELEVATION: 1,567'	

Making its way through State Game Lands No. 217, the Appalachian Trail corridor sits atop the spine of Blue Mountain. The expansive ridge is a prominent feature, dividing the state into distinct geological territories, separating the Great Appalachian Valley from the northern Susquehanna Lowlands and the eastern plateau regions. Roughly 10 miles west of the Lehigh River, the wooded mountaintop also forms the basis of the dividing line for several counties, separating the southern Berks and Lehigh Counties from the northern Schuylkill and Carbon Counties. The Appalachian Trail crosses this invisible, fabricated border several times on its rambling course across Blue Mountain as it visits chaotic, slanting stacks of stone, from which hikers can enjoy a view that surveys both sides of the ridge.

The hike detailed here follows the Appalachian Trail west from the Bake Oven Knob parking area, heading "southbound" on the trail to visit both Bear Rocks and the Knife's Edge. These two formations are physically quite different, with the broad, blocky stacks of Bear Rocks contrasting sharply from the thinner, skewed plates of Knife's Edge. Both, however, provide a sweeping view of valleys to the north and south. The trail from the parking lot starts very flat and easy but quickly gets rocky and stays that way for the majority of the hike. Also of interest on the hike are short, four-sided stone columns, standing upright in the woods. These columns mark the boundary of Carbon, Lehigh, and Schuylkill Counties, and are engraved with the county names on the corresponding sides.

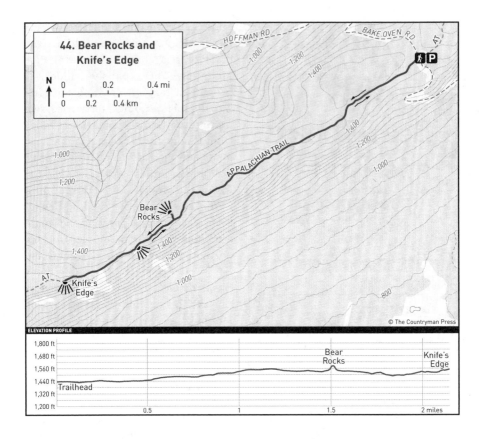

GETTING THERE

From the west, follow I-76 E. Take exit 226 and merge onto US 11 N toward Harrisburg. Keep right and in 2.2 miles merge onto I-81 N. Follow I-81 N for 36.8 miles, then take exit 89 and merge onto I-78 E. Drive for 34.6 miles. Take exit 35 for PA 143 toward Lenhartsville. At the end of the ramp, turn left onto PA 143 N. Drive for 12.1 miles, then turn left onto Mosserville Road. In 1.8 miles, cross PA 309 and join Mountain Road. Continue on Mountain Road for 2 miles, then turn left onto Ulrich Road. In 0.9 mile, Ulrich Road becomes Bake Oven Road. Continue uphill on Bake Oven Road, driving for 1.1 miles to reach the large gravel parking lot on the right side of the road.

The hike starts on Bake Oven Road,

northwest of Philadelphia. From the Philadelphia area, follow I-476 N. Take exit 56 toward Lehigh Valley. At the end of the ramp, keep left and follow signs for US 22 W/I-78 W toward Harrisburg. Continue onto I-78 W and take exit 49B toward Fogelsville. Merge onto PA 100 N and drive for 8.3 miles. Turn right onto PA 309 W for 0.3 mile, then turn left onto Bake Oven Road. Follow Bake Oven Road for 4.2 miles, and turn left at Church Road to stay on Bake Oven Road. In 1.8 miles, arrive at the large gravel parking lot on the right side of the road.

GPS Shortcut: Type "Bake Oven Knob Parking, Bake Oven Road" into Google Maps and set it as your destination. The large gravel parking lot is located at the top of the ridge on the right side of the road.

THE HIKE

Head west from the parking area, entering the woods on the white-blazed Appalachian Trail. The trail immediately passes behind a metal gate and begins following the rounded top of the mountain on a grass woods road. The terrain is easy on this old road as it navigates the flat ridgetop. After 0.4 mile, the Appalachian Trail turns to the left, leaving the road grade behind. The woods road continues straight on, so keep an eye out for the white blazes that guide you onto the Appalachian Trail.

Upon leaving the old road, the terrain becomes a lot rougher and the grade begins trending uphill on the narrowing trail. While the angle of ascent may be straightforward and relatively effortless, the terrain will add a touch of difficulty to the journey. The sharp, angular rocks that poke up from the rocky footpath will remain a constant for the rest of the hike, growing more and more prevalent as you advance. This type of hiking forces you

BEAR ROCKS

to carefully consider each step as you hop from stone to pointy stone. It is a great way to strengthen your ankles and test your balance, but it can become tiresome and frustrating very quickly. Take

LOOKING NORTH FROM BEAR ROCKS

SIGN MARKING THE SPUR TO BEAR ROCKS

graffiti mars the rock formation, helping to obscure the location of the blue blazes. Take your time and use common sense, however, and the top of the rocks should be easy to reach. From this elevated stone platform, pleasant pastoral views can be enjoyed looking to the north and south. The view to the south is slightly obscured by the treetops, but the view to the north is excellent. There are plenty of cracks and crevices to scramble around and explore here as well. Enjoy the towering stone and the view, and when you are ready to continue, follow the spur trail off the rock formation to head back to the Appalachian Trail.

Continue to follow the ridge on the Appalachian Trail heading southbound. Your course through the woods traverses small undulations, always on the jagged rocks. At one point roughly 0.2 mile away from Bear Rocks, there is a small enclosed vista that looks over the valley on the south side of the ridge. In another 0.2 mile, there is a dry campsite on the left side of the trail with enough room for two or three tents.

Immediately after passing the campsite, ascend a heap of thick stone slab that forms a tilting ledge that points north. This narrow, slanting spine of the ridge is the aptly named Knife's Edge. Carefully make your way up the rocks to reach the viewpoint here. The area is almost entirely exposed, with just a few shrubby trees providing cover from the sun and wind. The vista sits above a small scree field, peeking over the treetops to gaze at the pastoral patchwork farmland in the valley to the south.

When you are finished enjoying the view at Knife's Edge, turn around and follow the white blazes of the Appalachian Trail back to the parking lot on Bake Oven Road.

your time and shift your focus from the rugged terrain to the thick, serene forest around you.

You will start to see short stone columns a few feet off the trail as you make your way through the Appalachian Trail corridor. These markers denote the boundary line between counties, and they are engraved with the names of the different counties on the corresponding sides. On the southern side of the ridge sits Lehigh County. For the first stretch of the hike, Carbon County lies to the north, but after walking 1.3 miles from the trailhead, Carbon County ends and the Appalachian Trail follows the border of Schuylkill County instead.

Arrive at Bear Rocks 1 mile and roughly 100 vertical feet after turning off the grassy roadbed. This stately stack of weathered stone is located approximately 0.1 mile off the Appalachian Trail to the right, and it can be accessed by following a short blue-blazed spur that steeply ascends a jumble of slabby boulders to gain the summit. The blazes on this short spur are sparse and faded, making the route slightly difficult to follow. Additionally, an unfortunate amount of

Hawk Mountain Sanctuary

DISTANCE: 5.1 miles

DIFFICULTY: Very Difficult

HIKING TIME: 3 hours

TYPE: Loop

TOTAL ELEVATION GAIN: 1,077'

MAXIMUM ELEVATION: 1,520'

When Hawk Mountain Sanctuary was established in 1938, it was the first wildlife refuge devoted to the protection of birds of prey. The nonprofit organization was founded by Rosalie Edge, who leased the land four years earlier to stop hunters from killing migrating raptors for sport. Since then, the information collected by Hawk Mountain Sanctuary has been extremely valuable to scientists and conservationists studying changes in the raptor population of eastern North America. Raptor sightings logged by staff members, volunteers, and birdwatching enthusiasts are tallied and organized by species to provide a year-by-year overview of the population health and density of the majestic birds. From August to December it is very common to see throngs of birdwatchers on exposed portions of the mountain intently scanning the skies for various migrating birds of prey.

Hawk Mountain Sanctuary also maintains close to 10 miles of hiking trails that visit the rocky ridgetop and circle a small boulder field in the valley to the south. The hike described here drops into the valley on the River of Rocks Trail to explore the boulder field, then it climbs to the top of the ridge and leads back to a popular raptor sighting area by following the narrow spine of the mountain. The ridgetop trail visits several rugged overlooks and traverses areas of large, disordered rocks. Hikers will need to use both hands and feet to ascend at a few points. A few options exist to shorten the hike. Please note that Hawk Mountain Sanctuary is a privately owned, self-sufficient wildlife preserve that requires visitors to either pay a small entrance fee or purchase a membership to use the trail system. The sanctuary does not allow dogs on their trail system.

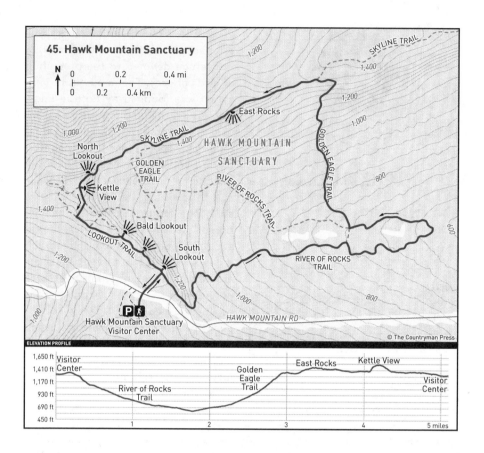

GETTING THERE

From the west, follow I-76 E. Take exit 226 and merge onto US 11 N toward Harrisburg. Keep right and in 2.2 miles merge onto I-81 N. Follow I-81 N for 36.8 miles. Take exit 89 and merge onto I-78 E toward Allentown. Drive for 28.5 miles. Take exit 29 for PA 61 N toward Pottsville. At the end of the ramp turn left onto PA 61 N. Follow PA 61 N for 4.5 miles and turn right onto PA 895 E, continuing for 2.5 miles. Turn right onto Hawk Mountain Road and drive for 2.1 miles, heading steadily uphill. Turn right into Hawk Mountain Sanctuary and follow signs to the parking lot and make your way to the visitor center.

From the east, follow I-78 W. Take exit 40 onto PA 737 N toward Krumsville. At the end of the ramp, turn right onto PA 737 N. Drive for 5.3 miles. In Kempton turn left to stay on PA 737 N for another 0.5 mile. Turn left onto PA 143 S and drive for 0.4 mile, then turn right onto Hawk Mountain Road. Drive for 6.7 miles, then turn left into Hawk Mountain Sanctuary. Follow signs toward the parking area, and proceed to the visitor center.

GPS Shortcut: Enter "Hawk Mountain Sanctuary" into Google Maps and your GPS will direct you to the trailhead.

THE HIKE

Before beginning the hike be sure to stop at the visitor center and pay the admission fee. Trail maps are also available from the center, and they are recommended if you plan on altering the route described in this entry. After leaving the visitor center, head down the wide gravel path that leads toward Hawk Mountain Road. Cross the road and go through a wooden gate to enter the trail system on the orange-blazed Lookout Trail, passing a restroom building immediately. Head up a short, relaxed incline following the wide, easy trail for approximately 0.1 mile to arrive at the South Lookout. The South Lookout gazes out over the boulder field to the southeast in the valley below. When you are ready to continue, turn down the red-blazed River of Rocks Trail, which breaks off the Lookout Trail to the right, just before reaching the South Lookout vista.

Upon joining the River of Rocks Trail, the terrain becomes much more rugged and challenging, with lots of roots and rocks sticking out of the ground along a narrow, moderately descending tread that drops into the valley. In 0.2 mile, the trail bends to the left in a wash of jumbled boulders, continuing to descend. A few hundred feet beyond the turn, an Adirondack-style shelter can be seen off in the distance on the right side of the trail. The shelter is maintained by Hawk Mountain Sanctuary, and it is available for use only by members who reserve and pay in advance. Keep heading downhill on the River of Rocks Trail, going into the heart of the valley, winding through the woods and scrambling over a slew of chunky boulders. Go straight across a dirt service road that intersects the trail and continue to descend. The trail goes over a wooden footbridge that spans a small stream and enters a rhododendron stand immediately afterward. Roughly 0.7 mile in, as the elevation change

THE RIVER OF ROCKS TRAIL

starts to relax, an exposed boulder field will begin to come into view on the left side of the trail. The boulder field, created by periglacial activity during the Pleistocene period, is the namesake of the River of Rocks Trail, providing not-so-subtle hints as to why the terrain along the footpath is so rough.

The forest up until this point has been almost entirely deciduous, but in the valley, small white pines and the occasional hemlock start to fill in the landscape. You will cross several small seasonal streams as you advance, especially during rainy periods and in the springtime. The rocks that slow your progress can usually be used to traverse these watercourses without getting your feet too wet, but this rule does not always hold true. In a few instances, it may appear as though the only place

SURVEYING THE COUNTRYSIDE FROM THE NORTH LOOKOUT

there is not a stone to step on is precisely where you need to place your foot.

At the 1.3 mile mark, the River of Rocks Trail intersects with the Golden Eagle Trail, which breaks off to the left, heading across the boulder field and entering the woods on the other side. If you turn left onto the Golden Eagle Trail here, you will shorten the hike by 0.9 mile. Turn right, continuing to follow the red blazes and head gradually uphill on the remains of a wide, grassy woods road for less than 0.1 mile, then turn left and leave the road grade behind, resuming your course on the narrow, difficult tread. At certain points through this section of the sanctuary the trail advances over portions of trail so rocky that the only place to paint blazes is on the rocks themselves. The route is very well-marked, but in these areas it can be easy to drift off the trail, so pay attention to which way the blazes point. As before, the trail crosses a few seasonal runs as you circle the boulder field, and it continues to descend gradually.

At mile 1.8, briefly exit the evergreen forest as the trail curves to the left around the far eastern tip of the boulder field, where the trees seem to be growing straight out of the rocks. Continue following the red-blazed trail, which reenters mixed forest on the northern side of the boulder field. The trail is still very challenging on this side of the rocky expanse, and instead of descending, it begins to gain elevation at an equally mellow angle. In 0.3 mile after starting the relaxed ascent, enter a dense stand of rhododendrons and cross the same stream twice, both times with the aid of footbridges.

In another 0.1 mile, the River of Rocks Trail reconnects with the Golden Eagle Trail. Turn right onto the yellow-blazed Golden Eagle Trail and begin ascending moderately for 0.4 mile up the side of the ridge. The trail soon becomes much steeper, crossing a few more wet areas as it climbs. Sometimes the trail resembles an old road grade, but more often than not it follows the same jumbled terrain you traversed near the boulder field. Once the angle of ascent starts

intensifying, the trail narrows to the span of a generous singletrack and the terrain becomes a little smoother.

Just before the 3-mile mark, the Golden Eagle Trail bends to the left abruptly and ends a short distance later, where it meets with the Skyline Trail on top of the ridge. Turn to the left and begin following the blue-blazed Skyline Trail, heading west along the ridgetop. The trail on top of the ridge is relatively flat and easy at the start, but 0.2 mile after leaving the Golden Eagle Trail, the blue blazes of the Skyline Trail lead up a short, steep, rocky climb. After the short ascent, the ridge narrows to a very thin spine of stone. Take your time on the rough terrain and continue along the crest of the ridge. In another 0.2 mile, arrive at the East Rocks summit. An excellent viewpoint here gazes south, over the boulder fields in the valley toward The Pinnacle, a prominent point on the neighboring ridge. The hike to The Pinnacle is described in the next entry.

Beyond East Rocks, the trail follows the rugged spine of the mountain for 0.3 mile, occasionally arriving at exposed areas that peek above the trees to glimpse far-reaching views to the south and north. At mile 3.7, the trail descends a short distance as the ridge broadens. In 0.2 mile, approach the junction with the other end of the Golden Eagle Trail. The Golden Eagle Trail descends to the left, heading back into the valley. Instead, keep right and continue to follow the Skyline Trail, lazily skirting the base of a clumpy rock formation. The Skyline Trail goes up and over another ledge similar to the East Rocks formation, then it begins a very steep climb up crude stone steps under the shade and cover of hemlocks and rhododendrons. This portion of the trail requires the use of both hands and feet, and it is fairly exposed, so use caution and advance carefully.

Arrive at the North Lookout a short distance past the 4.2 mile mark. From this exposed stone precipice, a sweeping panoramic view of the surrounding

THE PINNACLE AS SEEN FROM EAST ROCKS

LOOKING OUT OVER HAWK MOUNTAIN SANCTUARY

ridges and countryside can be enjoyed. This is a popular area for birdwatching, so expect the vista to be crowded, with large groups of people excitedly peering through binoculars in search of migrating birds of prey in the sky above. Continue into the woods on the other side of the vista, and pick up the orange blazes of the Lookout Trail, which descends from the vista on comparatively easy terrain, passing a wooden walkway, the Kettle View, and a pit toilet past the North Lookout.

Roughly 0.1 mile after leaving the exposed vista, the Lookout Trail reaches the junction with the Escarpment Trail, which breaks off to the left. If you are still in the mood to clamber over rocks and enjoy viewpoints, turn left onto the Escarpment Trail; otherwise, continue to follow the wide, easy Lookout Trail on

your way back to the parking area. Both trails head in the same direction and are roughly the same length. The difference is that the Escarpment Trail navigates the lip of the mountain on very rocky terrain that features several short ups and downs, whereas the Lookout Trail follows a much easier, much more direct course. The Escarpment Trail rejoins the Lookout Trail in 0.2 mile. Follow the orange-blazed trail downhill at a relaxed rate, passing the Bald Lookout, Ridge Overlook, and River of Rocks Overlook.

At the 4.9-mile mark, arrive back at the South Lookout you visited just before dropping into the valley on the River of Rocks Trail. From here, turn right and head toward Hawk Mountain Road and the visitor center. You will arrive back at the parking area in 0.2 mile.

Pulpit Rock and The Pinnacle

DISTANCE: 9.2 miles

DIFFICULTY: Difficult

HIKING TIME: 4 hours

TYPE: Loop

TOTAL ELEVATION GAIN: 1,197'

MAXIMUM ELEVATION: 1,614'

Widely regarded by many Appalachian Trail thru-hikers to be the two best viewpoints in the state of Pennsylvania, Pulpit Rock and The Pinnacle offer excellent views of Berks and Lehigh Counties. The vistas, which are located on property owned by the Hamburg Borough Watershed, sit east of the Furnace Creek–fed Hamburg Reservoir. A tract of private land near Pulpit Rock is accented by a collection of telescope domes that are owned and operated by the Lehigh Valley Amateur Astronomical Society. The society occasionally hosts night sky viewing events that are open to the public. The wooded land supports the Appalachian Trail as well as a handful of other footpaths, most of them repurposed from service roads.

The hike to Pulpit Rock and The Pinnacle follows the Appalachian Trail northbound on uneven, rocky terrain. The course features a fair amount of elevation change initially, giving way to a relatively flat ridgetop walk through the forest. Just before beginning the ascent, the Appalachian Trail passes Windsor Furnace Shelter, an Adirondack-style shelter intended for thru-hikers and other backpackers. This is the only area on the lands of the Hamburg Borough Watershed where overnight camping is allowed. If you plan to stay overnight, be sure to contact the city offices of Hamburg Borough to register your vehicle to avoid being towed or ticketed. Additionally, please be aware that this hike is extremely popular. The parking area is routinely full and the summit can be quite crowded on summer weekends, so plan on hiking The Pinnacle during the week if you want to avoid crowds. Overflow parking is available at certain points along the road leading to the trailhead.

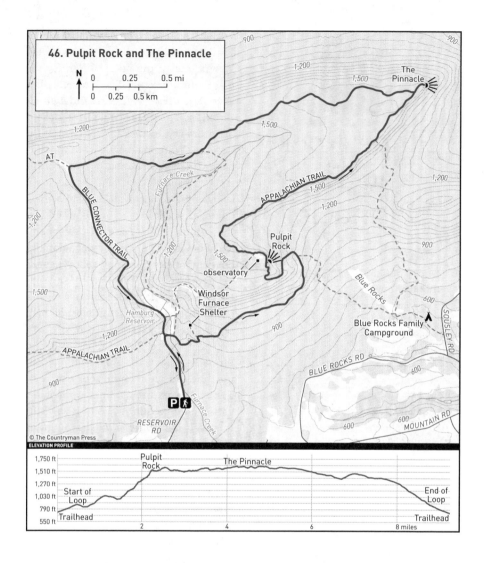

46. Pulpit Rock and The Pinnacle

GETTING THERE

From the west, follow I-76 E. Take exit 226 and merge onto US 11 N toward Harrisburg. Keep right and in 2.2 miles merge onto I-81 N. Follow I-81 N for 36.8 miles. Take exit 89 toward Allentown and merge onto I-78 E. Drive for 29.4 miles. Take exit 30 toward Hamburg, and at the end of the ramp turn right onto N 4th Street. Drive for 0.5 mile. Turn left onto Old US Route 22 and drive for 2.2 miles. Turn left onto Reservoir Road and

pass under the highway. In 0.9 mile, you will arrive at the parking area next to the Hamburg Reservoir Pumphouse. If the parking lot is full, park alongside the road. Take care not to not obstruct traffic or disobey road signs.

From the east, follow I-78 W. Take exit 35 for PA 143 toward Lenhartsville. Turn left at the end of the ramp and follow PA 143 N for 0.7 mile. Turn left onto Mountain Road and continue for 2.9 miles. Turn right onto Reservoir Road and follow it for 0.4 mile to where it ends at the

Hamburg Reservoir Pumphouse. The hike starts from here. If the lot is full, parking is available along the roadside, but be sure not to block any access roads.

GPS Shortcut: Type "Pinnacle Trail Head, AT Access" into Google Maps and your GPS will navigate to the parking area, located near the borough of Hamburg.

THE HIKE

From the parking area at the end of Reservoir Road head north, passing by an information kiosk and ducking behind a metal gate to join a wide gravel road. Follow the blue blazes along this flat road grade, which trends very gradually uphill. In 0.2 mile, another gravel road breaks off to the right, leading toward a utility building near the flow of Furnace Creek. Stay to the left and continue following the blue blazes for another 0.2 mile, at which point the gravel road bends to the right and meets with the tread of the Appalachian Trail, a junction marked by a wooden sign. Merge onto the Appalachian Trail and begin

HIKING ALONG THE APPALACHIAN TRAIL

TRAIL SIGN POINTING TOWARD THE VISTAS

to follow its white blazes. The trail stays on the wide gravel road grade and very quickly crosses a small bridge that goes over Furnace Creek. Arrive at a fork in the road on the other side of the creek. Turning to the left leads toward the reservoir, while the Appalachian Trail enters the woods on the right. Keep right and follow the Appalachian Trail.

The historic white-blazed trail descends a short distance beyond the fork, then it curves to the left and begins a gradual ascent on wide and bumpy tread, passing a small stream that feeds into a marshy pond. Arrive at a signed trail intersection about 0.3 mile after meeting with the Appalachian Trail. Going straight ahead from this point for 0.1 mile on a blue-blazed connector trail will lead to the Windsor Furnace Shelter, which features a picnic table, a privy, and room for several tents. Turn right

THE VIEW FROM PULPIT ROCK

to stay on the Appalachian Trail. After passing the spur toward the shelter, the trail climbs gradually and consistently on increasingly rocky terrain, meandering through mixed forest dotted with short, shrubby mountain laurels.

The trail briefly levels out at the 1.1 mile mark, continuing on the flat course for roughly 0.3 mile before dipping in elevation a short distance and then begins a moderately steep ascent. You will come to another blue-blazed trail that leads to the Blue Rocks Family Campground after 0.3 mile of climbing. Stay on the white-blazed trail and continue to ascend steeply on a winding course that bends first to the left, then to the right. At 2.1 miles in, the Appalachian Trail makes an abrupt, easily missed right-hand turn, leaving the relatively wide path. Take the right turn to follow the Appalachian Trail. From here, continue over several large boulders and

a flight of steep stone steps that twists and turns toward the top of the ridge. It can be easy to drift off the trail here, so pay close attention to the blazes to avoid missing a turn, and to discern the correct route on the intense rocky climb.

Reach the top of the ridge at the 2.2-mile mark. A short distance after passing through a gap in the rocky crest, the Appalachian Trail arrives at a small clearing. To the left is a grassy private observatory area, with several telescope domes owned by the Lehigh Valley Amateur Astronomical Society. On the right is Pulpit Rock, one of two vistas on this hike. The viewpoint faces the northeast from the top of a small cliff, surveying the surrounding hills and the Blue Rocks boulder field below, which contrasts sharply with the forest all around it.

After leaving Pulpit Rock, the Appalachian Trail continues along the rocky ridgetop, circumnavigating a vast, sloping depression on the wooded rim. The trail passes a radio tower in 0.3 mile, then follows some small, rolling ups and downs. At mile 2.9, toward the end of the arcing course, the Appalachian Trail passes through a corridor walled in on either side by craggy boulders. Immediately afterward, it arrives at a junction with a red-blazed connector trail. The red-blazed trail breaks off to the left and meets with another trail that descends toward the reservoir. You want to keep right and follow the white blazes through a cluster of jumbled boulders, resuming a northeastern bearing.

The narrow trail advances along the edge of the broad ridge on rough, undulating terrain, hemmed in by dense brush. In 1.1 miles, a yellow-blazed trail will appear from the right. This trail descends steeply into the valley and eventually leads to the Blue Rocks Family Campground. Go straight past this footpath and follow the Appalachian Trail for another 0.4 mile. At this point, you will reach a very large talus pile. The Appalachian Trail turns to the left here, but a sign in front of the talus pile points in the opposite direction toward The Pinnacle. Turn right and follow the blue-blazed spur for 0.1 mile, emerging from the tree cover onto the exposed viewpoint at The Pinnacle. You will want to set aside plenty of time to enjoy the vista, which faces east. This large, broad point on the end of the ridge offers expansive 180-degree views of the surrounding farmland and the nearby ridges. It is a popular destination to catch the sunrise. There are numerous places to sit all along the edge of the outcropping. The ledge is known to support a variety of snakes that like to bask on the sun-warmed stone, so pay attention to where you step. Additionally, the narrow shaft of a vertical cave opens on the northern end of the vista. Take care to peer into the darkness at a safe distance,

HAMBURG RESERVOIR

PASTORAL SCENERY SEEN FROM THE PINNACLE

as a fall into the cave would certainly require swift medical attention.

When you are finished enjoying The Pinnacle, head back up the blue-blazed spur trail toward the talus pile, then continue along the Appalachian Trail heading west. The terrain remains extremely rocky for 0.3 mile, eventually giving way to a woods road which, while not completely void of rocks, is much smoother. Generally speaking, the woods road is wide enough that you can easily avoid any patches of pointy rocks. The Appalachian Trail passes several vernal ponds before entering a corridor of mountain laurels, pines, and hemlocks.

At 6.3 miles, the trail enters a large, grassy clearing and meets with another blue-blazed trail that appears to the left. This trail descends to the reservoir in 1.4 miles, meeting with the previously mentioned red-blazed trail after 0.3 mile. It then continues along cobbly terrain that mirrors the flow of Furnace Creek. The course described here will eventually lead to the reservoir, but turning here to follow the blue-blazed trail will shorten the hike by 0.5 mile. Continue straight on the Appalachian Trail, exit the field, descend gradually for 0.3 mile, then head up and over a short hill at an equally relaxed angle.

In 1 mile after leaving the field, the Appalachian Trail turns to the right, extending for another 960 miles to where it ends at Mount Katahdin in Maine. Instead of continuing along the Appalachian Trail, turn left and pick up another blue-blazed trail, heading south on a grassy woods road. The trail assumes a nearly flat grade, trending downhill on a fairly straight trajectory for 0.7 mile before bending to the right and zigzagging downhill on a moderately steep slope for 0.6 mile.

Arrive at the reservoir and continue descending, passing the outlet channel and a metal barrier a short distance later. Emerge from the woods onto the gravel road you started the hike on. Retrace your footsteps down the gravel road, reaching the parking area in 0.4 mile.

Governor Dick Park

DISTANCE: 5.7 miles

DIFFICULTY: Moderate

HIKING TIME: 2.5 hours

TYPE: Loop

TOTAL ELEVATION GAIN: 696'

MAXIMUM ELEVATION: 1,148'

Lancaster County businessman and philanthropist Clarence Schock took over his father's business at the age of 30, between 1895 and 1896. The company, then named the Schock Independent Oil Company, produced lumber, charcoal, kerosene, and other oil products, partially operating on land outside of the borough of Mount Gretna, where he and his wife also owned a summer home. The land their summer home was located on is purportedly named after a man named Dick who worked the forest as early as 1880, chopping trees and monitoring the smoldering charcoal piles. Over the years he became known as Governor Dick due to his skill and prowess in the trade, and the name stuck to the area. Clarence and Evetta Schock cared deeply for the surrounding communities that supported their business, and they made arrangements so that after their deaths their fortune would benefit the general public of those communities in the form of a trust that funded local schools.

Clarence and Evetta Schock, who passed away in 1955 and 1956 respectively, made the mountain that their summer home occupied open to the public as early as 1936. Today, Governor Dick Park is operated by Lebanon County, and the park is open to the public for recreation and educational purposes. Governor Dick Park features more than 18 miles of trail and is a very popular destination for bouldering, mountain biking, and hiking. The hike described here follows a circuitous route throughout the park, passing several huge boulders and stopping by a 66-foot-tall observation tower that overlooks the forest. The vast network of trails running through the park allows for numerous options for route customization. With the exception of the Horseshoe Trail and two other minor connectors, each

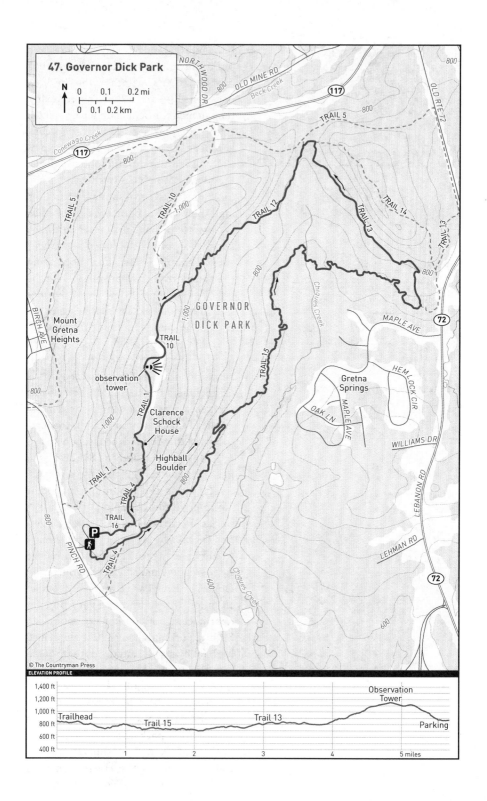

47. Governor Dick Park

N
0   0.1   0.2 mi
0   0.1 0.2 km

NORTHWOOD DR
OLD MINE RD
Beck Creek
117
800
800
800
OLD RTE 72
TRAIL 5
800
Conewago Creek
117
800
TRAIL 5
TRAIL 10
1,000
TRAIL 12
800
TRAIL 13
TRAIL 14
TRAIL 13
800
72
BIRCH AVE
Mount
Gretna
Heights
800
1,000
TRAIL
10
GOVERNOR
DICK PARK
1,000
Chiques Creek
MAPLE AVE
HEMLOCK CIR
observation
tower
TRAIL 1
TRAIL 15
Gretna
Springs
OAK LN
MAPLE AVE
Clarence
Schock
House
WILLIAMS DR
1,000
Highball
Boulder
800
TRAIL 1
TRAIL 4
TRAIL
16
LEBANON RD
LEHMAN RD
800
P
PINCH RD
TRAIL 4
600
72
Chiques Creek
600
600

© The Countryman Press

ELEVATION PROFILE

1,400 ft
1,200 ft
1,000 ft   Trailhead   Observation
800 ft   Tower
600 ft   Trail 15   Trail 13   Parking
400 ft
          1   2   3   4   5 miles

trail is numbered and blazed with a color and shape unique to that trail alone, and a plastic stake marks the beginning of each trail. For the uninitiated, it can be a little overwhelming to navigate this trail system. For these reasons it is highly recommended that hikers acquire a copy of the trail map. Trail maps can be downloaded from the park's website, or they can be picked up from the Clarence Schock Environmental Center.

GETTING THERE

From the west, follow I-76 E. Take exit 266 for PA 72 toward Lebanon/Lancaster. At the end of the ramp, turn right onto PA 72 S. Follow PA 72 S for 0.9 mile. Turn right onto Cider Press Road and drive for 0.4 mile, then turn right once more onto Pinch Road. Drive 1.7 miles. The paved parking area will be on the right side of the road, outside of the Clarence Schock Environmental Center.

From the east, follow I-76 W. Take exit 266 for PA 72 toward Lebanon/Lancaster. At the end of the ramp, turn right onto PA 72 S. Follow PA 72 S for 0.9 mile. Turn right onto Cider Press Road and continue for 0.4 mile, then make a right onto Pinch Road. Drive 1.7 miles. The parking area will be on the right side of the road, outside of the Clarence Schock Environmental Center.

GPS Shortcut: Type "Governor Dick Parking Lot" into Google Maps and your GPS will direct you to the parking area, located in front of the Clarence Schock Environmental Center.

THE HIKE

Park in the gated circular parking area outside of the environmental center. The area features a few picnic tables, a pavilion, and some pit toilets. To begin

THE 66-FOOT OBSERVATION TOWER

the hike, walk halfway down the driveway toward Pinch Road and make a left-hand turn onto Trail 15, which is marked with white diamonds. Immediately go past a depressed clearing and enter the woods, following moderately rocky terrain. Approximately 0.2 mile in Trail 4, which is marked with red diamonds, appears from the left and joins with Trail 15. The two trails share tread for a short distance, passing close to a few interesting boulders. Trail 4 turns to the left next to a bench in 0.1 mile, while Trail 15 turns right. Follow the white diamonds of Trail 15 to the right, and begin descending moderately.

MEANDERING THROUGH THE FOREST ON TRAIL 15

As you follow Trail 15 downhill, you may notice that the soil in this part of the park is exceptionally dark. This is a result of the charcoaling process that was carried out on the land decades ago. Continue along the winding course of Trail 15, through thick, deciduous forest composed of maples, oaks, beech, and tulip poplar trees, as well as a large quantity of shrubby spicebush. The trail passes several large boulders over its course, some of which bear white chalk markings on their cracks and edges. These marks are from bouldering, which is a style of rock climbing. Climbers typically ascend no more than 40 feet,

without the use of harnesses or ropes. At the 0.7 mile mark, an impressive 22-foot-tall monolith can be seen on the left side of the trail. This is the Highball Boulder. It is not uncommon to see fearless boulderers attempting to climb the sheer, flat face of this imposing piece of stone.

At 0.2 mile down the trail from the Highball Boulder, make a sharp turn to the left, then a short distance later turn sharply to the right. The terrain gets progressively more rugged the farther away from the environmental center you get, with lots of roots and rocks complicating the footpath. Trail 15 has a reputation as having the most difficult terrain in Governor Dick Park, so take your time and place your feet carefully.

The trail continues through the rocky forest, eventually leveling out for the most part. At mile marker 1.7, Trail 15 dips while passing an oddly shaped stack of boulders to the left, skirting the base of the rocky cluster. Unless you are hiking during a drought, it is usually possible to hear water running underneath the rocks at this point. Keep hiking and cross a wooden footbridge that spans a seasonal run a short distance later. The trail crosses two more footbridges that go over Chiques Creek in another 0.4 mile, just north of a marshy area. For the next 0.6 mile beyond Chiques Creek, Trail 15 follows a serpentine course that regularly twists and turns through the forest. Pay close attention to the blazes to make sure you stay on the trail.

At mile 2.7, the white diamond-blazed Trail 15 ends at the junction with Trail 13. Turn left onto Trail 13 and begin following its course, which is marked with green diamonds. The trail ascends and descends at random intervals that are never terribly steep or prolonged. The terrain is still rocky and the tread is fairly narrow as it leads along the base of a thickly wooded hill to the left. After 0.9 mile, Trail 13 meets with the start of the yellow circle–blazed Trail 14. Turn left here and continue to follow the green diamonds of Trail 13 downhill for less than 0.1 mile to arrive at another intersection. Trail 12, which is marked with blue diamonds, breaks off Trail 13 at this junction. Turn left once more and follow the blazes of Trail 12. The blue diamond–blazed trail heads uphill moderately for 0.9 mile, passing through two or three wet, muddy areas. The climb, while not terribly rocky or tiresome on the whole, does navigate a few stretches of steep, rough slope.

At the 4.5-mile marker, the blue diamond trail meets with the wide tread of Trail 10. Turn left onto Trail 10, which is blazed with a red and white rectangle, and follow it for 0.1 mile. Turn left onto the red rectangle–blazed Trail 2 at this point, continuing to follow wide woods road grade. Arrive at the observation tower in 0.2 mile, at mile 4.8. The unique concrete tower can be climbed via a series of internal ladders that lead to the caged-in platform on its top. A 360-degree view can be enjoyed from the top of the tower that surveys the countryside surrounding the park. Be aware that the tower area is a very popular attraction, which features several picnic tables and benches, and is occasionally quite busy and crowded.

Continue on the wide gravel road past the tower. This is Trail 1, an unmarked fire road. Although it is not blazed it is very easy to follow, passing a few benches over the next 0.3 mile. At mile 5.1, the fire road meets with Trail 4, which breaks off to the left. Trail 4, which briefly shared tread with Trail 15 at the beginning of the hike, is marked with red diamonds. Turn onto Trail 4 and begin following its blazes on much

narrower tread. The red diamonds lead past the ruins of the Clarence Schock Tower House a short distance after leaving the fire road. There is not much left of the house, except for a few crumbling bits of foundation. Still, it is an interesting piece of history that remains culturally significant to the area. Beyond the Clarence Schock Tower House ruins, Trail 4 descends moderately at first, quickly becoming steep, winding, and rocky for 0.4 mile.

Just after mile 5.5, turn right onto the Trail 16, also known as the Interpretive Trail. This easy, smooth trail is marked with white circles. It splits in a very short distance. Keep left at the split and continue along its tread for a little over 0.1 mile to arrive back at the environmental center and the parking lot.

HIKING OVER BOULDERS AT GOVERNOR DICK PARK

48

Kellys Run Loop

DISTANCE: 5.9 miles

DIFFICULTY: Difficult

HIKING TIME: 3 hours

TYPE: Loop

TOTAL ELEVATION GAIN: 1,243'

MAXIMUM ELEVATION: 731'

Managed by the Lancaster Conservancy, Kellys Run Nature Preserve sits on the eastern shore of the Susquehanna River and is flanked by the Pinnacle Overlook Nature Preserve to the northwest and the Holtwood Nature Preserve to the south. Lancaster Conservancy acquired 55 acres of land for the preserve when a local man, Thomas Stuart, donated his property; and the other 430 acres were a gift from PPL, Talen Energy, and Brookfield Renewable Partners. Kellys Run, the namesake for the tract, is a scenic and serpentine creek that flows through the preserve, draining directly into the Susquehanna River. A small but robust network of hiking trails adorns the land. The most prominent of them is the Conestoga Trail. This 63-mile foot-path connects the Horseshoe Trail with the Mason-Dixon Trail.

This hike follows the Kellys Run Trail as it loops through the preserve. For about half of its length the Kellys Run Trail shares tread with the Conestoga Trail, following a course beside the run itself through dense rhododendrons that cling to the steep gorge walls. Incredibly beautiful at any time of year, Kellys Run is popular for its deep reflecting pools and rocky precipices that line the water's edge. About halfway into the hike, an optional out-and-back segment follows the Conestoga Trail along a bluff on the edge of the Susquehanna River, leading to the Pinnacle Overlook. Not to be confused with The Pinnacle in Berks County, Pinnacle Overlook features a magnificent view of the wide, gentle bends of the Susquehanna River from a fenced-in perch and a craggy rock outcropping.

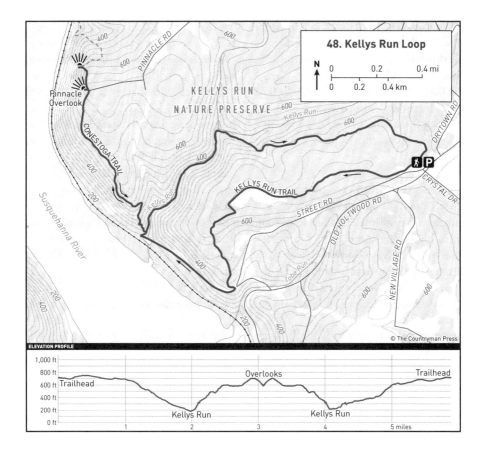

GETTING THERE

From the west, follow I-76 E. Take exit 242 to merge onto I-83 S. Continue for 21.8 miles on I-83 S. Take exit 18 for PA 124 toward Mt. Rose Avenue. At the end of the ramp turn left onto PA 124 E and drive for 1.4 miles. Turn right onto PA 24 S, then in 0.7 mile turn left onto Windsor Road. Follow Windsor Road for 4.4 miles, then make a right onto N Penn Street. Cross PA 624 and rejoin Windsor Road, continuing for 1 mile. Turn left onto PA 74 S and drive for 14.2 miles. Turn left onto PA 372 E and drive for 4 miles. Turn left onto Crystal Drive and follow it for 0.7 mile to reach the parking area, a gravel lot in front of a pavilion at Holtwood Recreation Area.

From the east, drive I-76 W. Take exit 328A, merging onto US 202 S. Follow US 202 S for 11.4 miles and take the exit for US 30 W toward Downingtown/Coatesville. Follow US 30 W for 20.7 miles, then turn left onto Swan Road. In 2.7 miles, turn left onto Green Street and cross a set of railroad tracks. Make the next right onto Valley Avenue and drive for 1.2 miles. Turn left onto Noble Road and follow it for 0.2 mile, then turn right onto Upper Valley Road. In 2.3 miles, Upper Valley Road becomes Valley Road; and 6.6 miles afterward Valley Road becomes E State Street and merges with PA 372 W. Follow PA 372 W for 4.8 miles, then turn left onto Friendly Road. Follow Friendly Road for 0.7 mile, then rejoin PA 372 W and drive for another

4.2 miles. Veer right onto Old Holtwood Road and drive for 0.9 mile to reach the parking area, a gravel lot in front of a pavilion at Holtwood Recreation Area.

GPS Shortcut: In Google Maps, search for "Holtwood Recreation Area" and set the result as your destination.

THE HIKE

Join the Kellys Run Trail in front of the picnic pavilion that sits at the north end of the parking lot. The trail is marked with blue blazes, and it runs to the left and the right from Holtwood Recreation Area. Turn to the left and follow the blue blazes going west, following a wide grassy trail that is level and well-graded.

DEEP IN THE KELLYS RUN RAVINE

The Kellys Run Trail passes underneath two power line swaths, the first immediately after leaving the parking area, and the second in 0.3 mile. In another 0.3 mile, the blue-blazed trail meets with a red-blazed footpath to the right that follows a northward trajectory, bisecting the Kellys Run circuit and connecting to the other half of the loop. Go straight past this junction and continue to follow the Kellys Run Trail with its blue blazes that adorn wooden posts through the open and airy expanse of a large field. The trail meanders gently through the clearing, turning to the left at its far end to skirt the edge of the woods for a short distance before turning right and reentering the tree cover at the 1-mile mark.

After leaving the field, the Kellys Run Trail begins to descend moderately, bending to the left and advancing along narrow singletrack tread through forest thick with brush. You will pass a few oddly placed wooden benches as you make your way downhill. In 0.4 mile, arrive at the gated end of Old Pinnacle Road and Street Road. Cross the road here and turn right to go behind the metal gate and continue to descend steadily, following the paved surface of a buckled, crumbling roadbed. This disused road is a strange part of the Kellys Run Trail, though it provides partially obstructed views of the Susquehanna River, which lies approximately 500 feet to the left.

In 0.5 mile after joining the old paved road, the trail approaches the shore of Kellys Run and a railroad line, bypassing the remains of a dilapidated bridge by turning off the pavement to the right. Cross Kellys Run on a string of short stepping-stones. Turn right on the other side and start to head upstream. Immediately after turning, however, the Kellys Run Trail meets with the Conestoga

HIKING PAST TUMBLING WATERS ON KELLYS RUN

Trail. Turning onto the Conestoga Trail here will lead to the Pinnacle Overlook, climbing strenuously to the top of the wooded riverbank. If you want to skip the hike to the Pinnacle Overlook, stay straight and continue following the blue-blazed Kellys Run Trail and the continuation of the orange-blazed Conestoga Trail upstream. Doing so will shorten the hike by 2.2 miles.

To visit the Pinnacle Overlook, turn left and begin following the orange blazes of the Conestoga Trail very steeply uphill on rocky terrain, weaving your way in between several large boulders. The orange blazes meet with an old woods road grade about halfway up the riverbank. Turn right onto the woods road and climb uphill moderately for about 200 feet, arriving at a junction with a few different trails. Turn left and leave the road, resuming the steep, arduous ascent. The grade of the Conestoga Trail relaxes after roughly 0.3 mile of intense climbing, then continues ascending moderately on narrow, rocky sidehill tread 300 feet above the Susquehanna River. Meander through oaks and sparse pines on this elevated route, passing a few clearings on slanting stone faces that provide patchy views through the trees. The Conestoga Trail joins another woods road grade past this area, leveling off for a short distance, then continuing the steady ascent on the wide tread. Arrive at the Pinnacle Overlook at the 2.8 mile mark. From this fenced-in clearing, an impressive, far-reaching view can be seen of the bending Susquehanna River, looking northward. There is a gravel parking area here, a few picnic tables, and benches too. Roughly 0.1 mile up the Conestoga Trail is a similar viewpoint on top of an exposed cliff. To reach this rugged vista, follow the orange blazes north and descend on a moderately steep dirt road grade in between the steep drop-off to the left and an old stone fence on the right. The rocky vista will be on the left, a short distance off trail on an obvious herd path. When you are finished at the Pinnacle Overlook, turn around and retrace your footsteps on the Conestoga Trail to head back to Kellys Run.

Turn left onto the blue-blazed Kellys Run Trail and follow the flowing water upstream on a pleasant creekside path. The Conestoga Trail shares tread with this footpath for the remainder of the hike, so you will see occasional orange blazes interspersed with the blue blazes. The trail crosses the water at a few points, making use of well-placed stepping-stones to advance through the V-shaped ravine, heading gradually uphill. Kellys Run bends sharply in a few places, flowing around sheer walls of stone and over bouldery masses of rock, forming quietly singing cascades and broad, shallow reflecting pools. The hills on either side of the run are heavily populated with lush green rhododendrons, contributing further to the scenic nature of the area.

The blue blazes follow the flow of Kellys Run for 0.7 mile on rolling terrain,

VIEWPOINT OVER THE SUSQUEHANNA RIVER

VIEW OF THE MIGHTY SUSQUEHANNA RIVER LOOKING NORTHWEST

sometimes leading right beside the edge of the water and other times following it from a farther-removed course on the canyon wall. When you come to the confluence of two branches of Kellys Run, turn right and cross both streams, then continue to follow the flowing water uphill along the base of a towering rock wall. At 0.1 mile after the double water crossing, the Kellys Run Trail bends to the right and begins to climb a moderately steep incline, heading away from the water.

At 5.1 miles in, pass the northern terminus of the red-blazed connector trail you passed at the beginning of the hike on the right side of the trail. Continue straight on undulating terrain to follow the blue blazes, revisiting both of the power line swaths you crossed earlier. In 0.5 mile, upon exiting the second power line swath, the Kellys Run Trail enters a shady patch of forest composed of thorny underbrush, American holly, spruce, and white pine. Make your way through this short stand of dark, moody trees for 0.1 mile, emerging into a grassy field and climbing a short knoll.

At this point, the parking area and the pavilion will be visible in the distance slightly to the right. Follow the blue-blazed Kellys Run Trail for the remaining 0.2 mile to arrive back at your vehicle.

49

Wissahickon North Gorge Loop

DISTANCE: 5.2 miles

DIFFICULTY: Moderate

HIKING TIME: 2.5 hours

TYPE: Loop

TOTAL ELEVATION GAIN: 855'

MAXIMUM ELEVATION: 365'

Wissahickon Valley Park is a 2,042-acre city park managed by Philadelphia Parks & Recreation. The park largely follows the Wissahickon Creek Gorge, stretching north from the confluence with the Lehigh River. The park boasts an impressive 50 miles of trail, including the gravelly bike path tread of Forbidden Drive, as well as an assortment of more rugged footpaths that run throughout the gorge area on either side of the creek. Home to many historic bridges, houses, and monuments, Wissahickon Valley Park is an immersive haven from the busy city and is deeply relished by its many visitors.

This hike follows a number of trails through the Wissahickon Creek Gorge on a narrow loop that heads south along the water's edge. The route skirts the foot of several large rock formations and passes both the Rex Avenue Bridge and the Thomas Mill Covered Bridge. The second half of the hike heads north, following trails that travel the top of the gorge, primarily on rolling forest terrain. Many intersecting trails exist, should you wish to shorten or lengthen the hike. A detailed map of the park trail system is available for purchase from the Friends of the Wissahickon, a nonprofit organization that, since 1924, has played an integral part in the protection and recreational development of the park.

GETTING THERE

From the west, follow I-76 E. Pass exit 326 and stay straight to merge onto I-276 E. Take exit 333 toward Norristown and keep right at the end of the ramp to merge onto W Germantown Pike. Follow Germantown Pike for 3.6 miles. After crossing straight over W Northwestern Avenue, Germantown Pike

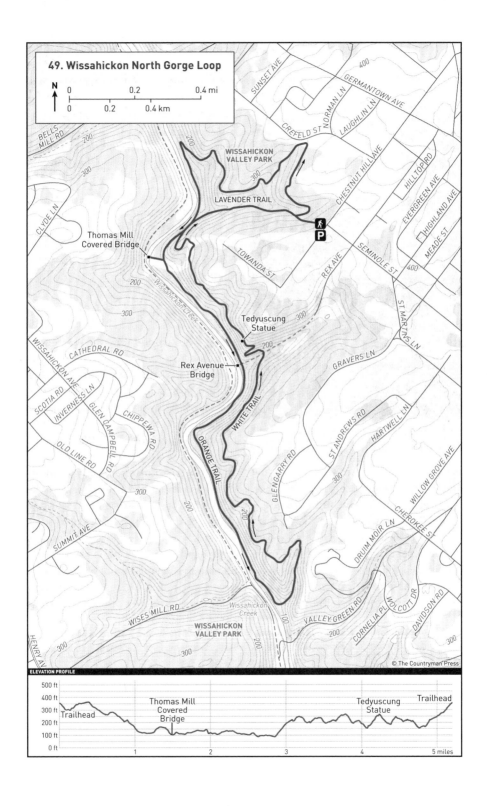

49. Wissahickon North Gorge Loop

N

0   0.2   0.4 mi
0   0.2   0.4 km

BELLS MILL RD

SUNSET AVE

NORMAN LN

CREFELD ST

GERMANTOWN AVE

LAUGHLIN LN

WISSAHICKON VALLEY PARK

CHESTNUT HILL AVE

HILLTOP RD

EVERGREEN AVE

HIGHLAND AVE

LAVENDER TRAIL

CLYDE LN

Thomas Mill Covered Bridge

TOWANDA ST

REX AVE

SEMINOLE ST

MEADE ST

Wissahickon Creek

Tedyuscung Statue

ST MARTINS LN

CATHEDRAL RD

Rex Avenue Bridge

GRAVERS LN

WISSAHICKON AVE

SCOTIA RD

INVERNESS LN

GLEN CAMPBELL RD

CHIPPEWA RD

WHITE TRAIL

ORANGE TRAIL

GLEN GARRY RD

ST ANDREWS RD

HARTWELL LN

WILLOW GROVE AVE

OLD LINE RD

SUMMIT AVE

CHEROKEE ST

DRUIM MOIR LN

CORNELIA PL

WOLCOTT DR

DAVIDSON RD

HENRY AV

WISES MILL RD

Wissahickon Creek

WISSAHICKON VALLEY PARK

VALLEY GREEN RD

© The Countryman Press

ELEVATION PROFILE

500 ft
400 ft
300 ft
200 ft
100 ft
0 ft

Trailhead

Thomas Mill Covered Bridge

Tedyuscung Statue

Trailhead

1   2   3   4   5 miles

THE TEDYUSCUNG STATUE PEERING OVER THE GORGE

Lane. In 0.5 mile, turn left on McCallum Street. Follow McCallum Street for 0.5 mile, then turn right onto W Mermaid Lane and continue for another 0.5 mile. Turn left onto St Martins Lane and follow it for 0.8 mile. Turn left onto Seminole Street and drive 0.3 mile to where it ends. Turn left onto W Chestnut Hill Avenue. The trailhead will be on the right in 200 feet. It is marked by a sign and an information kiosk.

GPS Shortcut: Type "Wissahickon Valley Park Chestnut Hill Parking" into Google Maps and your GPS will direct you to the trailhead.

THE HIKE

Enter the woods on the Lavender Trail, heading north from the parking area, and begin descending on a wide, bumpy path, aided by a handful of shallow steps. After 0.1 mile, at a four-way intersection, turn right and continue along the Lavender Trail. Walk a short distance upstream alongside a small watercourse that eventually empties into Wissahickon Creek. Turn to the left and cross the stream on a bridge and begin a short, gradual ascent on easy terrain. The forest in this area is composed primarily of oaks, beeches, and maples. A fair amount of English ivy grows all around here as well, covering the ground and creeping up the trees that populate the park.

Turn left just before the Crefeld Street trailhead and descend into a ravine, passing a large culvert and another creek bed on the right. In 0.2 mile, after a moderately rocky drop in elevation, arrive at another trail intersection. Turn right at this point and cross the creek bed on a footbridge to remain on the Lavender Trail. The trail climbs to the top of a hill and drops

becomes Germantown Avenue. Follow Germantown Avenue for 1.2 miles, then turn right onto W Chestnut Hill Avenue. Drive 0.4 mile, where the parking area will be on the right side of the road, 200 feet past the junction of Seminole Avenue.

The hike starts from the Chestnut Hill trailhead of Wissahickon Valley Park, northwest of center city Philadelphia. From downtown Philadelphia, follow I-76 W. Take exit 340B for US 1 N toward Roosevelt Boulevard. Merge onto US 1 N and drive for 1.5 miles. Take the exit toward Wissahickon Avenue N. Follow the ramp and merge onto Roberts Avenue, then keep right and merge onto Wissahickon Avenue. Drive for 2.9 miles. At this point Wissahickon Avenue turns right and becomes W Allens

down the other side, following rocky terrain and crossing a drainage channel on another wooden footbridge. A short distance later, at the 1-mile mark, reach the end of this leg of the Lavender Trail. Turn left onto the Orange Trail here and begin following it on the eastern bank of Wissahickon Creek. The terrain on the Orange Trail is rocky and rough, forcing you to clamber over blocky boulders as you continue downstream. In 0.2 mile, cross a concrete bridge that spans the stream you crossed earlier, just before it drains into Wissahickon Creek. The trail climbs moderately on the other side of the stream, entering a grove of hemlocks and rhododendrons. In 0.1 mile after the water crossing, arrive at a trail intersection with another leg of the Lavender Trail, which cuts back sharply to the left in the opposite direction, and the White Trail, which ascends a moderately steep incline ahead and to the left. Veer to the right to stay on the Orange Trail.

In another 0.1 mile, after descending a flight of stone steps, the Orange Trail comes to an old dirt road. Looking toward the creek on this dirt road, one can see Thomas Mill Covered Bridge, the only remaining covered bridge in Philadelphia. A small constructed waterfall is downstream just past the covered bridge. Continue on the Orange Trail as it mirrors the flow of Wissahickon Creek, ascending and descending at short, punctuated intervals for the next 0.5 mile, navigating the wooded bank and passing several interesting rock formations. Descend a flight of rustic steps and pass under a stone archway at mile 1.9 to reach the Rex Avenue Bridge. Similar to the Thomas Mill Covered Bridge, the Rex Avenue Bridge

THOMAS MILL COVERED BRIDGE

connects to the smooth gravel tread of Forbidden Drive on the other side of the creek. Cross Rex Avenue and go over a narrow stone walkway, continuing to follow the orange blazes. Over the next 0.9 mile, your course follows rugged terrain through thick forest that gives the illusion that you are much more secluded than you actually are.

At mile 2.8, the Orange Trail turns quickly to the left and meets with the White Trail. Turn left onto the White Trail, then veer to the right in about 100 feet where the White Trail splits, and begin ascending on a wide, gravel road. The gravel road, which climbs gradually but steadily for 0.2 mile, follows the edge

CREEKSIDE ASCENT ON THE WHITE TRAIL

of a small stream that empties into Wissahickon Creek. Turn left near the top of the gorge to stay on the White Trail, leaving the gravel road. In contrast with the low-lying tread of the Orange Trail, this portion of the White Trail meanders along the top of the creek gorge on moderate terrain near the drop-off. In 0.2 mile after turning off the gravel road, the other leg of the White Trail meets with your current course. Cross a drainage ditch on a plank footbridge and continue following the White Trail, descending to Rex Avenue once more at mile 4.

Go straight across Rex Avenue and bend to the left, climbing steeply up the hill on the other side. The trail climbs a moderately steep incline, switchbacking here and there to facilitate an easier ascent, regaining the top of the gorge in 0.2 mile. Pass a descending spur trail quickly after resuming your walk on top of the gorge. At the end of this short spur, down a steep flight of steps, is a very tall statue of a Native American man that peers over the gorge toward the west. The statue is commonly referred to as Tedyuscung after a Lenape man who worked to negotiate land rights for his people in the 1700s. While the statue of Tedyuscung stands in honor of an entire people group, he is something of a historical fallacy, being inaccurately portrayed in the ornate feather headdress worn by Native American tribes west of the Mississippi.

If you visited the statue, return to the White Trail. Keep following the White Trail for 0.4 mile to reach a busy trail intersection. Go straight, following the trajectory of the White Trail, crossing the remains of a sloping dirt road, then turn left 90 degrees at a bench that surveys the gorge. This cluster of marked trails and unofficial herd paths can be

IMPRESSIVE STONEWORK NEAR THE REX AVENUE BRIDGE

confusing to navigate, so pay close attention and take your time here. After turning at the bench, the White Trail curves around to the right for 0.1 mile, descending to the junction with the Orange Trail and the Lavender Trail you passed previously. From this junction, bear right onto the Lavender Trail.

Follow the Lavender Trail for the last 0.5 mile, ascending gradually on rooty, rocky terrain beside a small stream. After 0.4 mile, another leg of the Lavender Trail meets with your course from the left. Stay straight for a short distance to arrive at the four-way intersection the hike started on. Turn right here, ascend the wide path, and in approximately 0.1 mile arrive at your vehicle.

John Heinz National Wildlife Refuge

DISTANCE: 4 miles

DIFFICULTY: Easy

HIKING TIME: 2 hours

TYPE: Loop

TOTAL ELEVATION GAIN: 31'

MAXIMUM ELEVATION: 12'

Once a vast wetland spanning nearly 6,000 acres, Tinicum Marsh shrank significantly down to about 200 acres due to the explosion of industrialization and development that occurred after World War I. Today, the John Heinz National Wildlife Refuge protects the remaining marsh, which is the largest remaining freshwater tidal wetland in Pennsylvania and an important habitat for a wide variety of bird species. The refuge, originally known as the Tinicum Wildlife Refuge, grew through charitable donations to the City of Philadelphia and was awarded National Natural Landmark status in 1965. Seven years later, in 1972, the Department of the Interior absorbed a total of 1,200 acres of land that included the refuge and established the Tinicum National Environmental Center. The name was changed in 1991 to honor the work of Henry John Heinz III, who, among many others, worked to preserve the marsh from urbanization.

The hike described here wanders John Heinz National Wildlife Refuge on an easy circuit that visits two boardwalk areas, a handful of wildlife blinds, and a two-tier observation deck. The small trail system is popular with cyclists, runners, hikers, birdwatchers, and photographers due to the quantity of birds who either nest in and around the marsh or visit on their migratory journey. With almost a complete lack of elevation change, smooth terrain, and a large number of places to stop and enjoy the scenery, John Heinz National Wildlife Refuge can be enjoyed either as a quick afternoon excursion or as a relaxing, protracted wildlife experience. Consider bringing a pair of binoculars. Note that the trails are not blazed, but they are signed and easy to follow regardless.

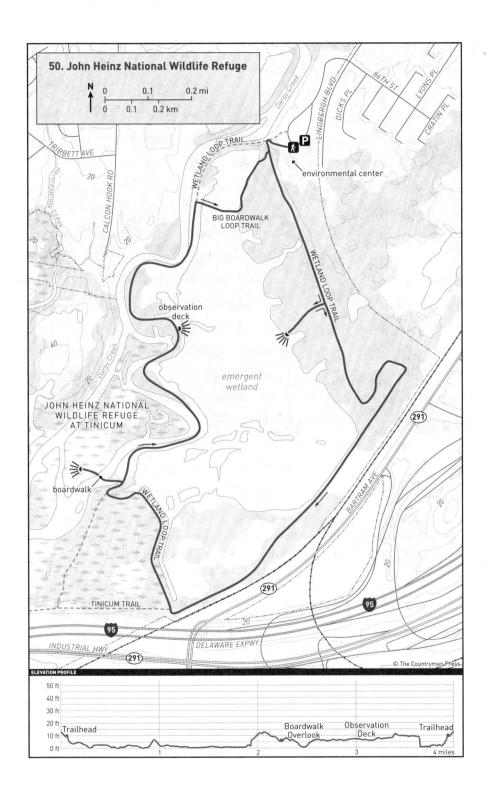

50. John Heinz National Wildlife Refuge

N

| 0 | 0.1 | 0.2 mi |
| 0 | 0.1 | 0.2 km |

Darby Creek

TRIBBETT AVE

LINDBERGH BLVD.

DICKS PL.

86TH ST

LYONS PL.

CRATIN PL.

CALCON HOOK RD

Hermesprota Creek

20

20

20

WETLAND LOOP TRAIL

environmental center

P

BIG BOARDWALK LOOP TRAIL

WETLAND LOOP TRAIL

40

20

observation deck

Darby Creek

emergent wetland

JOHN HEINZ NATIONAL WILDLIFE REFUGE AT TINICUM

291

BARTRAM AVE.

20

boardwalk

WETLAND LOOP TRAIL

TINICUM TRAIL

291

95

95

20

INDUSTRIAL HWY

291

DELAWARE EXPWY

20

© The Countryman Press

ELEVATION PROFILE

50 ft				
40 ft				
30 ft				
20 ft				
10 ft	Trailhead		Boardwalk Overlook	Observation Deck	Trailhead
0 ft		1	2	3	4 miles

BOARDWALK OVER MARSHY WATER

GETTING THERE

From the west, follow I-76 E. Use the left lane to take exit 347A toward Penrose Avenue/PA 291. Continue onto S 26th Street and in 0.9 mile turn right on Penrose Avenue. Follow Penrose Avenue for 2.4 miles, then turn right on Island Avenue. Drive for 0.4 mile. Turn left onto Bartram Avenue and continue for 0.3 mile. Turn right onto S 84th Street. Follow it for 0.7 mile, then turn left onto Lindbergh Boulevard. In 0.3 mile, turn right into John Heinz National Wildlife Refuge. The hike starts from here.

The hike starts from the parking lot outside of the wildlife refuge, southwest of downtown Philadelphia. From downtown, follow I-676 E and keep left toward Chester to merge onto I-95 S. Follow I-95 S for 7.2 miles. Take exit 14 to merge onto Bartram Avenue. Follow Bartram Avenue for 1.1 miles. Turn right onto S 84th Street and follow it for 0.7 mile. Turn left onto Lindbergh Boulevard and drive for 0.3 mile. Turn right into John Heinz National Wildlife Refuge. The hike starts from here.

GPS Shortcut: Enter "John Heinz National Wildlife Refuge at Tinicum" into Google Maps and your GPS will navigate to the trailhead.

THE HIKE

Walk west from the parking area on a paved pathway, passing the environmental center, an information kiosk, and picnic area underneath a pavilion. As you approach a pit toilet building, turn left and duck behind a metal gate to pick up the wide, gravel tread of the Wetland Loop Trail. The route the trail follows lies to the left of the emergent wetland, advancing along level, well-graded trail, meeting with a spur trail on the right in 0.4 mile. This short, 0.1-mile spur leads to a scenic viewpoint that gazes over the water. Visit the vista if you wish, then return to the gravel trail and continue your hike.

For the first portion of the hike, the Wetland Loop Trail follows a fairly straight trajectory, but at 0.9 mile the trail begins to bend to the left, heading away from the body of water. In 0.2 mile, however, the trail begins to curve back to the right, arriving at the marshy edge of the wetland very shortly thereafter. Similar to the first leg of the hike, this portion follows a fairly straight shot on flat, gravelly terrain, navigating a narrow strip of land in between the water to the right and a swamp, train tracks, and the highway on the left. There are several places on the trail to look out over the water through clearings in the cattails, as well as several benches (that may or may not be flooded) to stop and rest.

Continue following the edge of the water, then turn right and arrive at a trail junction 1.9 miles in. The Tinicum Trail heads to the left, while the Wetland Loop Trail continues going straight on. Keep straight on the Wetland Loop Trail and head away from the highway on a belt of raised road grade that bends and curves more so than before. The trail leads beside a bird blind in 0.3 mile and continues for 0.2 mile, passing the tread of another gravel road that comes

VIEW FROM THE OBSERVATION DECK

WILDLIFE BLIND ALONG THE WETLAND LOOP TRAIL

in from the left as the trail bends to the right. At mile 2.4, approach a short spur on the left side of the trail. Turning here leads approximately 0.1 mile to the end of a boardwalk, where a pleasant westward-facing view can be enjoyed, surveying a large portion of the tidal marsh. A covered area at the end of the boardwalk provides shade and seating to take in the view. When you are ready to keep hiking, head back to the Wetland Loop Trail and turn left, continuing on your previous trajectory.

The Wetland Loop Trail advances along the narrow strip of land, bending back and forth on level terrain for 0.5 mile, eventually arriving at a two-tiered observation deck built over the water, nestled among the cattails. This is an excellent place to stop and enjoy the view that looks northeast almost 180 degrees. Many birds call this area their home. When you are ready, continue walking the Wetland Loop Trail past the observation deck. At mile 3.4, the Wetland Loop Trail meets with the Big Boardwalk Loop Trail. From this point, you can either go straight and stay on the Wetland Loop Trail, or you can turn onto the Big Boardwalk Loop Trail and go across the water. For the purposes of this hike, turn right and follow the boardwalk over the water, reaching the other side in roughly 0.1 mile.

On the other side of the boardwalk, bend to the left and follow a narrow, singletrack trail north for 0.2 mile, arriving at the broad tread of the Wetland Loop Trail, very near to where you started the hike. Veer left onto the gravel terrain and leave the narrow trail, passing behind the gate and turning right. From here, walk the paved path for about 0.2 mile to arrive back at the parking area.